AVENGING ANGELS

By the same author

A Writer at War: Vasily Grossman with the Red Army 1941–1945 (2005)
(with Antony Beevor)

*Defending the Motherland: The Soviet Women Who
Fought Hitler's Aces* (2015)

LYUBA VINOGRADOVA

AVENGING ANGELS

SOVIET WOMEN SNIPERS ON THE
EASTERN FRONT (1941–1945)

With an Introduction by Anna Reid

*Translated from the Russian by
Arch Tait*

MACLEHOSE PRESS
QUERCUS · LONDON

First published in Great Britain in 2017 by

MacLehose Press
An imprint of Quercus Publishing Ltd
Carmelite House
50 Victoria Embankment
London EC4Y 0DZ

An Hachette UK company

First published in the Russian language as Ангелы мщения. Женщины-снайперы
Великой Отечественной by Azbooka-Atticus Publishing Group in 2017

This publication was effected under the auspices of the
Mikhail Prokhorov Foundation TRANSCRIPT Programme
to Support Translations of Russian Literature

A CIP catalogue record for this book is available
from the British Library.

ISBN (HB) 978 0 85705 196 7
ISBN (TPB) 978 0 85705 197 4
ISBN (Ebook) 978 0 85705 198 1

Designed and typeset in Quadraat by Libanus Press, Marlborough
Printed and bound in Great Britain by Clays Ltd, St Ives Plc

In memory of my friend, Anna Sinyakova (Mulatova)

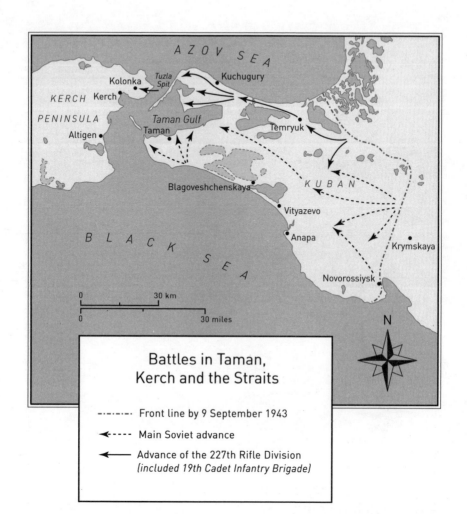

AZOV SEA

KERCH PENINSULA

Kolonka
Tuzla Spit
Kerch
Kuchugury

Taman Gulf
Taman
Altigen
Temryuk

Blagoveshchenskaya
K U B A N

Vityazevo

B L A C K   S E A
Anapa
Krymskaya

Novorossiysk

0   30 km
0   30 miles

N

Battles in Taman, Kerch and the Straits

–·–·–·– Front line by 9 September 1943

◄---- Main Soviet advance

◄——— Advance of the 227th Rifle Division
(included 19th Cadet Infantry Brigade)

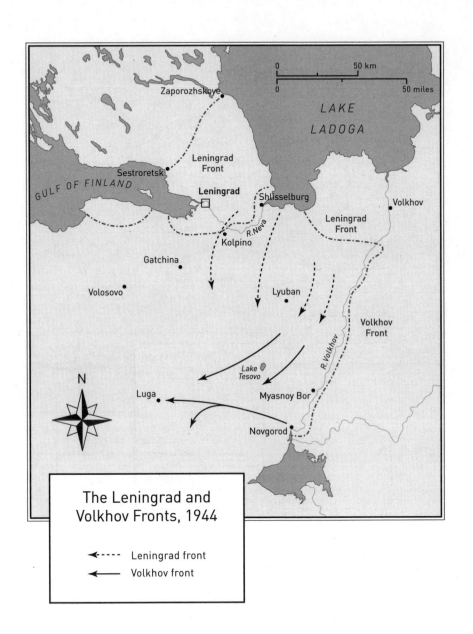

0   50 km
0   50 miles

LAKE LADOGA

Zaporozhskoye

GULF OF FINLAND

Sestroretsk

Leningrad Front

Leningrad

Shlisselburg

Volkhov

Leningrad Front

R. Neva

Kolpino

Gatchina

Volosovo

Lyuban

Volkhov Front

R. Volkhov

Lake Tesovo

Luga

Myasnoy Bor

Novgorod

N

The Leningrad and Volkhov Fronts, 1944

◄----- Leningrad front
◄——— Volkhov front

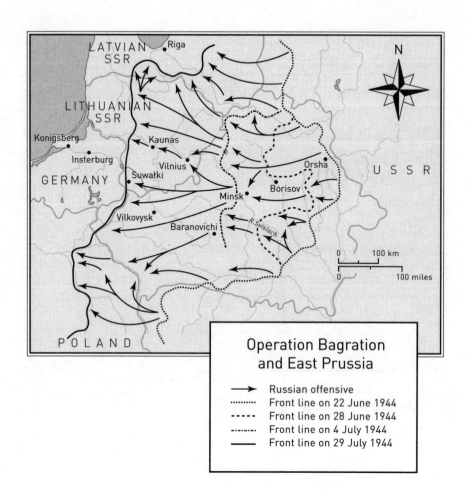

**Operation Bagration
and East Prussia**

→ Russian offensive
········· Front line on 22 June 1944
- - - - - Front line on 28 June 1944
-·-·-·- Front line on 4 July 1944
——— Front line on 29 July 1944

LATVIAN
SSR
Riga

LITHUANIAN
SSR

Konigsberg

Insterburg

GERMANY
Kaunas

Vilnius
Suwatki

Vilkovysk

Baranovichi

Minsk

Borisov

Orsha

USSR

R.Svisloch

0   100 km

0   100 miles

N

POLAND

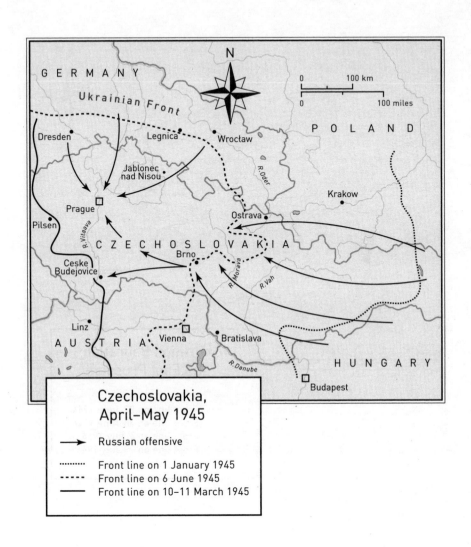

Czechoslovakia,
April–May 1945

→ Russian offensive

·········· Front line on 1 January 1945
- - - - Front line on 6 June 1945
——— Front line on 10–11 March 1945

Contents

List of Illustrations

Introduction

Anna Reid

The Soviet Union sent more women into combat during the Second World War than any other nation before or since. Estimates vary widely, but one can safely assume that a minimum of 570,000 women served in the Red Army during the course of the war, and more likely 700,000–800,000. Add in female partisans and volunteers to civilian militias, and the total rises to around a million.

In the chaotic weeks following the German invasion of June 1941, Soviet women, like men, volunteered in huge numbers, queuing to register for whatever war work was available. Though an estimated 20,000 were able to join up immediately, simply by personally approaching local commanders, the majority were initially channeled into factory or civil defence work. Full-scale conscription of women into the military did not begin until March 1942, to make up for enormous losses suffered during the initial German Blitzkrieg and the defences of Moscow and Leningrad. By 1943, however, women were fully integrated into all services. Most acted in relatively traditional roles: as nurses, secretaries, drivers, telephonists, signallers, mechanics and cooks. But a substantial minority took up arms: as anti-aircraft and machine-gunners, sappers, scouts, bomber and fighter pilots and aircrew, snipers, tank crew and ordinary infantry. They won promotion as the war progressed, so that by 1945 female platoon, company and even battalion commanders were common enough to attract little comment.

Nowhere else did women fight in anything like these numbers, if at all. In Britain, though over half a million women wore uniform, the only ones allowed actually to operate weapons were 56,000 "Ack-ack girls" who manned mixed-sex anti-aircraft batteries from the summer of 1941 onwards.

Though the "girls" quickly proved their worth, they met with considerable official opposition, and remained symbolically banned from triggering their guns' firing mechanisms. Prompted by the British example, America secretly trained 395 female anti-aircraft gunners from December 1942. But the experiment was abandoned within a few months, for fear, according to the head of army personnel, that neither "national policy nor public opinion are yet ready to accept the use of women in field force units".

In Germany, the National Socialist ideology of "children, kitchen, church" for women was so strong that they were not fully mobilised even into civilian war work until 1943. They were not drafted into the army until 1944, and as late as November of that year Hitler issued an order reiterating that no women be weapons trained. Three months later, with the Red Army at the gates of Berlin, he finally authorised the creation of an all-female infantry battalion, with the aim of discouraging desertion from the crumbling Wehrmacht. It had not yet formed when Germany surrendered.

Various explanations have been put forward for the Soviet Union's unique willingness to use women in combat. Cultural and historical factors may have played a part: the long roll-call of female revolutionaries under the last two tsars, the tens of thousands of women who served on the Bolshevik side during the Russian Civil War, the Soviet constitution's (theoretical) embrace of sexual equality. The overwhelming factors, however, were probably simply Soviet women's own strong incentive to fight – they had seen their own country invaded, and friends and family killed – and the military's desperate need for extra manpower, following near-overwhelming losses in the opening months of the war.

Avenging Angels is a companion volume to Lyuba Vinogradova's earlier *Defending the Motherland: The Soviet Women Who Fought Hitler's Aces.* Both centre on her interviews with women who took on some of the war's most high-profile combat roles – as fighter and bomber pilots, and as snipers. Vinogradova's concern is not to assess their contribution to the war effort, nor to Soviet gender politics, but to capture their individual stories, the particular lived experiences that are left out of conventional top-down military history writing. What, she wants to know, was being a sniper on the Eastern Front actually like?

Even for young women raised amidst the turmoil and hardships of Stalin's Russia, joining the army came as a social, emotional and physical shock. At training school, peasant girls from dirt-poor villages had their cherished braids lopped off, and encountered tea and bed linen for the first time in their lives. Gently raised students from Moscow's Conservatoire found themselves taking orders from illiterate Tatar shepherds. Once at the front they had to learn to deal not only with enemy fire, but with cold, gnawing hunger, lice, oversized boots, rudimentary sanitation and sexual assaults by drunken male officers.

Like their male counterparts, most female snipers found their first "kills" traumatic, particularly because they were administered not during the heat of battle, but during periods of static warfare, when the victim emerged from his trench to wash or clear snow. Some were transferred to non-combat jobs, but the rest grew used to killing, competing to increase their "tallies". During assaults they doubled as infantry, running forward and firing with the men, or as medics, moving the wounded and administering first aid. Many, of course, were killed or wounded themselves. Overall casualty rates are unknown, but judging by the sample Vinogradova gathers here, they were very high. Most of her interviewees had lost multiple "sniper partners" by the end of the war.

On demobilisation, women were expected to revert to traditional gender roles. As *Pravda* put it in March 1945, they had "very energetically proved themselves as pilots, snipers, submachine gunners. But they don't forget about their *primary duty* to nation and state – that of *motherhood*." The return to civilian life was hardest in the countryside, where post-war famine, caused by a combination of food requisitioning and poor harvests, killed somewhere between 1 and 1.5 million. Everywhere, female veterans learned to keep quiet about their war service, lest neighbours deride them as discarded "front-line wives". (Members of America's Women's Army Corp were similarly insulted, routinely labelled sluts or lesbians.) Like their whole age cohort, they were lucky if they found husbands, the large majority of their male contemporaries being dead.

As well as paying tribute to a unique class of soldier, Vinogradova's work makes an important contribution to today's debate about what roles women should play in warfare. As the U.S. Air Force officer and historian Reina Pennington points out, "At a time when there is still wide debate about whether women *can* serve in combat and what they *might* do if allowed to serve, we are still surprisingly ignorant about what women actually *have done* in wartime combat situations." To remedy that, there are no better exemplars than the soldiers whose stories are collected here.

Preface

In September, autumn is just beginning in Krasnodar. The sky is blue, the city's trees heavy with ripe fruit, and the sun, although lower in the sky, is still warm. When you come there from autumnal Moscow, you immediately feel more alive, especially if there is someone warm and kind waiting for you. In Yekaterina's apartment there was also borshcht waiting for us, the real borshcht you find only in Ukraine and the southernmost parts of Russia, and "wee blues" (aubergines to a Russian), and slices of bread and baloney and tea with chocolates, and stories and more stories. Our new friend, who a week ago had not known we existed, welcomed us like family. Almost ninety years old and limping heavily from a severe wound suffered at Sevastopol, she bustled round the apartment carrying cups and dishes. Her round, pleasant face was wreathed in smiles. She was pleased to have visitors, and talked endlessly about the war, about herself, her sons, her grandchildren, about her city and her neighbours and friends.

We had come to Krasnodar because, seventy years ago, Yekaterina Terekhova, Katya Peredera as she then was, had been a sniper in the war, with a tally of thirty Germans killed or wounded. I had already met many women snipers. I had drunk tea with them, listened to their tales of sniper school and the front line, and about life after the war. My heart went out to them, I pitied them in their old age and infirmity, but all the while I was listening out for an answer to one particular question: were they tormented by the thought of the lives they had taken?

The sharpest, most clear-cut answer I got to that was the one Yekaterina vouchsafed, on behalf both of herself and, I felt, the rest of her comrades. She was telling me about some lunatic sectarian preacher who had latched on to her and called upon her, in view of her great age, to lose no time repenting her sins. To this she had said in surprise,

"What sins do I have? I have never stolen anything. I have never killed anyone." This kind, sweet woman had spent her life trying to help people in the entirely peaceable profession of a doctor, and she had not the slightest doubt that the whole of her existence had been occupied by doing good, including the time when she was at the front. In fact, especially then.

How many of my generation, the "children of perestroika", would go out today to die for our country? How many would be willing to kill for it? We would do well to try, at least partly, to understand the young women, contemporaries of our grandmothers, who took up arms in that war. This book is an attempt to see the Second World War through their eyes.

LYUBA VINOGRADOVA
JANUARY 2017
MAPUTO, MOZAMBIQUE

Chapter 1

"You're my little girl! How will you survive there without borshcht?"

Searchlight beams run across the night sky and meet, having caught their target, a small, slow biplane, which in this light looks like a helpless silver-winged moth. Its pilot and navigator are blinded by the unbearable light. One more second, and the plane is on fire.

Comrades of the doomed crew are able to watch the burning plane from the ground, as the night bombers' target is not far away tonight. Girls clad in flying suits watch in a daze as the ball of fire starts falling slowly; the pilot and navigator don't have parachutes so will only survive by a miracle. The chief of staff Rakobolskaya rushes to the log book where flights are registered in order "to see who is burning".

Four of the crews sent by Rakobolskaya to bomb the Blue Line in the Kuban on that terrible night never came back. After the search for them proved in vain, Rakobolskaya wrote to the families of the eight girls to tell them that they had gone missing. Polina Gelman, whose best friend, the navigator Galya Dokutovich died that night, kept waiting for a long time for Galya to come back, until eventually she accepted the loss and decided that if she survived the war and if she ever had a daughter, she would call her Galya.

The 588 all-female night bomber regiment continued to retrain navigators as pilots, and mechanics as navigators in order to make up for the losses. New crews were now engaged in the fighting and the advance towards the powerful chain of fortifications on the Taman Peninsula dubbed the Blue Line was replaced for a while by battles in the air. The Soviet side was pulling together resources for a new offensive.

This was the third year of war on the Eastern Front. The fighting, unprecedented in its scale, causing incalculable destruction and claiming millions of lives, was at its fiercest. But by the August of 1943 the Red Army had seized the strategic initiative. The turning point had been the Battle of Stalingrad, followed by the breach of the Leningrad encirclement and victory in the Battle of Kursk. Memories were still fresh of the disaster of 1941, the rapid German advance resulting in the encirclement and capture of a great part of the regular Soviet army, colossal casualties and the loss of great territories, major industrial centres and key agricultural regions. Before Stalingrad it was hard to believe in victory. After Kursk, victory began to feel like a real possibility. Two or three girls among Katya Peredera's comrades in the sniper platoon were even convinced that if their dispatch to the front was delayed they would not get the chance to cover themselves with glory as the war would soon be over.

The Germans, compelled to retreat in the spring of 1943 from the Caucasus, were determined at all costs to hold the Taman Peninsula – both to shield the Crimea and as a bridgehead for new attacks. Rounding up local women and children to work for them, they created an almost impregnable line of fortifications from the Sea of Azov to the Black Sea, exploiting the potential of the terrain – marshes and lagoons in the northern sector, and mountainous, forested terrain in the south – and in the middle built multiple rows of fortifications with minefields and barbed-wire entanglements in front of them. The Germans called this line the Gotenkopf, or Goth's Head, but the Russians had kept the Blue Line, the name the Germans had used in their early planning. The Soviet North Caucasian Front's spring offensive had failed to have a major impact owing to a lack of resources. Continuing for a week, it succeeded only in moving forward a short distance to the Cossack village of Krymskaya on the approaches to the Blue Line.

Katya Peredera first came here, to the area around the Cossack village of Kurchanskaya, in August 1943. The front line was only three kilometres away and the no-man's-land between the German and Russian positions was a treacherous expanse of lagoons and nameless small islands.[1]

Katya had arrived together with 19 Cadet Infantry Brigade, to which her sniper platoon was attached. Such platoons were a great novelty: so many snipers had been trained by 1943 that whole platoons of them, around thirty soldiers apiece, were being sent to accompany regular units. These platoons were considered extremely valuable, even if they consisted, like Katya's, exclusively of girls.

At first, everything was relatively quiet. They were on the defensive. Only occasionally did a burst of rifle fire come from the reed beds, and in the mornings the Germans staged "five-minuters", a short spell of untargetted artillery shelling.[2] The girls had been familiarised with front-line rules and local conditions: no marching in columns; when you needed to move, you stooped down and moved one at a time, often scuttling across open ground. If a "Frame" appeared, a German Focke-Wulf recon-naissance aircraft, you hit the ground. (The girls instantly hated the Frame for forcing them to muddy their uniforms.) If you needed water to drink or wash with, you headed for the nearest shell or bomb crater, of which there were plenty. Water in the lagoon, an immense area of shallow water, was unfit for drinking, bitter and salty. Only those few girls who had grown up in the vicinity of lagoons could drink it with impunity (and felt very superior to their weakling sisters as a result).

Their platoon was accommodated in nine dugouts, and again, as in Medvedovskaya where they had been trained, the girls made the place more civilised with reeds from the lagoon. These were fashioned into beds, used to line the dugouts' ceilings to prevent soil trickling down, and as floor coverings. They also used reeds to make campfires.

Forces were being built up ready for the new offensive, but in the relative peace before it was launched seventeen-year-old Galya Koldeyeva, the youngest girl in the sniper platoon, would quietly sneak off to bathe in the shallow lagoon. Nikolai Zainutdinov, a good, brave, if uneducated, Tatar lad, became the girls' guardian and mentor. He had learned to shoot accurately while tending flocks of thousands of sheep in the steppe. Wolves often attacked, and the shepherd became expert at despatching them.[3] Trained as a sniper at the front, Zainutdinov rapidly earned respect; so much so, indeed, that he was put in charge of a platoon. When he found the snipers entrusted to his care were girls, he was undismayed. Because he was so tall, the girls called him One-and-a-Half Ivans, made fun of his less than impressive education, sulked when he "imposed discipline", but in general got on well with him.[4]

There were endless dogfights in the air above them, anticipating the offensive that began on 10 September 1943. 19 Brigade was not immediately drawn into it; instead they watched the troops mass before they were sent forward. For several days in early September new units had been arriving, while others left for the front line. In the evenings shots would ring out in the vicinity of the girls' dugouts, one, or two, or three. Then, almost immediately, one or other of them would emerge. This was a pre-arranged signal, calling the girls out for a tryst, sent by soldiers who were not allowed into their female comrades' quarters. These brief en-counters and walks by the lagoon rarely led to anything serious; passions flared, but the next day or the day after, the boy's unit, after its brief respite, would go forward to the Blue Line. Only a few exchanged addresses and continued their romance by correspondence. Katya Peredera barely had time to chat to likeable Sergeant Lyova. Their plan to dally in an empty dugout was thwarted by the stern and vigilant One-and-a-Half Ivans, who was there in a flash to enquire, "And where might you be going?" He shooed them away and threatened to write to their parents.[5] The next morning, Lyova was wounded in the eye and Katya heard no more of him.

The girls had no illusions: they knew an offensive was imminent and that many of these soldiers would die. They had heard about the earlier fighting here. "We had not encountered fortifications like these ones in Kuban. Here they were dug in, everything was underground. They had thoroughly prepared it all in advance and clearly had no intention of leaving. It took us two days to walk the 10 kilometres of the Blue Line," a soldier who fought there recalled.[6] Even now, seventy years later, search parties are finding and re-burying bodies. They rarely manage to identify them: in November 1942 soldiers' Bakelite capsules containing an identifying slip of paper were abolished. The authorities had decided that the instruction booklet carried by every soldier could serve the same function although, of course, this was not the case: the books rapidly mouldered, or deteriorated in water. In the view of many researchers, the motive for abolishing the capsules was that the government preferred its millions of casualties to remain anonymous. "That had many advantages. There was no need to bury them, no need to pay a pension to bereaved families who had lost their breadwinner, and they wanted to conceal the huge scale of the losses."[7] In spite of these obstacles, the search parties are sometimes successful: people who feared remaining unidentified after they were killed would scratch their names on a comb, a spoon or mess tin, or make medallions for themselves out of spent cartridges.

The guitar was in splinters. Thank God, its owner, Olga Korotkevich, had survived the shelling, but she was wounded and it looked serious. Olga was fun, loud, "all-singing, all-dancing", the best singer in their platoon. When she left home to learn to be a sniper, she took her guitar with her and was inseparable from it, even right at the front. Now, her face contorted with pain, she asked repeatedly, "Where's my guitar?" "Don't worry, Olga, you'll get your guitar!" Olga's sniper partner was Katya Peredera, and she was being as reassuring as she could while hastily, and not very expertly, bandaging her wound. She needed to get Olga out, and fast.[8] There was fierce fighting all around them: this time the Red Army would succeed in breaking through the Germans' Blue Line.

The 19 Cadet Infantry Brigade had suffered a great deal in the September offensive of the North-Caucasian Front. The platoon of female snipers, who acted as ordinary infantry soldiers during the advance, also suffered casualties. In the course of a few days at Temryuk their platoon of thirty-three was reduced to twenty-three.[9]

Katya was right: Olga survived and bought another guitar, but she did not return to the front, and was crippled for the rest of her life.

Katya's new sniper partner was Zhenya Makeyeva, a tall, handsome girl, dark-eyed and dark-skinned, sharp-tongued, sociable and courageous. Zhenya became Katya's closest friend: they were inseparable until 7 May 1944, when Zhenya was killed, and Katya was unable to bury her.

Most of the girls in Katya's platoon had been conscripted in Krasnodar, a big city in the south of Russia close to the Black Sea, but Katya and Zhenya were both from Kropotkin in the Krasnodar province. They lived in different parts of the small Kuban town and so did not know each other before meeting up at sniper school. Like the other girls in the platoon, they were called up immediately after the Krasnodar region was liberated in February 1943.

The Germans had reached Kropotkin on 4 August 1942. The town was built on raised ground, and Katya and her family looked down the valley towards the Caucasus and saw German units advancing. When they broke through, Katya, though never faint-hearted, jumped down into the cellar without bothering to use the ladder. She sat there, joined by her mother and sisters, while the Germans drove into town in cars and on motorcycles. When the girls emerged to see what was happening, the troops were already in the streets, plundering, taking eggs and milk from the housewives and shooting hens.[10]

Katya remembered the occupation as a time of fear and hunger, although she did not personally witness any atrocities. The only terrible thing that happened immediately after the Germans entered was the execution of a small number of retreating Soviet soldiers whose carts were intercepted.

After that, things seemed to settle down. Many of the townspeople were happy to help the Germans, and pro-German companies of Cossacks and Crimean Tatars roamed the streets. People who had been at odds with the Soviet regime before the war went to work in the police or local administration. "The worst thing I remember," a Krasnodar resident recalls, "was a canvas-covered truck driving up and thirty or forty people in fascist uniforms piling out. All of them were speaking Russian."[11]

Workers, if they had a job, just went to work as usual under the German occupation: they had a family to feed.[12] The Germans tried to catch anyone in the Soviet resistance and atrocities were taking place nearby, but Katya's family knew about it only through rumours. The Germans demanded milk and eggs from the townspeople. They made expeditions by motorcycle to remote villages and farmsteads that still had a lot of poultry, and would take away live ducks and geese. The village boys quickly learned that when they heard motorcycles coming they should take long rods and drive the birds down to a river, lake or stream to wait for the uninvited guests to depart. Otherwise, the Germans let local people get on with their lives, although they made it plain that they regarded them as subhuman. Sometimes they did not simply requisition food but exchanged it for "their ersatz" (the word refers to surrogate, inadequate, replacements of foods such as butter or bread, and was borrowed by the Russian language from German during the war). Not a few of the local people said – some openly, others in private – that if the Germans just gave them land to farm, life under them would be better than under the Soviets.

Kropotkin was liberated by Soviet troops after heavy fighting some six months later, and soon Katya and many of her contemporaries received conscription notices. Boys of her age had already been conscripted in 1942. Many girls had no wish at all to go to the front, and hid with their grandmothers or other relatives. Katya enlisted as a matter of conscience: she knew that many of the boys in her class had already been killed.[13] The country had lost so much of its male population during the first two years of the conflict that it now had no choice but to start using women in the army, on an even larger scale than before. In a country that proclaimed 100 per cent equality of the sexes, it did not seem strange to anyone that an extensive mobilisation of women for the army should take place. There are no reliable statistics as to the number of women who served in the Red Army during the Second World War; women went down in the lists of their units together with men. The estimates range from 500,000 to nearly a million. Apart from serving as secretaries, nurses, telephone operators and cooks, women were also employed as signallers, aviation technicians, personnel of anti-aircraft artillery and machine-gunners. Marina Raskova's female pilots became famous throughout the land. There were also female tank crews and marines. From 1943 onwards, thousands of young female snipers appeared at the fronts. Some researchers later claimed that the decision to train women as snipers was made on the basis of serious research proving that women had the potential to be better snipers than men, because they were calmer and more patient. In fact, the main factor that played a role here was the desperate shortage of men.

Most of Katya Peredera's new friends, including herself, had only a very vague idea of what their future role as a sniper would entail, and were curious to find out what the training was going to be like. A group of about a hundred girls, enough to form a company of snipers, were given a ride in open railway goods trucks full of salt, and brought to Krasnodar. The ancient city, the beautiful capital of Kuban, which occupied the land of the ancient Bosporan Kingdom by the Black Sea, was severely damaged. The factories had been blown up by the N.K.V.D. ahead of the German arrival, and even worse destruction was to be wrought by shells, bombing, and arson by the Germans before they were driven out.[14]

From Krasnodar, the prospective snipers were taken to the Cossack village of Medvedovskaya, a peaceful spot at the confluence of two rivers, with small white houses set in orchards and with huge vegetable gardens. Here they were to be trained. They were billeted in a pigsty, there being nowhere else, and the girls accepted that with a war going on this was no time to be picky. They cleaned out the pigsty and made themselves mattresses from the plentiful reeds in the lagoon. They put the mattresses by the walls, wooden benches in the middle, hung a sheet of paper with the day's routine on the wall, and were ready to begin their new lives.[15] Women's uniforms were not standard issue for the Red Army at that time so, like hundreds of thousands of others who had been enlisted already, they were given hugely oversized men's uniforms and boots.

Their tunics came to the knees of the shorter girls and their boots kept falling off. You could cry about it, or laugh. Along with all other girls at the front, they were given a cropped haircut like boys. For centuries, a plait coiled round the head had been the pride and joy of Cossack girls, and most of the snipers-to-be had never cut their hair. Parting with these plaits was very upsetting, and many wept and begged to be excused the sacrifice. The sergeant, lame from his time at the front, referred to orders from above and was unrelenting.[16] Their hair remained a source of anguish until the end of the course, and when it was over they had it permed in Krasnodar for the first and last time in the war.

After a few theory lessons, the battle-hardened sergeant taught them everything he thought they would need to know at the front. The trainee snipers began square-bashing and had shooting practice in a gully. Targets were set up and the sergeant taught them how to aim and manage the recoil – the strong jerking movement of the rifle that followed the shot. That, however, was only the half of it: he also taught them the camouflage skills essential for a sniper ("a sniper should be invisible!"), and even had them sitting underwater in the lagoon breathing through a straw.[17] It is a wonder they had the strength for such strenuous training, because their food was terrible, often consisting of nothing but barley porridge, which was cold and "turning blue" well before it ever reached them at the firing range. Katya recalled her mother's lamentation as she saw her daughter off to the front: "You're my little girl! How will you survive there without borshcht?"[18]

The culture and traditions of Kuban are closer to those of Ukraine than of Russia, and neither before nor after the war could Katya imagine a life without borshcht. Her mother found a way to cheer her daughter up by coming to see her in Medvedovskaya, covering the 150 kilometres on foot and by getting lifts in trucks. She arrived together with the mother of Zhenya Makeyeva. Nobody knows how they met or who told them their daughters were in Medvedovskaya, but Katya and Zhenya were aware that their mothers were coming to see them, and prepared a welcome. They asked the local women to let them wash the tunics they had muddied during training exercises, and stitched on clean undercollars. Their mothers brought a little food, but it was already in short supply even in Kuban. Zhenya's elder brother was fighting (and he too would not return from the war). Katya's mother told her that her elder sister, Nina, was currently serving somewhere nearby as a nurse.[19]

In May the weather warmed up and flowers appeared. The girls picked posies and their barracks was untypically fragrant for the army.[20] At the end of May, they were given blank cartridges and dummy hand grenades for an exercise: the snipers' mission was to destroy an enemy assault group that had supposedly broken through to the railway, and liberate the station. By all accounts the dummy operation was a great success. At the end of their training, they heard they were to be examined on theory, drill and shooting by a front-line commission. This was to include Lyudmila Pavlichenko, a sniper who, before she was injured, had also been fighting on the North Caucasian Front. They had heard and read a lot about her in propaganda leaflets: she was said to have "exterminated more than 300 fascists", so it was a great disappointment for the girls and their mentor the sergeant when the celebrity failed to turn up.

Chapter 2

"Who would think of powdering their nose in a war?"

In late August 1942, almost every Soviet magazine, and many in the West, reported an amazing visit. Soviet front-line fighters had arrived as part of an official Young Communist League delegation to an International Student Assembly in the United States. There was much more to the visit than that, however. The delegation was to stay in the US for several weeks, travelling all over the country and addressing a wide variety of audiences in order to draw attention to the perilous situation on the Eastern Front.

There had never before been, and would not be for many decades afterwards, so much interest and friendly feeling towards the U.S.S.R. as in the autumn of 1942. Russia, which until very recently had been considered a rogue state, a secretive, backward, aggressive colossus that had made a pact with the Germans and attacked neighbouring countries in order to seize territory, was now being viewed quite differently. It was a land desperately fighting a powerful and ruthless aggressor. Communists and trade unionists in the U.S. and Europe demanded that their governments should support Russia more effectively. The Germans had captured a huge swathe of Soviet territory and were fighting for Stalingrad: if Russia lost that battle it could lose the war, and the consequences of that could affect the whole world. People followed the news from the Eastern Front eagerly. Russia was on everybody's mind and many families identified closely with the victories of the Red Army.

There could not have been a better time for a delegation from the U.S.S.R. to visit the U.S., and this one included two highly decorated front-line fighters. The head of the delegation was, predictably, not a war hero but a bureaucrat, Nikolai Krasavchenko, the propaganda secretary of the Moscow Young Communist League. He was involved, at least administratively, in forming groups to be dropped behind the German lines, which was sufficient for him to be introduced to American audiences as a partisan fighter.[21] Two other members of the delegation were snipers who, before the outbreak of war, had been students: Hero of the Soviet Union Vladimir Pchelintsev and Lyudmila Pavlichenko.

Why were two snipers chosen, rather than two pilots or tank commanders? Most probably because at that moment the other branches of the Red Army were suffering a seemingly unbroken series of conspicuous reverses at the hands of their opponents. The sniper movement, on the other hand, was something to shout about. The Germans feared Russian snipers and the Soviet press devoted a great deal of space to them, often exaggerating their exploits. Moreover, these two personable young snipers were outstanding representatives of authentically Communist youth. Both were educated, having gone straight from university to the front, were ideologically primed, and more than capable of speaking on varied topics. Both had an affiliation with the N.K.V.D., the much-feared Soviet secret police, Pchelintsev through his unit and Pavlichenko through her father.[22] They were people who could safely be sent abroad.

Vladimir Pchelintsev gives a detailed account of that trip to the U.S. At the time of the visit he was already a famous sniper on the Leningrad Front, and rightly considered one of the founders of the sniper movement in the Red Army.[23] The trip came as a complete surprise to him. The 22-year-old sniper had just been recalled from active service to work at the sniper school near Moscow. He was woken during the night and taken to meet Nikolai Mikhailov, first secretary of the Young Communist League's Central Committee. Mikhailov immediately explained the reason for the summons, but Pchelintsev could not believe his ears. He was to be sent to America? For a moment he was taken aback. "Have I misheard? Did he just say something about America? How can I possibly go to America when there is a war on?"[24]

Mikhailov confirmed that, yes, he was to go to a student assembly being held in America. Pchelintsev still could not believe it, and merely grunted. To him America was as remote as Mars. "American imperialism" embodied all the horrors of capitalism, with corrupt morals, endemic racism, a decaying economy and venal press. People believed the propaganda unquestioningly, because almost nobody had ever been to America, or indeed anywhere outside the U.S.S.R. Soviet people did not travel abroad. In fact, peasants, who represented the bulk of the population, did not have even internal passports, so could not travel outside their own collective farms, the Soviet pseudo-cooperatives that had been forced upon the nation's peasants with rigid, and costly, brutality.

Right now, however, Vladimir Pchelintsev reflected in perplexity, the fate of the country was in the balance. How could they just go off to America? He had little time to ponder the matter. In Mikhailov's office the next day he met Lyudmila Pavlichenko, whom he had seen before at the sniper school in Veshnyaki, and a tall young man, Nikolai Krasavchenko. They were taken to see Georgiy Alexandrov, director of the Propaganda Department of the Soviet Communist Party's Central Committee, who explained to them the great importance of their trip, and were then immediately kitted out for their journey. Within a few hours, uniforms for Vladimir and Lyudmila had been made to measure at the store that was usually reserved for Soviet generals, on to which their lieutenant's insignia of rank were sewn. They were given dapper civilian clothes, underwear, shoes and coats of a quality they could never have dreamed of before. They were supplied with delicacies to surprise the capitalists with, and a substantial amount of currency so they would not have to borrow money from anyone.

Soon they were flying a long, complicated route with numerous landings in order to bypass German-occupied countries. They flew via Tehran, where they were struck by the dazzling shop windows in the wealthy centre of the city and the multitudes of extremely persistent beggars; and through Cairo, where there were more beggars, but also the pyramids and a shop selling watches, where Pchelintsev acquired a Swiss chronometer, a piece of equipment essential for any sniper. In Cairo, the members of the delegation saw "ingenious white cupboards" at the Allied airbase, which turned out to be refrigerators. These were quite unknown in the U.S.S.R. At a reception in Lagos, at the time the capital of Nigeria, the representatives of the U.S.S.R. decided the black waiters must be wearing white gloves to serve the guests in order to prevent them from being disgusted by their skin colour. In Accra, the capital of the Gold Coast, at a reception given by the British governor, Vladimir tasted a strange fruit that filled his mouth with "a disgusting, soapy taste" and made him feel sick. It was out of the question to spit it out, so he just had to swallow it. That was his first encounter with a grapefruit. Vladimir liked a "tricky fruit the size of a small melon and with peel like the skin of a crocodile, with thorns and sharp needles", its flavour was "a cross between an orange and a strawberry" He would learn later that it was a pineapple.

Then "a leap across the ocean" and a short stop ("We could hardly believe it") in Brazil, where the plane was fumigated against the plague and they had "some glass tubes" stuck in their mouths: thermometers, which they were also seeing for the first time. They flew along the coast – Brazil, French Guiana, Devil's Island, Suriname, Venezuela – and landed on the island of Trinidad. They could not tear themselves away from looking at the Caribbean through the portholes: "The colour of the water was amazing." On the fourteenth day of their journey they reached Washington. They were taken straight to the White House where, it was announced, as a special honour, the Soviet delegation would stay overnight.

The president was away, but they were looked after by Eleanor Roosevelt personally, who made a big impression. Upright, tall and elegant, with a "rather coarse face" heavily marked by wrinkles, she was an intelligent, erudite woman whose influence in society did not depend on her position as First Lady.

The next morning the delegation found a "huge crowd of journalists and photographers" waiting for them at the Soviet Embassy, and were blinded by flashbulbs. Indeed, flashbulbs attended them everywhere they went on the tour, and it was not long before they were being bombarded by the assembled journalists' initial questions. The public wanted to know everything about the Soviet delegation, especially the snipers, and particularly Lyudmila. To Western ears, the word "sniper" had unpleasant overtones: a sniper was a marksman who killed stealthily rather than in a fair fight. Now America had an opportunity to make the acquaintance of an attractive young woman who had ambushed and murdered over 300 people.

On 29 August 1942, many newspapers reprinted a brief report to the effect that,

> Twenty-six-year-old Lieutenant Lyudmila Pavlichenko, a bewitch-
> ing warrior princess who has the highest individual score among
> the best snipers of the Red Army, yesterday did two things she could

never have imagined when, a few weeks ago, during the defence of Sevastopol, she shot her 309th fascist.

1) She arrived in Washington, becoming the first Amazon of the Red Army to visit the capital of the United States.

2) She spent the night at the White House as a guest of President Roosevelt and America's First Lady.

Miss Pavlichenko has been awarded the Order of Lenin and wounded on four occasions.[25]

She really did not look like a killer. It fell to Pavlichenko and Pchelintsev to blow away quite a few stereotypes. Here were Red Army officers, communists, snipers with tallies of hundreds of victims, appearing before the American public as perfectly normal, likeable young people. The enigmatic girl sniper was, naturally, the centre of attention.

As Pchelintsev recalls, "the trickiest, and sometimes downright impertinent, questions were directed at Pavlichenko. There were no bounds to the journalistic fraternity's curiosity." "Do girls wear lipstick at the front line and what colour do they prefer?" "Which brand of cigarettes do they smoke?" "Will Miss Pavlichenko agree to have her portrait on cigarette packs? The company is prepared to pay a million dollars!" "What underwear does Lady Pavlichenko prefer and what colour does she like?"[26]

Pavlichenko was bashful at first, but soon overcame her shyness and thereafter was never short of a pithy reply. Once she had learned how to handle impudent questions, she stopped being defensive and went on the attack. A number of brief video clips of the trip have survived,[27] and it is enough to watch them for a couple of minutes to see the kind of girl she was, with a delicate face and expressive eyes, lively, sharp-tongued, and with a distinctive south Russian accent. "I have to say honestly that she was quite good with people. Guests and hosts were very taken by her smile and unaffectedness. Nikolai and I were no match for her," Pchelintsev recalled.[28]

Nevertheless, it was hard work. Every step of the way there was

35

incessant attention from the press: flashbulbs, questions, curiosity about every detail. The newspapers reported that she had had to take a break from giving speeches to have a gold front tooth replaced by a white one – while that was being done she could not speak on the radio because of a whistling sound she made.[29] They wrote about her stocky figure, her high "Russian Army boots", and her demure olive-green uniform. The press opined that it did not fit her very well. They reported, to the indignation of the Soviet embassy, that her skirt was the wrong length and that, were it shorter, Pavlichenko's figure would look better. They commented that the Soviet sniper was not very tall, that she was rather "solid", even "plump". Pchelintsev himself remarks in his memoir that the beer, of which they were drinking a lot because of the heat, caused her problems: "Our Lyuda began putting on weight."

Who knows, perhaps the Soviet diplomats, when they saw Pavlichenko in real life or in newspaper photos, may have been anxious that the capricious Western public might start to doubt whether this stout young woman could really crawl for hours on her belly, and sometimes go for several days without food – some of her duels with German snipers, she told people, could last a day or more.

However, enthusiasm for the girl sniper far outweighed any criticism or ridicule. Young Russians like her were currently seen to be saving the world from fascism, so journalists wrote about her enchanting smile, her eyes shining like cold stars in her lovely face, and quoted the bold, witty answers she gave to their tricksy questions.

"Lyudmila was never short of an answer," Pchelintsev noted enviously. "Her education in the history faculty stood her in good stead." She answered directly and vividly, and people remembered her responses. When asked about cosmetics, she retorted, "Who would think of powdering their nose in a war?"[30] As for underwear and the length of her skirt, she replied it was of no interest to her how long her skirt was or whether or not she had silk underwear under it. "This is a Soviet uniform, and I wear it with pride."[31] To the question she was asked in front of a huge audience in Chicago as to why she, a girl, had chosen such a profession, she gave a response which was subsequently to be quoted hundreds, indeed thousands, of times, "Gentlemen, I am twenty-five years old and I have already managed to kill 309 of the fascist invaders. Do you not think, gentlemen, that you have now been hiding behind my back for rather too long?"[32] The crowd froze for a moment, but then exploded in a great roar of approval.

The young people had, of course, found themselves addressing more conservative, even hostile, audiences, for example, on the campus of the University of Pittsburgh.[33] Where the audience was working class, however, the Soviet representatives, and especially Lyudmila, were received rapturously. The U.S., Canada, the United Kingdom . . . meetings, rallies, interviews. The tour lasted two months. From newspaper articles, radio and television interviews, and quotations from Pavlichenko's speeches to U.S., then Canadian, and later English, audiences people were able to gain some idea of this heroic woman's biography.

By now, anyone interested in her story knew that Pavlichenko was twenty-five (in fact she had just turned twenty-six, because she was born on 12 July 1916), that she had completed her schooling while simultaneously working at a factory as a polisher, enjoyed gliding and shooting under the auspices of the quasi-military Osoaviakhim sports association, and had volunteered for the front at the outbreak of war, despite having just one more year of her history course at Kiev University to complete.

She opened her tally as a sniper in August 1941, before twice suffering concussion as well as a minor injury. Despite that, Pavlichenko managed to raise her tally to 187.

After the fall of Odessa, the Independent Maritime Army, of which she was a member, was sent to reinforce the Crimea, and Lyudmila Pavlichenko spent eight months defending Sevastopol. This was where the major events in her career as a sniper occurred. Together with her partner, she destroyed an enemy observation point, trained novice snipers, and regularly fought duels with German snipers. Pavlichenko accounted for thirty-six of them. During one of these duels she lay in the same position for twenty-four hours, stalking a cautious enemy. When, at dawn on the second day, she finally managed to spot and shoot him, Pavlichenko took from the corpse not only his rifle but also his sniper's logbook, which revealed that he had begun his career as a sniper at Dunkirk and that, by the time he met his match in a Russian girl, he had despatched 500 of his opponents' soldiers and officers.

At Sevastopol Lyudmila was again wounded and concussed. In all she had three wounds and four cases of concussion. She was evacuated by submarine to Novorossiysk, where she was hospitalised. Upon her discharge, the military command decided Lyudmila Pavlichenko's life was too valuable to risk, and she was transferred to a sniper school to train others.

Lyudmila Pavlichenko told enthralled Western audiences that the Germans knew of her existence and feared her. They even invited her by loudspeaker to go over to their side, promising to make her an officer and give her chocolates and cakes.[34] She described having to lie motionless in one place for 15–20 hours (even in winter). She described how four marksmen were sent specially to assassinate her, and how she managed to despatch them all. She brought their identification documents and four assault rifles back to Soviet troop positions. She described how the Germans had threatened they would cut her into 309 pieces, one for every enemy soldier she had shot, when they caught her.[35]

In America the delegation was a sensation. Paul Robeson sang for them, Woody Guthrie wrote a song about Lyudmila Pavlichenko, and she recalled how the great Charlie Chaplin, "in front of everybody, carefully sat me down on a sofa and began kissing my fingers. 'It's just incredible,' he kept saying, 'that this little hand has killed Nazis, has scythed them down by the hundred, without missing, at close range.'"[36]

In Britain, where a year and a half previously nothing of the sort would have been imaginable, the Soviet delegation, and particularly Lyudmila, found a no less rapturous welcome waiting.

On 6 November 1942 the *Derby Evening Telegraph* described Lyudmila Pavlichenko inspecting a company of the Home Guard in London. "Wearing the uniform of a Red Army sniper, Lieutenant Lyudmila Pavlichenko today jumped out of a car in front of the Ministry of Information. Without more ado, she inspected a Home Guard company drawn up in her honour . . . She marched down the line in her high Russian boots, periodically stopping to take someone's rifle, draw back the bolt and look down the barrel. When photographers asked her to aim it, she spun round towards them and took aim at the leading photographer."

"Girl Sniper Receives Three Gifts from Brits", reported the *New York Times* on 23 November, describing another rapturous reception accorded the heroine by an audience of 2,000 women.[37] A girl from an arms factory presented her with a revolver to use against the enemy. An Oxford student gave her history books she would find useful in her studies after the war, and a housewife gave her a silver teapot as a symbol of life in peacetime. During the meeting, more than £350 was collected for medicine and bandages for Russia. The pupils from a home for disabled children, having no money, donated their collection of rare butterflies.

There were, of course, many people who were concerned about the morality of exalting a sniper, even if the sniper was a young and extremely brave woman. What nobody doubted was the veracity of her story. The times were such that neither in the U.S.S.R. nor in the West did anybody ask awkward questions. Today, however, they are somewhat harder to avoid.[38]

In its October 1942 issue, *New Advance*, a Canadian magazine for young people, published an article by Jesse Storey, a delegate to the International Student Assembly. Writing about the Soviet delegation, Storey said,

What a remarkable woman Red Army Lieutenant Lyudmila Pavlichenko is! I learned an interesting fact that helps us to better understand her anti-fascist temper at a breakfast in the White House which Mrs Roosevelt gave for the Canadian delegation. We were in the reception room, chatting casually with Mrs Roosevelt, when she suddenly said she had received the Soviet delegation there the day before. One of the questions Mrs Roosevelt asked Lyudmila was, how could she, a woman, bring herself to shoot at Germans after seeing their faces in her sights? American women find that difficult to understand! Lieutenant Pavlichenko replied tersely, "I have seen with my own eyes my husband and child killed. I was next to them."

This story is quoted here from Pchelintsev's memoirs.[39] Did he know that was untrue? Pavlichenko told another Western reporter after the war that she had recently had a son. That too is far from the truth. In 1946, Pavlichenko's son, Rostislav, was fourteen years old. Lyudmila gave birth to the boy at the age of fifteen, and her marriage to a student called Alexey Pavlichenko, who was older than her, immediately collapsed. As a result of the scandal the family had to move from the town of Belaya Tserkov' to Kiev. The boy was raised by his grandmother, allowing Lyudmila to work, study and go off to fight. Pavlichenko's biographers studiously avoid all mention of Rostislav, who lived an unhappy life in the shadow of his famous mother. He does not fit into the edifying story of the girl sniper.[40] Even the guidebook to the Novodevichiy Cemetery, where Rostislav Pavlichenko is buried next to his mother, omits any mention of how they were related.[41]

Russians are superstitious. They believe, for instance, that if you lie that are ill, you will assuredly fall sick. As for the death of one's child, no one would dream of lying about that. The Canadian journalist may have made a mistake, or Pchelintsev may have misunderstood him, but other statements and stories of Lyudmila Pavlichenko also give rise to serious doubts.

What are we to make of the tale she told of how she regarded the 300th German she had killed as a birthday present to herself? Lyudmila Pavlichenko's birthday was 12 July, but Sevastopol had already been captured by the Germans at the end of June, and even the main Soviet news agency, the Informbyuro admitted the city's fall in its bulletin on 3 July. According to Soviet sources, Pavlichenko was evacuated with serious injuries, but no wounded soldiers were evacuated from Sevastopol after mid-June. Pavlichenko herself in her memoirs, published for some reason only in 2015, mentions that she was evacuated on 22 June 1945.[42] Even if she and her biographers have got the date of her injury and evacuation wrong and she did indeed give herself a birthday present of her 300th enemy soldier on 12 July, when did she find the time to kill another nine? If we are to believe Pavlichenko's account, German propagandists shouted through a loudspeaker that they would cut her into 309 pieces ("Which meant they knew my tally!" she claimed). She must logically have remained at the front long enough after her birthday for the Germans to have discovered her tally.[43] But where was this all taking place if Sevastopol had long since fallen?

Celebrity came to Lyudmila Pavlichenko suddenly, and only after her personal tally had supposedly reached nearly 200 enemy soldiers killed. It has to be said that the story, as related in the very first publication about Pavlichenko in the national Soviet press, is odd. The article was in the form of a letter from a certain Sergeant Grigorov, who had suddenly decided to tell the country about the exploits of the woman who had achieved the highest personal tally of all Soviet snipers. Why had no reporter been sent out earlier? In her memoirs, Pavlichenko says that at that time no one really knew what snipers did on the front line, and that in any case they were not very cheerful and talkative people, unlike, for example, machine-gunners. Nina Onilova, a machine-gunner in the same regiment, had a lot written about her.[44]

In his letter, Sergeant Grigorov described the following episode: Lyudmila spotted a German observer hiding in some bushes and started to stalk him. He was an experienced soldier and it was difficult to get him in her sights. She waited. First, the German showed her a helmet on a stick, but the "keen-eyed Young Communist League member" did not fall for that. Next, "a domestic cat suddenly walked along the path. This was unusual. An inexperienced marksman might have been distracted, started staring at the cat, and enabled the observer in the meantime to do his work." Needless to say, the Young Communist League member did not fall for the trick with the cat either. But the story was not yet over. There next appeared "a funny dog that stood up on its hind legs". Not even that distracted the sniper. (This appears to be the only known instance of cats and dogs being used in this way against a sniper.) Finally, "straight out of the ground there rose a cunningly made effigy of a fascist soldier in full uniform and with a rifle. That was informative: the effigy could not have popped up by itself, it could only have been raised by a human being. That told her there was a German here, and that meant he would shortly become visible." Finally there was the glint of binoculars and Pavlichenko "smoothly pulled the trigger". The German's "nose pecked forward and he rolled downhill."[45]

Oleg Kaminsky, a Russian historian, undertook the first serious research into the veracity of the tales of the supersniper. He found some oddities in the stories of her earliest days at the front. Pavlichenko's account of the fighting in Odessa describes a completely different district from the one in which, according to the documents, her regiment was fighting. Lyudmila Pavlichenko claims that General Ivan Petrov personally ordered her to select and lead a platoon of snipers.[46] In 1941 and 1942, however, the Red Army did not yet have any sniper platoons. Moreover, by the time Pavlichenko's front-line career was over she held the rank only of sergeant major, which would have precluded commanding anything larger than a squad. Pavlichenko also told the tale of how the Germans once sent in a whole platoon of their snipers to take on her platoon, and how a duel ensued between the Soviet and German snipers.[47] This is implausible: the Germans at that time also had only lone snipers, and not many of those; there could be no question of whole platoons of them.

Determined to solve the riddle of Lyudmila Pavlichenko, Kaminsky turned to the awards list of her unit and made a surprising discovery.

Pavlichenko, who had supposedly "shot 187 fascists", had not even been decorated for the fighting at Odessa. How was that possible, given that, in order to raise morale, not only soldiers who had distinguished themselves in some way, but also cooks, clerks, and artists in front-line brigades were decorated? Snipers were awarded a medal for ten enemy soldiers killed or wounded, and an Order of the Red Star for twenty. Raising your tally to seventy-five was enough to secure you the title of Hero of the Soviet Union. Why did Pavlichenko get nothing? During the defence of Sevastopol, she was said to have raised her total to 260 in just six months. For this, she was finally only awarded a medal "For Merit in Battle", and her first Order of Lenin only much later when, after the fall of Sevastopol, she was in hospital. In her memoirs Pavlichenko mentions the award to Nina Onilova and says she was not envious, because all that really mattered was that the enemy soldiers she and Nina had killed would never fight again. As regards Vladimir Pchelintsev, who was fighting on a different front but at the same time as Pavlichenko and whose tally was only half her own, Pavlichenko explains his success (rank of senior lieutenant and the star of a Hero of the Soviet Union) as being due to the fact that he was a man and, unlike her, was good at staying on the right side of the authorities.

Why did this woman, about whom, until the fall of Sevastopol, nobody knew anything, become famous so precipitately? Was it because the top brass, who until then had overlooked her spectacular successes in battle, suddenly came to their senses? A more likely explanation is that the defence of Sevastopol, during which there were many instances of genuinely outstanding heroism, had ended in disaster. The Independent Maritime Army, which Lyudmila Pavlichenko never mentioned in her interviews, ceased to exist after Sevastopol: it had been annihilated. Forced back by the Germans to the sea, people resisted desperately, expecting help to arrive at any moment and that they would be evacuated by ship. None came. A handful of people managed to fight their way through to the mountains. More than 100,000 were wounded, died, or were taken prisoner. That disaster, just one of many in the first year of the war, further undermined morale in the army and the Soviet population. Heroic role models were needed, including women, because at just this moment the U.S.S.R.'s leaders, recognising the impossibility of fully replacing the huge losses incurred, adopted a policy of mass conscription of women into the army.[48] In order to give the name of Pavlichenko more substance and lustre, she was finally, on 16 July 1942, awarded, not the gold star of a Hero of the Soviet Union, which was the highest Soviet decoration, but the second highest – the Order of Lenin. She became a Hero of the Soviet Union only after the tour of the United States and Great Britain.

If the biographers are to be believed, Pavlichenko was evacuated from Sevastopol (by submarine!) because of a serious facial injury. She wrote herself that it was to her cheekbone.[49] But why, in that case, is there no trace in the photos taken during her tour abroad, only a couple of months later, of even a scar on her smooth young face? Why do we never read in the memoirs of her fellow soldiers in the regiment anything about Lyudmila Pavlichenko? It is certainly true that nearly all of them were killed, but surely a handful at least who had fought with her in battle must have survived? Those who fought in the Maritime Army, some even in the regiment where she served, write about the heroic reconnaissance of Maria Baida;[50] about Nina Onilova,[51] awarded two Orders of the Red Banner and, posthumously, the star of a Hero of the Soviet Union; about Zoya Medvedeva,[52] who followed in the footsteps of Onilova; about the scout Annushka,[53] who was captured and tortured by the Germans; but of Pavlichenko there is no mention. Moreover, according to Pavlichenko's biographer, it was the appearance of memoirs of participants in the defence of Odessa and Sevastopol in the second half of the 1970s that prompted her to start work on her own.[54] Was that perhaps because her name was nowhere to be found in the accounts of commanders and those of her regimental comrades?

Why did Pavlichenko almost never show off her shooting skills during the tour of America? In his memoirs, Pchelintsev writes that, wherever they went, people could not wait to see how well Red Army snipers could shoot. In all the arms factories supplying weapons to the Soviet Union they were given firearms and urged to pull the trigger. In every case, and very willingly, this was done by Pchelintsev. He was a dazzling marksman and had been a sniping enthusiast even before the war. He tells of one instance: "One time in Washington, the situation made it impossible just to laugh it off, and plainly one of us was going to have to defend the honour of the uniform. Of course, the reporters wanted Lyudmila to demonstrate her skill. We had some difficulty persuading them it would be more appropriate for me to do so."[55] Pchelintsev only once mentions Lyudmila shooting during the visit, and describes her performance as "slapdash".[56]

I suspect these questions will remain unanswered for ever. As if Lyudmila Pavlichenko had not confused the issue sufficiently, her biographers duly piled in, even mentioning her "sniper's record book". If such a book exists, it is a forgery, because they appeared in the Red Army only in 1943, when her sniping career was already over.

Pavlichenko's memoirs read like a novel. Before the war, a young woman completed the training course at the Osoaviakhim sniper school in Kiev, having previously been a member of her factory's shooting club. (After her first attempt, the head of the club told her she had an exceptional talent.)[57] She went off to the front as a volunteer and soon proved an excellent sniper. Sometimes with a platoon, sometimes with a partner, and sometimes entirely on her own, she went hunting in no-man's-land, but would also venture far behind enemy lines, killing soldiers and officers, enemy headquarters staff and snipers. Almost every tale about another successful "hunt" concludes with a description of Sniper Pavlichenko, alone or with colleagues, searching the bodies of dead enemies and enemy premises for trophies, apparently wholly unconcerned that anyone might still be alive in there or that the Germans might send in reinforcements.[58] Such descriptions are rarely found in any other stories about the operations of other snipers, and neither is the detail that, when inspecting the bodies of victims, this girl sniper would identify her own kills from the signature bullet wound she inflicted on the bridge of the nose or in the temple.[59]

Her relations with the powers that be figure prominently in the book. If her memoirs are to be believed, Pavlichenko was greatly admired by General Petrov, who gave her an individually inscribed sniper rifle and appointed her to command a platoon.[60] But her connection with Petrov was the least of it. Before they set off for America, Pavlichenko and the other delegates were given words of encouragement by Comrade Stalin personally (something the other participants, for some reason, do not mention). When he asked if there was anything else they needed for the journey, Pavlichenko replied that she would need an English textbook and dictionary. She would want to know the Allies "as closely as she knew the enemy".[61] Evidently the books she was given by the great man helped her dramatically – in her memoirs Pavlichenko says she often spoke English during the trip, something not mentioned by any of the reporters, Western or Soviet.[62] She would doubtless have needed her English for intimate conversations with America's First Lady. Pavlichenko tells how she fell into the water while sailing on a boat on the pond at the Roosevelts' estate, to which the delegation was invited as a sign of special favour. Eleanor Roosevelt invited her to her bedroom, and personally cut down and hemmed pyjamas for her while Pavlichenko was taking a shower and drying her clothes (for some reason she had nothing to change into). The president himself arrived in a wheelchair, having come to his wife's part of the house because she was late for dinner. He found the two women chatting like old friends. At the sight of him, the Russian sniper, whose clothes were still drying, jumped to her feet, clutching a towel to her loins, and blurted, "I do beg your pardon, Mr Roosevelt!"[63]

Needless to say, on her return from America the famous sniper found herself in Stalin's office once again, but this time on her own. She had been invited as someone familiar with the Roosevelts. ("'Tell me what kind of people they are . . .' the commander-in-chief asked Lyudmila, taking a long drag on his pipe.")[64] When Lyudmila Pavlichenko asked permission, at the end of the conversation, to return to the front, the Leader took a pencil and did some calculations on a piece of paper to show the sniper that she could do the country much more good by staying at the rear and training new fighters.

After the war, Lyudmila Pavlichenko graduated from Kiev University but did not become a historian, neither did she become an instructor in marksmanship. She worked in the General Headquarters of the navy, and, later, in the War Veterans Committee, evidently without making any great impression at either. She smoked incessantly and, it was rumoured, drank too much.[65]

When she went to visit a friend, Lyudmila would sometimes tell her schoolboy son stories about the war, including one that invariably horrified him. In order to set up a sniper position where she could be well camouflaged, Sniper Pavlichenko would sometimes crawl over the battlefield and pull dead bodies into a heap. She would then take up position behind them. Sometimes someone's dead hand would slip on to her face, and Pavlichenko would move it back.[66] I am not even sure how to comment on this.

All the records of the Maritime Army, in which Lyudmila Pavlichenko served, were lost when the army was destroyed. No documents have survived confirming Pavlichenko's tally or even that she was listed as a sniper by her regiment. Almost all we know about her is based on her own words, which are full of contradictions.

We could go through other stories about the most famous Soviet female sniper, but it is more rewarding to talk about others: women whose names are to be found in the records of their divisions, in lists with numbers in their "tallies", most often ones or twos. They did not go probing no-man's-land, did not climb trees or make raids behind enemy lines. Taking up position before dawn at an embrasure in the trenches, they would spend hours peering, with eyes watering from the strain, through binoculars and the sights on their rifle at the German front, waiting for just a single victim to stray into their sights. That kill was worth the long hours of waiting in frost or heat, rain or blazing sun, thirsty and hungry. "Kill the German!" Soviet propaganda ordered them, in the words of the leading political writer of the time, Ilya Ehrenburg. They saw no other way of saving their country and getting back their normal lives.

Chapter 3

"Look at the family she's from. And we're just ordinary!"

By the autumn of 1943, Lida Larionova, a sniper on the Volkhov Front near Leningrad, although already a seasoned infantrywoman, had killed only one German. This dark-haired eighteen-year-old from the north of Russia, with her high cheekbones, was one of hundreds of women trained on sniper courses while continuing to do their "day job" on the front line. Most of them were from the Leningrad and Volkhov Fronts where, until spring 1943, the situation was often one of stalemate, so there was little excuse not to train.

It is in this kind of static, trench warfare, when both sides are building up their forces by remaining on the defensive, that snipers come into their own. They harry the enemy relentlessly, keeping him constantly on the alert, unable to raise his head above the parapet of the trenches, afraid to run across open ground. Without inflicting major damage, because losses as a result of sniper fire are rarely substantial, snipers wear enemy soldiers down psychologically.

In the Red Army, the sniper movement began in the darkest days of the war, in autumn 1941 on the Leningrad Front. It was not a policy launched from above, but devised by marksmen like Vladimir Pchelintsev who had trained on shooting ranges before the war and now saw an opportunity to do something, at least, to unsettle the Germans, who were subjecting Leningrad and its defenders to a merciless siege. It was not long before the top brass saw the value of the movement, and a large-scale campaign was mounted in both the national and army press and among the troops. It became fashionable to train as a sniper. Successful snipers were the pride of their units.

Vladimir Pchelintsev is considered to have been one of the pioneers. A year after opening his tally as a sniper at Nevskaya Dubrovka, Pchelintsev was in New York, thinking back to that autumn day in 1941 when "the faltering voice of the battalion commander whispered, 'Give it to him!'" The German had come down to the Neva for a bucket of water and was 400–450 metres away, a distance from which, on a firing range, Vladimir was guaranteed to hit the target. Now, though, when he had the German in his sights, his hands were trembling. And then he "understood with total clarity what the problem was: in full view of everyone, he was about to kill a human being." Ordering himself to cast off such sentimentality and remember all the many, many Soviet people he had seen killed and wounded since the beginning of the war, Pchelintsev fired.[67] A second German ran to the aid of the man who had fallen, and the battalion commander now shouted at the top of his voice, "Get the second one too! D'you hear me, Pchelintsev, hit the second one!" Vladimir soon found himself the centre of attention, with reporters turning up to his unit. His letter to Vezhlivtsev, another sniper, challenging him to a contest, and Vezhlivtsev's reply were printed in the front-line newspaper. Other snipers piled in. Now there were articles about socialist competition between snipers. (In the U.S.S.R., "socialist competition" was encouraged in every sphere of life.) Snipers shared experiences and told their stories. The front-line newspapers reprinted each other's reports and the national newspapers reprinted those of the front-line newspapers. The movement spread. Soon snipers' rallies were being held, intended to boost the morale of the troops.

"While the German army continued until 1940 to use the old, pre-war optical sights, the Red Army developed a modern sniper rifle and trained huge numbers of snipers. Russian snipers acted alone, as a sniper and observer team, as sniper pairs, and even in whole companies of up to sixty snipers."[68] The German sniper who wrote that said his Russian counterparts caused the Germans a great deal of trouble at the beginning of the war, and in 1942, when the war had become more static as the German advance slowed down and both sides spent long intervals of time in defensive positions, they became a real menace. Perhaps he was exaggerating, but the passage gives a sense of the fear Russian snipers instilled in the enemy.

As the sniper movement developed, marksmen, of whom, thanks to Osoaviakhim, there was a plentiful supply in the army, saw they could play an important part in the war effort and become a military elite, on a level with pilots and tank crews. They could be confident of being provided with the equipment they needed, which consisted of no more than a sniper's rifle. (The most popular model was the Mosin, which had a telescopic sight providing fourfold magnification.)

At the end of 1941, 48-year-old Nina Petrova from Leningrad finally got her opportunity to work on her speciality in the war. A physical education and sports instructor for the Spartak sports club, a Master of Sport who had trained sharpshooters, she was sent to the front as a nurse. For a long time the army was reluctant to take her on even in that capacity because of her age. Petrova, however, finding herself close to the front line and defending her hometown, was just waiting for an opportunity to prove that, even though approaching fifty, as someone who before the war had drawn crowds of onlookers at shooting galleries, she should properly be employed at the front as a sniper.

She eventually got her hands on a sniper's rifle, and the commander permitted her to go "hunting" in her spare time. A nurse in a field hospital has little enough of that, but the commanders finally woke up to the asset they had once they saw her tally begin to mount. From then on until her death in 1945, Petrova ran front-line sniper courses, took her trainees out to shoot at the front and, of course, went hunting herself.[69]

Thousands of rank-and-file soldiers who never trained with Osoaviakhim before the war, trained at the front and aspired to being given a sniper's rifle, production of which was steadily stepped up as the conflict wore on. Lida Larionova, a simple country girl, who until recently had not known the meaning of the word "sniper", also mastered the profession. She had not completed her secondary schooling or been to sniper school, and she knew nothing at all about ballistics but, like Nina Petrova's trainees, learned everything on a course at the front.

Lida was called up in September 1942. Her village in Vologda Province was poverty-stricken as only villages in the north of Russia can be, where the soil is poor and the summer is very short. Bread had long been a luxury, and there was virtually nothing to eat but potatoes and turnips. Seeing Lida on her way to the army, her mother cooked potatoes in their skins and gave her dried potato and dried turnips (they also prepared these in larger quantities and forwarded them to the front in lieu of tax). Her mother wrapped it all up in a cloth and put the bundle in a basket along with Lida's only decent dress. She had nothing else to give.[70] Lida's younger sister, Afanasiya, known to the family as Faya, was in her early teens, but walked the thirty kilometres to the enlistment office in Babaevo with her sister. Their aunt was waiting for them there and accompanied them to the army office. She was crying. Faya was puzzled by her tears because she was sure the war would soon be over and Lida would come home a heroine. In fact, she envied her.

Faya also desperately wanted to get to the front, but was too young. She was, however, old enough for the "labour front". Babaevo was on the front line, and Faya, who was only fourteen, along with others her age, was taken to work to support it. She loved school, but now that had to wait. Teenagers were sent to fell and transport timber, which fuelled the small steam locomotives serving the front. The stokers on the locomotives were also teenagers. They slept on the floor, and were so badly fed that the emaciated boys and girls soon became exhausted. They were sometimes issued black soap, but washed only their hair, saving soap by washing the rest of themselves with oatmeal. Faya had felt boots, but they were patched and had holes. The bombing was terrible, and caused the horses to bolt. She remembered one time she was lying on the ground among the birches, bombs were falling, and she said over and over again, "Lord, let me get through this!" There were a lot of wolves that year and they were just as terrifying. The horses would also bolt if they scented a wolf, and a chill would run through the young girl's heart. Faya hated the wolves more than the Germans. When she saw Germans at close quarters, her main emotion was pity. There were so many German prisoners in Babaevo during that first year of war, and they were totally unprepared for the Russian winter, skeletally thin, ill, and with only "thin hats and coats". The children brought them cranberries, which the Germans, who gave the children tobacco in return, ate to stave off scurvy. When the children brought the fruit, the Germans would queue quietly, without any pushing and shoving. Many of them were to find their last resting place in a large German cemetery nearby.[71]

On the day they were to leave for the army, there were many girls from surrounding villages at the army office, from Babaevo and even Borisovo, fifty kilometres away. They were informed they would be going to Vologda to be trained as nurses. When they arrived at the Volkhov Front, there was a lull in the fighting and Lida quickly got used to her new surroundings and role. There were not many wounded, and there was time for singing and dancing. The young accordionist was a good musician. The main song he played was "Katyusha", as well as more recent favourites such as "The Dugout" and "Your Blue Shawl". Lida was embarrassed that the girls from the towns knew all the steps for these tunes, while she knew only Russian folk dances.

Taking advantage of the relative calm, the soldiers were given a lot of political indoctrination, and also offered courses for learning new military skills. The most popular were for machine-gunners and snipers. Lida wanted to learn a new profession, so she applied for the sniper course and was accepted. It was short but intensive, and started with drill.

They seemed to do a lot of running, and also had to jump over a skipping rope, but their main occupation was shooting. By now it was May, warming up, but they were still in greatcoats as the supply units always took time issuing uniforms for the new season. They learned to shoot standing up and lying down, with the target set at 100 or 200 metres, and often moving. This was even more difficult, because you had to make swift calculations about angles and speed. She was not very good at first, but was taken in hand by the young commander when he found out they were from the same part of the country. Lida thought he was very nice, and wondered whether or not he was married. "Neighbour," he promised, "I'll teach you to shoot a fly in the eye."[72]

Anya Sheinova was on the course with Lida, and she too was at the front as a nurse. They were put into a pair and trained together. This was the standard practice for the Red Army. One partner in the pair carried out observation and covered their partner, while the other one shot. Partners swapped roles on a regular basis: one's eyes quickly got tired from observing intently. Lida and Anya started going out "hunting" together, seeking potential victims each time but afraid to pull the trigger. On the day that Lida did eventually open her tally she found it very difficult to kill the German who appeared in her sights. He was quite close and, as she had been taught, Lida aimed at his head. She knew that it was only when the distance was greater that you should aim for the chest, to give yourself a better chance of hitting the target. He was young. "I saw him slump forward," Lidia Larionova recalled many decades later. Horrified, she jumped out of the trench and ran all the way back to the medical unit. "I've killed a person!" she screamed. The sergeant who had sent the two of them to that position laughed and pulled her cap down over her eyes. "You've killed an enemy," the nurses said, congratulating her, but Lida sobbed her heart out.

Lida wrote home that she had a warm, new fur jacket, felt boots and padded trousers and that they were well fed. To ragged, hungry Faya it felt as if her sister had won the lottery. While there was no fighting, Lida and her friends even managed to get their hair permed in a small local town. But then there came the offensive – the operation that finally broke the siege of Leningrad and liberated the Leningrad province. When the Leningrad and Volkhov Fronts linked up, "We had other things to think about than perms." In the offensive Lida once again became a nurse, on the order of her commander. She and Anya found themselves in the middle of the fighting at Myasnoy Bor, a village whose ominous name meant Flesh Woods and where, in summer 1942, 2 Assault Army had perished in the encirclement. Now, though, in 1943, Lida was with troops liberating the settlement. She remembered how young some of the boys were, seventeen-year-olds called up to the army earlier that year. They were raw, inexperienced, and were all killed.

Lida was grateful to their commanders, who kept women away from the thick of the fray. She knew that if she had been at the front throughout the war, she would never have come back alive – to attack with the infantry meant certain death. Nikolai Nikulin, a gunner fighting in that area, remembered a girl sniper just like Lida who lost her life during the offensive: "We ran on. A place where the trenches crossed. From down below came a frightened voice: 'Run as fast as you can! This area is under fire.' We went on even further. We were worn out and had to slow down. In one of the trenches we saw a corpse that had lost its legs, with red stumps instead of knees. Long hair, a familiar face. 'Look, that's the girl sniper from our neighbouring company. The one who sang so well! Damn!' the soldier ahead of us exclaimed as he leapt over the body."[73]

"Prepare to receive wounded!" Lida and Anya were ordered during the fighting at a station in Novgorod Province. Anya, who considered herself a sniper, not a nurse, just said, "I'm going to the front line," and left. Nobody disciplined her afterwards. Lida was more obedient and continued to tend the wounded. She swam across the River Velikaya under fire, and had to lie flat, unable to raise her head during intense bombing somewhere in Lithuania, where they were forced to lie in the snow almost all day. She would probably have found killing her second German less traumatic than the first, but did not go back to being a sniper. That was not for her, Lida decided. Women aren't meant to kill.

The Soviet military authorities disagreed, however, and in May 1943 decreed that large numbers of girls should be trained as snipers at a special college.[74]

Anya Mulatova was drafted into the army in summer 1943. Her conscription papers were delivered and, unlike some other girls she knew, she made no attempt to hide. To begin with she was not sure why she was called up when others were not, but when she saw that no papers were sent to Larisa, the daughter of the director of the Zagotzerno[*] grain mill, she drew her own conclusions. "Well, look at the family she's from," Anyuta said to herself. "And we're just ordinary . . ."

In the enlistment office, to which she went with a friend from her village of Simanshchina in Penza Province, they were told about a recent appeal from the Young Communist League Central Committee to girls of their age, and given to understand that even though they had been conscripted, they could nevertheless consider themselves to be volunteering, which is what was entered in their papers. For the rest of her life Anya duly said she had volunteered.

Anya Mulatova had completed ninth grade at school in Simanshchina and was very keen to complete tenth. She loved her school, but it was requisitioned as a hospital. She and her classmates helped to retrieve the pupils' desks, the teacher's desk, and the globe of the Earth, which was the sum total of the school's equipment. The Germans were at the gates of Moscow, and very soon casualties were arriving at the school. For a time there was even a wagon at the station with wounded soldiers who had nowhere else to go. Anya and her friends went to read letters to them and sing songs, and did what they could to help the nursing staff. The injured soldiers (many of whom had "serious, terrible wounds") greatly appreciated their visits.

---

[*] Soviet organisation dealing with the procurement of grain.

Anya sang well. She had a plain face with small green eyes and a nose that was not exactly refined, but she was tall and well proportioned, and had a mane of curly brown hair that she formed into ringlets, white skin and rosy cheeks. Many of the wounded found her pretty. Like other girls, she had her own special patient to look after, Vladimir Shevelyov from Moscow. This official initiative, for the civilians to take care of a particular wounded soldier, became very popular. They wrote to each other for a while afterwards and, when she was sent to sniper school, she visited his mother and aunt in Moscow.[75]

The school ceased to be used as a hospital but was not reopened and, to help support her family, Anya worked at the collective farm as a bookkeeper. It was not she who saved the family from starvation, though, but her sister, Liza, who worked in the Zagotzerno office. Lisa allocated some of the oil cake waste (what remained after oil was squeezed from sunflower seeds) to feed poultry, and some she took home. The family sifted the waste, pounded it in a wooden mortar, and baked it into flatbreads. These loaves, together with their own potatoes and pumpkins, were their staple diet.

Anya's younger brother, Vladimir, suffered most from hunger. He was a growing boy who, having heard about pilots delivering food to people who needed it, longed to become one himself and drop a whole sack of flour down to his family.

Anya did not recall any very elaborate farewell as she left for the army. There were no tears from her mother, and in all the commotion her departure passed almost unnoticed. Her mother did not know she was enlisting as a sniper, and if she had it would have meant nothing to her because she was completely illiterate and could not read the newspapers. She had too much work on her hands to spare any time for crying. She started worrying about her daughter only later, when she received her letters from the front, which Anya's siblings read to her: "Dear Mother, It is night and I am standing in a trench. How I miss my warm, soft bed."

When she heard she was going to sniper school, Anya was neither particularly pleased nor dismayed. If she was to be a sniper, fine. Quite what that involved she did not know, but Anya decided that what would be would be, and that what she was told to do, she would do. She wouldn't have minded being a signaller. The only thing she did not want to be was a nurse, because she was afraid of blood.

Girls from all over the U.S.S.R. were brought to the Central Women's Sniper Training School, which was modelled on existing sniper courses and opened at Veshnyaki in Moscow Province. Among them were many very committed patriots, and not a few, like Klava Panteleyeva, had surreptitiously added a year to their age to get into the army. Others, like Tonya Zakharova, had seen young men, whom they had married just before the war, disappear off to the front, and were eager to go there themselves to be closer to them. Most of the girls, however, had been conscripted and had no choice in the matter.

One of these involuntary volunteers was Kalya Petrova. The war had already started when she completed her secondary education in the industrial town of Lunino, near Penza. She wanted to be a German teacher like her mother, but the war decided otherwise. The main priority was to stave off starvation, and Kalya decided to work for the time being in an arms factory where there were decent rations, and think again later. Her father and sister were already at the front and her mother, in order to feed herself, was selling off her possessions.

Life at the factory was hellish. The food was terrible, and the aunt she was living with in Penza was unwilling to cook the food that Kalya had received on her rations coupons. They were given almost no days off, but when one was suddenly allowed, her mother went to extraordinary lengths to feed her daughter properly. When she had eaten until she could eat no more, Kalya rolled on the floor with a terrible stomach ache. It was no easier for the other girls (all the workers at the factory were girls), but Kalya was one of the first to rebel. Having put up with the life for a year, she simply ran away. Her mother was horrified. The secret police had long held suspicions about their family: Kalya's mother was a merchant's daughter, her husband had been a lieutenant in the tsarist army. Both categories were considered highly suspicious by the N.K.V.D. and constantly risked arrest and imprisonment. In the 1930s both parents had often been called in for questioning. The family lived in constant fear. What might happen now Kalya's mother could not imagine; people working in arms factories were considered to have been mobilised, and to walk out was tantamount to desertion. Kalya knew a girl who had been sent to prison for doing the same thing, but decided she could put up with it no longer. Her mother thought of a solution. She went to a former student of hers who was now working at the enlistment centre and asked for her daughter to be accepted as a volunteer. Kalya Petrova, who knew nothing whatever about shooting and had never had the slightest interest in the sport, was sent off to train as a sniper.[76]

"During the war years, the Young Communist League Central Committee conducted seventy-three youth mobilisation campaigns. Of the 800,000 young people they sent to the armed forces, 400,000 were girls," official publications proudly declared.[77] Now that Soviet myths have been debunked, we know that many of these young women were not in fact volunteers. Though this does not detract from the debt of gratitude their country owes them, it is worth remembering that many who were conscripted in those years and sent to work as signallers, snipers and anti-aircraft gunners could have made just as significant a contribution to the cause in the rear. Who can say how many children were unable to go to school during the war because there were no teachers in the villages?

In 1942, Klava Shilo was a schoolgirl, one of six children in a family her mother raised in direst poverty. All her life her heart was pained when she thought back to February of that year, when her favourite teacher, Lyubov Alexandrovna, was seen off to the front. The young teacher had been evacuated from Kursk to Klava's village of Yeginsai just before the arrival of the Germans, leaving her mother and sisters to suffer under the occupation. One time, right there in the classroom, overcome with sadness, she wept as she put her hand on Klava's head and said she looked just like the little sister she had left behind with the Germans. Shortly afterwards, the teacher was called up; that Sunday the pupils of Yeginsai came to see her on her way as she was driven on a sledge through the village. Klava's mother had knitted warm mittens for the teacher. She asked them to halt the sledge, and invited Lyubov Alexandrovna into their house. An oil lamp lit the room where her mother was cutting up a pumpkin to cook for the next day. Klava's brothers and sisters were sitting round the table nibbling pieces of raw pumpkin. The teacher was delighted with the mittens and said thank you very warmly. As she got up to leave, she reached out towards the heap of raw pumpkin and asked if she could take a little. Klava's mother scooped a mug of *kvasha** out of the pot for her to drink. She wrapped some grits made from maize and grain husks in a piece of newspaper, and put the raw pumpkin right in her new mittens. When she looked down at the teacher's feet and saw that all she had to wear that harsh winter was a pair of ordinary shoes under galoshes, her eyes filled with tears, but she just had nothing more to give. When Klava's mother came out to see Lyubov off, though, she brought some homespun sackcloth and tucked it round Lyubov's legs, stuffing the improvised garment with hay. Later, the teacher wrote to tell them she was at Stalingrad, but after that there were no more letters. "The war swept away all trace of her," Klava's mother sighed. [78]

Chapter 4

"Mummy, why are there all uncles and only one auntie?"

As they left to join the army, the prospective snipers took only their oldest clothes with them. They knew they would have to throw them away at some stage. After several days in quarantine, the new cadets were led to the bathhouse by women in uniform, the section commanders. The girls

* Fermented mixture of rye or buckwheat flour with water and malt.

were dressed in whatever had come to hand and had absolutely no idea how to march. They had shawls on their heads, and boots, half-boots, or even ordinary shoes on their feet. Yulia Zhukova thought they looked like gypsies. They broke ranks, and talked loudly to each other as they walked along, sharing impressions of their new situation. Nobody paid any attention to the commanders, who were struggling to maintain at least some semblance of order.[79]

Local women were standing on the pavements, looking on pityingly as the future snipers passed. Some of them were keening, or made the sign of the cross over the girls, but most just stood there silently. Many of the girls pulled off their hats, scarves or mittens as they walked along and threw them to the crowd, not wanting to waste them when someone else could make good use of them. They were told that they would get their army uniforms after washing at the bathhouse. Some of the girls held on to their warm things, and were wise to do so: woollen socks and mittens came in very handy at the front. A red scarf Sasha Shlyakhova kept as a reminder of home, though, was to compromise her camouflage and cost her her life.[80] At the bathhouse their army uniforms were waiting, and they were "a right spectacle" as they tried to find items the right size.[81] There was also "a whole brigade of hairdressers" waiting to cut their hair short. Anya Mulatova felt a pang of regret when her locks were cut off and fell to the floor like heavy sausages, but took it in her stride. Goodbye then, sausages. Klava Panteleyeva just found her comrades' and her own new look comical: their boys' haircuts, with a short forelock, and then the men's uniforms, which were too big for them, made them look like clowns. On the day of the shearing, Klava's partner, Marusya Chigvintseva, was ill and escaped the cropping. When they were marched through the streets of Podolsk, some children standing at the roadside shouted, "Mummy, why are there all uncles and only one auntie?"[82]

Anya Mulatova found herself in the second cohort of the Central Women's Sniper Training School. With over 700 trainees, it was the largest of the three cohorts that had studied at the school. The first cohort had graduated and had been sent to the front in June 1943. There were rumours that an entire sniper platoon, thirty-three girls, had drowned when their launch sank on Lake Ladoga.[83] That summer, girls were being sent to the school from all over the U.S.S.R.: municipal enlistment offices selected those with excellent eyesight, giving priority to any who already had shooting practice, and sent them to Veshnyaki in groups of around ten. Not all were accepted on arrival: there was another commission to examine them at the school. And of the twelve "keen-eyed girls in good health" who left Dzhambul in Kazakhstan with Klava Loginova, only nine were selected. The rest were sent to specialise in other areas and were upset: they believed they had been specially chosen for the course as active Young Communist League members with experience of sharpshooting.[84]

There was nowhere suitable at the sniper school for a shooting range so a new location had to be found. The students spent the summer camping in the village of Amerevo, some of them living in a shed, while others, like Anya Mulatova, lived in tents in groups of ten or eleven. Anya made friends with her new colleagues in the company, tall girls, "Queens" like herself. The girl snipers were grouped by height from the outset, and some of the companies immediately acquired an unofficial name, coined either by Nora Chegodaeva, who had been in charge of the women's sniper courses which preceded the school, or by "important generals" on the Personnel Committee, one of whom, wiping his eyes with a handkerchief, laughed as he looked at a girl of diminutive stature, "Where do they get these little pencils from?"[85] From then on, some were Pencils, some were Queens, while girls in between had no permanent nickname. As a result, the schoolmates they remembered tended to be girls of similar height to themselves, with whom they lived and studied. Of her friends at the new Podolsk school who became posthumously famous, Anya Mulatova remembers only two, both tall: Roza and Tanya. Tanya Baramzina was a "not particularly likeable village girl, very ideologically minded, who never stopped talking".[86] Everyone was surprised that she wore spectacles while shooting. Anya and her friends discussed how, given her poor eyesight, she could possibly have been selected for sniper school, and agreed it could only have been because of her work for the Party or Young Communist League. Anya heard in 1944 that Tanya had been killed, but learned the details only after the war. Tanya Baramzina had been redeployed as a signaller when her vision became even worse, and met her fate as she defended a bunker with wounded soldiers against a Nazi assault. If we can believe the account of an injured soldier said to have miraculously survived (the Germans shot the others, but he pretended to be dead), the Germans tortured Tanya and then shot her with a grenade launcher. To begin with, the name of this communist martyr remained unknown, and she was simply called "the girl in a greatcoat".

The second sniper in their company of Queens who fought and died heroically at the front was Roza Shanina. Roza was a nursery school teacher from Arkhangelsk, a very tall, energetic, rosy-cheeked, blonde girl. She had big, limpid eyes, a pleasant face and a mane of hair, but Anya felt she was completely unfeminine. She had a rolling, masculine gait and was rather coarse, talking loudly with a strong regional accent. Anya was surprised to see an article in a front-line newspaper in 1944 that described Roza as a beauty, but kept her feelings to herself.[87]

Klava Panteleyeva, on the other hand, was small and belonged to the Pencils' company, the 7th. Being a short girl, Klava remembered only thin little Aliya Moldagulova of those who died heroically.[88] Aliya, an exceptionally active girl, was remembered by people in other companies too. Klava Loginova recalled encountering her on the first day. No sooner had they been brought to Amerevo than Aliya ran up and asked if they had had anything to eat. When she heard that they hadn't, she "ran off so swiftly" to find out what was going on.[89]

The trainees began settling into their new routine, their army uniforms and masculine hairstyles. Each girl now had a partner. They trained together as a pair, sat next to each other in the canteen and slept next to one another on bunk beds. The combination of being so far from their families at such a young age, and the tough new conditions into which they had been thrown, underlined the importance of having a friend who could cheer you up, and brought these girls very close to one another. At the front partners would often sleep together on one greatcoat and cover themselves with the other one. And if one of them got killed the other was likely to experience this as the biggest tragedy of the whole war.

From the first day of their life in the army they were shown no mercy. After reveille at six in the morning, they were taken two kilometres to the river to wash. The girls soon learned that relaxing in the canteen was a luxury they could no longer afford: the order to get up from the table was invariably given before any of them had really finished eating.[90]

The teaching was intensive. In the barracks there was theory, which included ballistics and the characteristics of their equipment. Drill and shooting practice took up the rest of their time. The girls spent a lot of time outdoors, whatever the weather. They were taught to dig different types of foxholes, to camouflage themselves and sit for long periods (as they might ahead of an ambush), to navigate terrain and crawl on their bellies. There were lessons in the additional skills needed for sniping: observation and the ability to commit the details of the landscape around them to memory, sharpness of vision and keeping one's hands steady. They were also taught unarmed combat techniques and how to throw a hand grenade.[91]

When they began training on the firing range, the young snipers had first to excavate deep trenches and emplacements, set up firing points, and build primitive defensive earthworks. How much soil they had to move using crude entrenching tools! Next came the actual training in shooting: they dug themselves in, camouflaged themselves, learned to move around by crawling and by dashing from one piece of cover to another, and they fired and fired and fired. "We were shooting at targets which were full height, from the waist upwards, from the chest upwards, targets that were running and fixed, in full view and camouflaged; we fired standing, lying and kneeling, supported and unsupported; we fired while moving and when stationary."[92] They were given as many cartridges as they needed, but after the firing had finished they had to pick up every single spent cartridge case. The girls were often crawling around together on their hands and knees in the mud, searching for missing cases to help one of their comrades. When they had learned to handle their weapon passably, their standard guns were replaced with sniper rifles.[93]

In September 1943, the school was moved from Amerevo to the former estate of Count Sheremetiev near Podolsk. The girls repaired the dilapidated buildings with their own hands. Klava Loginova and her comrades were allocated the former orangery. They mixed clay, carried bricks, and created quarters that began to feel acceptable. After the war, Klava put the experience to good use and built herself a house.[94] Bunks were installed, and each squad had their own "storey". "We lay side by side, like toy soldiers in their box," Yulia Zhukova remembered, but at least each of them had their own mattress and pillow (though they were only stuffed with straw), their own coarse grey army blanket, and even calico sheets and a waffle towel, always cleanly laundered.[95] For many village girls, this was a level of luxury that they had never experienced.

In the large family of Anya Mulatova (her father was a craftsman, so they had a better standard of living than most of their neighbours), all the children slept together on the floor on a purple homespun wool blanket that was a great favourite with fleas. Her mother and father had a bed behind a curtain. There was no question of bedlinen. Their mother sewed clothes for them from whatever piece of cloth was available, and was forever altering old clothes. One time Anya tore a piece out of a new dress while she was playing hide-and-seek and her mother beat her. Footwear was a constant problem. As soon as her sister Liza came home from school, she would take off her half-boots (which had heels), and their brother would put them on because he had none of his own.

In the mornings their mother usually made soup from millet, which they all ate from a shared bowl. Their mother added milk to it, their father began supping, and then the children were allowed to start. For dinner, they also had soup, potatoes, and sauerkraut. There was very rarely any meat, and on those rare occasions when there was, the first to eat would be her father and those of her siblings who were already working. The rest ate what was left.[96] By 1940, things were just beginning to improve, but then in 1941 the war began.

Deputy platoon commanders were, as a rule, also very young women who had done well in the first cohort and been kept on at the school. They drilled the girls diligently. Anyone who had not made their bed perfectly could expect extra fatigue duties: the straw mattress and sheet must be without a wrinkle, the pillows perfectly aligned, towels folded into triangles, with the bases of the triangles in a straight line.[97] If they failed to get dressed within the allotted couple of minutes, they would be ordered to "Stand down!" and the procedure would be repeated from the beginning.

Reunited after the war with women whose deputy platoon commander she had been, Zinaida Melikhova recalled various amusing moments and episodes, but the women remembered the time quite differently – her sternness, the drill, the extra fatigues . . . Melikhova never did go to the front. She was a very beautiful girl with a good figure and, in the opinion of her subordinates, "flirty". Without taking too much trouble to be discreet, she would kiss Odintsov, an officer she went on to marry, and got to stay at the school.[98]

They remembered the men as being very strict too. The platoon and company commanders were usually officers who had been wounded at the front. As far as they were concerned it was their duty to turn the girls, who had just come from civilian life, into soldiers. Klava Panteleyeva and her comrades were afraid of Panchenko, the director of tactics, who moved during exercises from one platoon to another. The moment the girls started to relax, they would hear, "Panchenko approaching!" Their task was to blend into the background so seamlessly that they could not be seen, and Panchenko kept them hard at it. Many years after the war was over, he came to a reunion of those who had graduated from the sniper school and admitted, "Girls, I had so much respect, and felt so sorry, for you."[99]

For some reason, what seemed most to lodge in their memories were episodes involving singing as they were marching. When they were tired, the girls would disobey orders and refuse to sing, whereupon they would be forced to do so. Anya Mulatova's company commander was Almazov, "a tall, handsome man, very stern". Not infrequently, terribly tired after marching the seven kilometres in each direction to the firing range and spending the whole day toiling away, they would be on their way to the canteen bareheaded and without mittens, dreaming only of covering the 300 metres to the warm hall, eating their dinner and after that getting back to their quarters and lying down, when Almazov would order, "Sing!" The exhausted girls would remain silent. Then Almazov would instead order, "Halt! To the right, to the left, five paces. Down!" And they would have to fall flat on their faces in the deep snow and crawl in the prescribed manner to the point indicated by the commander. Snow would be scooped up into the broad tops of their boots. Women in shawls and quilted jackets would stand by the roadside watching the young trainees and sighing sympathetically. If Almazov turned his back for a moment, the girls would get up and scuttle a couple of paces closer.[100]

Probably every girl who completed the course at sniper school could remember being punished for failing to sing on the march. An officer by the name of Ivanov, Taya Kiselyova's platoon commander, also had no time for insubordination. On one occasion, the girls were coming back tired from the firing range and remained silent when ordered to sing. They heard the order, "Down! Crawl!" This time the commander really had got a bee in his bonnet. Reluctantly they obeyed. There was rain and sleet, the girls' mess tins were clanking against their belts. At first they giggled, but then they started wailing. They were saved on that occasion by Kolchak, the school's director, who clearly thought that they had had enough. When their course ended, Ivanov, just like Almazov, made no attempt to conceal his affection and concern for them. "My dear, good girls," he said as he bade them farewell, "you take care of yourselves now!"[101] The harsh drills, these former front-line soldiers believed, would prepare their wards for the front, where their trials would be even harsher. They were right, and the girls would soon come to realise this for themselves.

There were, of course, some who just enjoyed humiliating other people. After the war, Yulia Zhukova really wanted to see her former platoon commander, Lieutenant Mazhnov, at one of their reunions and look him straight in the eye. Mazhnov did return from the war, but never showed up at any of the reunions. He must have known just how much the girls loathed him. He was a very ordinary, uneducated peasant and humiliated his subordinates, presumably to make himself feel big at their expense.

Out of all the merciless drilling and bullying, one episode stuck more than all the others in Yulia Zhukova's mind and made her really hate the platoon commander. One cold autumn day when they were out in the field on tactical exercises, the girls were "running through clinging mud that squelched underfoot and stuck to our boots". Mazhnov gave the order, "Down, forward on your bellies, crawl!" Yulia saw a huge puddle right in front of her, quickly sidestepped it and started crawling through the mud. But it was not to be. "Cadet Zhukova, stand up, return to initial position!" She flopped down straight into the icy puddle and started crawling.[102] Afterwards, their platoon commander explained that he was treating them in this manner for their own good. If Zhukova had behaved like that at the front, she would have been dead by now. To an extent he was no doubt right, but for the rest of her life, whenever she recalled the episode, Yulia Zhukova seemed again to feel "the cold, slimy mud seeping into the tops of my boots and into the sleeves of my greatcoat". Forcing her way through the thick mud, she swallowed tears of impotent rage and humiliation.

Their sergeants were mostly the best cadets from the first cohort. They were now to train the next cohort and go to the front with it as its officers. They were mostly a year or two older than the others, and responsible for maintaining order and discipline in the platoon. They were also answerable for property and firearms. If you had a good sergeant, life in the army could be just about bearable. She would help with your uniform if something was missing, and teach you to wind your leg wrappings properly, would understand if someone was unwell and, when necessary, say a kind word. Anya Matokh, who was killed in 1945, just days before victory was declared, was very popular in her platoon. A plump, calm girl from the Urals, she was a couple of years older than the rest of them, tried to make life easier for them, and did not neglect political indoctrination (important for the commanders but not so much for the girls themselves).[103] Anya Mulatova's platoon was less fortunate. Their Sergeant Shatrova was "small, dark, always looked angry" and treated her fellow soldiers abominably.[104] She too had been kept on from the first cohort to help with the second, and when they finished the course Shatrova went with them to the front. There she behaved no better than at the school. The girls under her command confirm that she treated them very cruelly, often finding fault for no reason. She was soon killed, and those who had been at the front with her asserted she had been shot by her own girls.[105] Anya Mulatova believed she might well have been.

People did witness or hear of similar incidents. Masha Maximova was not the least bit surprised when she heard the lieutenant who had been in command of their platoon at the school, "a really nasty bit of work", was killed by a bullet from someone on their side almost as soon as they got to the front. At the school, while harassing the girls crawling on their bellies, he was quite likely to step on someone's backside with his boot, remarking, "Lower, press yourself down lower. At the front this is going to be where you get wounded." "Serves him right," was all Masha thought.[106]

Sergeant Vashchenko was another woman greatly disliked by her subordinates. They considered her coarse and thoroughly unpleasant and, needless to say, often ignored her orders to sing on the way to the canteen. If she called out the name of one of the girls and demanded that she should sing, the reply might well be that she had lost her voice. Vashchenko would then lose patience and command, "At the double!", or find a way to spite them on the way back to the barracks. When they were nearly there, only a few metres separating them from warmth and rest, Vashchenko would suddenly order the girls to wade through a ditch and then proceed by crawling. "Stand up! Get down! Crawl!" The commands would rain down on them. They were all delighted when, one time, her bullying was witnessed by Commissar Nikiforova, who had arrived on a visit, and gave the sergeant a taste of her own medicine. Nikiforova very properly did not dress Vashchenko down in front of the trainees, but gave the order, "Dismissed!" She kept Vashchenko behind and made her give a thorough demonstration of how to crawl on your belly. Needless to say, this was instantly relayed throughout the school by a couple of highly amused witnesses.[107]

The food at the school was excellent, and they were to look back on it nostalgically at the front; most would continue to do so after the war. Though they couldn't expect any great delicacies, the portions were generous: soup and porridge and bread. They were at last able to eat their fill after the hungry years of war, seeing for the first time in a long while butter, sausage, cheese, sugar, and even real tea. For many, it was the first time in their lives that they had enough to eat. Many of them, indeed, had been on the verge of starvation in peacetime.

Those on duty in the kitchen would scrape clean what was left in the pot and give it to girls from their platoon. Quite often they would take this out to local women, who were starving and came begging for food with their children.[108] Some, like Klava Loginova and her sniper partner, Valya Volokhova, so wanted to have photographs to send home that they skimped on food for themselves in order to have something to barter (the trainees received no wages). Klava and Valya found a photographer in Podolsk and took sugar and bacon fat to exchange for photographs. They had intially tried taking him butter, but it melted, and the photographer himself tactfully suggested they might find it easier to bring lumps of sugar rather than the granulated variety. At first he was embarrassed and looked at the ground, urging them to eat it themselves, but eventually succumbed to temptation.[109]

And then there was Vera Barakina, blonde, blue-eyed, with delicate features, who each day after dinner collected every last scrap of bread from the table. She always felt they were underfed at the school. The mothers of girls who had gone to the front from Moscow or Moscow Province would come to visit and bring them something to eat. "How can they not share it?" Vera wondered furiously.[110] She was constantly hungry, having survived two winters of the Siege of Leningrad. During the first her father had been sitting on a chair in the kitchen when, without any warning, he died. His wife and her daughters held on. Vera, like her mother, was working in an arms factory and they received a daily ration of 250 grams of bread. They shared it with Vera's sister, who received only 125 grams because she had been wounded during the shelling and was unable to work. At the factory they were given soup made from flour, and they made soup at home with a mixture of flour and mud, while it lasted, which Vera dug up from the bombed-out ruins of a food depot on the bank of the River Neva. When stirred in the pot the mud, heavier than everything else, would gradually sink to the bottom after releasing the scraps of flour from the depot which had been hidden within it.[111] By the end of the second winter their strength was almost gone and they couldn't wait for spring, when the goosefoot and nettles that saved so many people from starving to death would emerge. Suddenly, a miracle occurred. Their mother came home from work one day to tell them they were all being evacuated, along with the factory. The girls were emaciated and indifferent to everything, but now showed signs of animation. Were they really going to get out?

Their mother died on the journey when, after crossing the frozen Lake Ladoga on a truck, it seemed they had reached safety. Vera and her sister dragged the body to a pile of others, and "we got back in the trucks and were taken on, to live." Until so recently that had seemed a forlorn prospect. At Manturovo railway station in Kostroma Province another miracle occurred: Vera and her sister were spotted by a distant relative who worked at the restaurant there. She went to meet all the trains bringing Leningraders. They stayed with her. Her relative got Vera a job as a cashier at the national savings bank but, just as she was getting used to having a full belly again, she was summoned to the enlistment office and told she would be joining the army. "I've been in the Siege," she protested. "Makes no difference," the officer said, and she could only murmur, "All right, then." After the war, when the others who had been in her regiment proudly said they had volunteered, Vera Barakina made no bones about it, and said openly that she had been far from pleased to have been sent to the front. She probably would have gone eventually to the enlistment office to volunteer, but then, in May 1943, she was still far too weak to even consider it.

After her experiences in Leningrad, even the front did not seem all that terrible. Many horrible things happened there: people were killed by shrapnel or bullets, her comrades were blown up by mines, and she herself was wounded twice, but Vera always said nothing in her life had been more dreadful than the Siege.

Their course was coming to an end, and during the political indoctrination sessions there was already talk about going to fight at the front. Vera Barakina was astonished when her sniper partner, Tonya Bulanenko, applied to be transferred to signals because she could not face being a sniper.[112] Tonya was a real sharpshooter but could not countenance actually firing at people. Vera had little doubt that being in signals would be a lot more frightening, crawling over open ground under fire, trailing a telegraph cable!

Many of the trainees dropped out in the course of those six months. Not everyone could cope with such a change in their way of life, or endure the heavy physical toll of trekking so many kilometres to the firing range and back in full gear (in the winter they had to make the same journey on skis), or life in the barracks. Many could not believe they would soon be fighting in the war and, moreover, as snipers. Back in the summer, when they were still at Amerevo, Zoya Nakaryakova from Perm went mad (or pretended to). First she began yelling at night, and then one afternoon on the road to the firing range she suddenly started shrieking, "Mama! Mama!"[113] At that she was promptly consigned to a psychiatric facility, and from there, it was said, to the secret police. Klava Loginova heard that after the war Zoya had been seen in Perm.[114]

Zoya was not the only one who did not make it to the front. There were others whose nerve failed. Two girls in Vera Barakina's company ran away. They were soon caught in Moscow, tried as deserters, and sent off to fight in a penal company. Vera heard no more of them. Another girl, on sentry duty at night, shot herself by taking off her boot and pressing the rifle trigger with her toe. "That would take some doing, shooting yourself with your foot!" the others whispered. They were all certain the girl must have done it because she was so afraid of being on guard on her own in the dark. They were all frightened of being on sentry duty, but many felt that members of the Young Communist League and future soldiers should be fearless and so were too ashamed to admit it. The dead girl was evidently no exception. Yulia Zhukova found guarding the ammunition store the worst detail at the school. Standing there at night by yourself was terrifying. The ammunition shed was some distance from the school building, in empty wasteland. There were bushes around and a deep ravine, also overgrown with bushes. At night when they were rustling you felt sure someone was sneaking towards you. Many years later, Yulia wrote, "You would lose your nerve, spin round, raise your rifle and shout, 'Halt! Who goes there?'"[115] The fear did not let go even after she had satisfied herself there was no one. "You would press your back against the wall and stand, peering into the darkness, waiting. Then you would force yourself to move away and walk round the store, a chill would run down your spine, and again you would be sure there was someone behind you. We were at war."

Chapter 5

"Why wash? It's dark, isn't it!"

Greetings from the front. Hello, my dear mother!
I got a letter from you today, which I hasten to answer. I should be able to write to you more often now.
I have no special news to tell you. I am by the sea, which is splendid. Life is varied, we do not stay long in one place, on the move all the time. It is good that the rain has not started yet. Although it is autumn, it is very hot here. So far all the girls are alive and well. My health is good enough too. Hello to everybody.
Your loving Zhenya.[116]

Zhenya Makeyeva's mother, like Katya's, was illiterate, and so the letter had to be read to her by Zhenya's younger sister.[117] Zhenya wrote to her mother in Kropotkin on 9 October. She and her comrades had only been at the front for a couple of months, but had already learned how to write home and let their families know where they were and what was happening to their unit without incurring the censor's wrath. When they read "by the sea", her family would have guessed Zhenya's unit had reached the Black Sea. "We do not stay long in one place" meant they were on the offensive. Soldiers often wrote that it was "hot" or "very hot" at the front, hinting that there was heavy fighting, but possibly Zhenya really was only writing about the weather. The most important news in the letter was that she and "all the girls" were safe and sound.
They got as far as Taman in the second wave of the offensive, without

experiencing any fighting. After the Blue Line was broken, the Germans retreated from the Taman Peninsula, putting up practically no resistance. The Red Army was pushing forward, clearing the Northern Caucasus of Germans and preparing for the liberation of the Crimea. Along the way, Katya Peredera became ill with malaria and, until she could be taken to hospital, periodically fell asleep while they were on the march, simply drifting out of consciousness. After treatment she caught up with the rest of them.[118]

They halted at Taman, preparing to cross the Kerch Strait. Although there was no longer anything permanent in their lives, the girls wasted no time before decorating their dugouts, which had been excavated in a gully, adorning their temporary quarters with what was to hand: little yellow flowers and tumbleweed.[119] They needed only a very short break, a lull in the routines of wartime, for youth and life once more to come into their own.

On 5 November, the sniper platoon was issued 300 rounds of ammunition per person and rations to last them five days. Where they were being sent nobody, of course, would say, but it was fairly obvious. The Germans had retreated over the Kerch Strait, and now it was time to pursue them.[120]

On 6 November they marched, carrying heavy loads, the thirty kilometres to the shore of the strait. Trucks were driving past with inscriptions on their sideboards reading "On to Crimea!" Soviet artillery was firing from the Chushka Spit in support of the Crimean landings, the army having been crossing the strait for several days already.[121]

The task facing the troops of the North Caucasian Front was to seize a bridgehead in the Crimea, which would become a base for further operations. The Kerch-Eltigen Landings, the largest amphibious operation on the Eastern Front during the Second World War, had begun on 31 October. The troops had a hard time of it because the Kerch Strait was narrow and shallow, making it impossible to use large ships. They had to be ferried by launches whose firepower was far inferior to that of the German vessels, which was "tantamount to pitching carts against tanks", as the commander of the fleet, Vice Admiral Lev Vladimirsky put it.[122] And, as People's Commissar of the Navy Nikolai Kuznetsov recalled, "We had often to make use of civilian craft completely unsuited to such operations, even rowing boats."[123]

On each of those first days they ferried several thousand troops under fire to the village of Eltigen, south of Kerch, and suffered heavy losses. No reinforcements could be sent to support the landing because two days later a tremendous storm broke, and when it was over, the Germans had blocked the approaches to Eltigen from the sea. "How are our sailors over there?" The girls from the women's night bomber regiment were very concerned for the marines fighting alone at Eltigen, soon dubbed the Land of Fire. The airwomen had made friends with the marines in October when that unit had been quartered next to their airfield in Peresyp.[124]

For the girls flying out to bomb the Germans on the opposite shore of the Kerch Strait, it was no distance at all: they could travel there and back in an hour. How far it was, though, for the seaborne troops! Day after day they were knocking rafts together, caulking boats and training, throwing themselves fully clothed and with their weapons into the icy water. When the girls were not able to fly because of bad weather (and there are many such days in Crimea in autumn), their "sailor boys" were invited to come into their heated house to warm up and dry out. Anya Bondareva fell deeply in love, although it is unclear whether that was with one particular marine or all of them at the same time. The other girls took a great liking to these brave lads too. When, one morning, Regimental Commander Bershanskaya announced they were to provide air cover for the marines who had made the crossing to Eltigen, they were only too happy to oblige.[125]

"The enemy is extending his beachhead at Kerch," the diary of military operations of the Wehrmacht's 5 Army Corps records on 6 November

1943.[126] Among the units making the crossing that day was an infantry regiment which had been allocated a women's sniper platoon. Their launch took four or five hours to cross, in terrifying conditions. Shells were exploding around their boat, which was carrying some fifty people, as the artillery bombardment continued relentlessly.[127] Many of the 570 Infantry Regiment, to which the snipers were attached, never made it to the far shore, drowning in ships sunk by the German artillery.

Alya Moiseyenko was wounded the moment she landed and was left on the beach to await evacuation back across the terrifying strait.[128] The rest were ordered to form a line and attack.[129] There was fighting to take the factory town of Kolonka. The following morning they were forced to retreat back to the shore when the Germans brought in fresh forces.[130] It was said there were a lot of Crimean Tatars fighting for them, which made the Red Army soldiers, furious at such treachery, fight even harder.[131]

The Soviet forces managed to capture the towns of Kolonka and Adzhimushkai on 14 November "after heavy fighting",[132] but with their resources exhausted they failed to extend the bridgehead. The Soviet troops on the Kerch Peninsula went on the defensive and would not be able to advance further until April 1944. Historians later wrote that the Soviet commanders were wrong in their evaluation of the situation and their adversary's strength. The objective therefore was not achieved, in spite of the great losses.[133] Another girl sniper from Kropotkin, Tanya Kostyrina, was killed in the battle for Adzhimushkai on 22 November. Neither Katya Peredera nor Zhenya knew her from Kropotkin or from the sniper school. Tanya and her friends had fled Krasnodar before the Germans arrived in 1942, and it is not known how she came to the front, but eventually she was trained in the front-line sniper courses. She was wounded twice, and both times returned to her unit.[134] In 1944, Tanya was posthumously awarded the title of Hero of the Soviet Union, and each year after the war Young Pioneers would plant red poppies at her grave in Adzhimushkai.

Katya Peredera's mother grew up in a deeply religious family, and as she watched her neighbours and colleagues receive notifications that their husbands or children had been killed in battle she began to pray for her daughters Katya and Nina to come back from the war alive. After the war, the whole country was to hear of another mother from Kuban, Yepistinia Stepanova, who lost all nine of her sons: Alexander, Nikolai, Vasiliy, Filip, Fyodor, Ivan, Ilia, Pavel and Alexander Junior. The eldest was killed in the Civil War, seven died in the Second World War, and the last returned from the war an invalid, later succumbing to his wounds.[135]

After the assault had stalled and the Russians started to occupy defensive positions, the regiment and its sniper platoon were taken off the front line and rested in the Adzhimushkai quarries. Their rest period soon ended and they were back to active service, but continued to live in the catacombs. The snipers' routine consisted of leaving the catacombs before dawn, equipped with their rifles, cartridges and knives. They carried water in a flask and some bread, sometimes also dried concentrate of foodstuffs such as millet porridge. As a rule, while on the defensive, half the platoon would be taken to the front line on any given day. Others were to be on duty on another day, or at times in the night, working as ordinary infantry soldiers. Once they reached the front trenches, the snipers would settle and set up a position: the embrasures were usually already there, the sniper just needed to see if the one she chose was properly camouflaged (with grass, tree branches, etc.), otherwise the Germans, who also had snipers, would spot her rifle. Once ready, the sniper just had to wait for a potential victim to appear. The partners in a pair took turns to watch the German front line through telescopic sights, since their eyes tired quickly and it was impossible for one person to be watching the whole time. When they saw a German, fired, and the German fell, another point was added to their tally, as long as the kill had been witnessed by other soldiers in the trench or an observer.

Meanwhile, above them the air battle at Kerch continued night and day. The snipers nicknamed the night bombers "Marina's girls",[136] aware that the women's bomber regiment created by the legendary Marina Raskova was at work.

On 1 December 1943, the logbook of the Wehrmacht's 5 Army Corps recorded, "All is more or less quiet on the ground. There is heavy fighting in the air. Particularly at Altigen and Kamysh-Burun. Planes are dropping supplies to the landing groups."[137] Only experienced pilots and navigators were taken on for the mission of dropping ammunition and food to the landing groups cut off at Altigen. The supplies had to be dropped from a height of less than 50 metres. Commissar Rachkevich addressed the assembled regiment, explained the situation at Altigen, and called for volunteers, but there was no real need: it was their "sailor boys", cut off from the main task force at Kerch and from the sea, who were dying at Altigen.[138]

Olga Golubeva kept remembering what an ageing lieutenant, whom everyone called Andreich, had said: "I just want to live till New Year ... And there has to be a tree for the holiday!" Olga so wanted to see these lads survive, to join them in celebrating the New Year, and for there to be a tree. They brought them "sacks", each shielded with oak planks and hooped with iron. Actually, it was stretching a point to call them sacks. "A heavy canvas sausage a metre in diametre, packed with all sorts of things, enveloped like smoked sausage in twine. In the middle was a loop for hanging it on the hook of the bomb rack."[139] With this bulky cargo, very heavy for a little Po-2 plane with its weak engine, Olga Golubeva flew with her pilot Nina Ulianenko across to the far, fiery bank of the strait. Putting on her lifejacket, which was supposed to inflate in water, Olga suppressed her anxiety, remembering the advice of Dusya Nosal, who had been killed at Novorossiysk and was the regiment's first Hero of the Soviet Union: "Leave your fears behind on the ground!" In low raincloud, Nina and Olga flew to the opposite shore. The wind carried them too far to the north, so they had to turn round and search for Altigen. They soon spotted it from the fires and constant plumes of explosions. They managed to drop the sack on their second circuit directly down to the white building of the school.

With each flight Olga felt more confident, and was soon shouting to the sailors as they came in low, "Chin up, lads! Hold on!" or "Look out, down there. Catch this one!"[140] Anna Bondaryova would drop love letters to all her sailor boys. When it was clear that no reinforcements would be forthcoming, those who had landed at Altigen fought their way through on 6 December to Mount Mithridat, which was in Soviet hands. The seriously wounded, who could not go with the others, asked to be given weapons and ammunition to cover their comrades' breakout.[141]

Rock: cold, sharp rock. Wherever you go there are rocks and darkness, impenetrable, black darkness. Underground caverns to right and left, in front and behind, endlessly. Above is twenty-five metres of rock and this huge mass weighs down on you and makes you feel claustrophobic, although there is so much room here that in places trucks and tanks can drive through, except where the vault or walls of the caves have been brought down by shelling.

How can you light up these vast caverns? There is little in the way of lighting. Many army units are billeted here and everyone lights the place as best they can. The ingenious make lamps out of anti-tank shells by pouring petrol into them and making a wick out of rags, or light a torch from kindling. Perhaps, though, it is for the best that many of the underground corridors and halls remain in darkness: any light would illuminate terrible scenes.

The further in one goes, the heavier the atmosphere. A smell of dampness and decay. Strewn on the ground are rags, papers and bones; many unburied human remains. The Red Army returned here only a couple of weeks ago. The walls are covered with writing: slogans, names. Nearly everyone who wrote them is dead now, and the handful who escaped the slaughter have been captured by the Germans.[142]

Here is a recess full of dead soldiers. They lie in their greatcoats, rifles by their sides. One is sprawled in the middle of the underground gallery, others along the stone walls, one is half-sitting, leaning against the wall, an eerie sight. The man describing this took part in five landing operations, but recalled that he saw nothing in the war comparable in horror with this. "We stood in silence, stunned. And then, in this truly sepulchral silence, Selvinsky[143] said, 'I don't know about you, but I can't go any further.'"[144]

It was impossible to forget the subterranean hospital. At a table sat a corpse in a white coat, as if even in death the doctor was continuing to work. Everywhere were stone graves of those who had died in the early days of the siege, when their comrades still had the strength to bury them.

The main body of the Soviet forces was evacuated over the Kerch Strait in May 1942. Some units, however, were given orders to fight to the last man; those few survivors who would later be able to talk about the tragedy would spend many years in the circles of hell, first in German concentration camps and then, many of them, in the Gulag, punished again for having surrendered.

By the time the caverns in Adzhimushkai had been recaptured, at the end of November 1943, the weather had turned cold and damp. Strong winds blew in from the Sea of Azov and rain turned the clay ground into a morass. The catacombs, to which the girl snipers' platoon was taken to rest, were, in spite of their ghoulish recent history, a welcome refuge: warm, dry, and very, very quiet. Sliding down an icy slope on their backsides as if on a playground slide, the girls entered a whole new world. All around, "campfires were lit and the air smelled of resin and burnt oil."[145] The shooting and the rumble of artillery fire were barely audible.

Gradually the girls settled in to this strange environment. They lit small fires, got hold of oil or, more often, petrol from the tank crews, for lamps made from anti-aircraft shells, or simply burned the hose of a gas mask, tucking it into a shell case. The hoses burned for a long time, emitting huge amounts of black smoke. "We were coughing up black stuff for the next six months," Katya recalls.[146] They collected flat rocks and made them into a table and even walls, creating a separate room for themselves. At last they were able to grab some much-needed respite, and sometimes they would not emerge from underground for several days at a time.

Water was in short supply. There was little of it even on the surface in Kerch. Whoever was on kitchen duty had to go up to fetch it from a cloudy well nearby. They tried to do so before dawn so as not to be seen by the Germans but sometimes, if there was not too much shooting, would go out when it was light. Katya was on duty with Lida Ryasina from Armavir one day, and Lida took the bucket out of her hands just as she was about to go up, saying, "You've been up so many times already. I'll go this time!" Lida did not come back down. Later, Katya heard she had been found severely wounded beside the well and taken to Kerch. She died there.[147]

After a week or two of rest, the commanders started taking the snipers up to the surface to hunt. A first group, just a few of them, went up. They were very warmly dressed, in quilted jackets and trousers, felt boots, and mittens that had a separate section for the thumb and trigger finger. They each carried a flask and a supply of bread. The land where their infantry regiment was deployed had been churned up by explosions, something they had not seen before, and Galya Koldeyeva reassured her partner that not every shell crater was a soldier's grave – they offered valuable shelter. That same first day, Galya and her partner Anya managed to shoot two "mules", Germans pulling a water bottle on a sledge, and later Galya managed to take out a machine-gunner.[148] Katya Peredera and Zhenya Makeyeva opened their tally the following day. The Germans were close here, only 150 metres or so away, and their faces were clearly visible in their sights. The snipers had to stay in their trench (one of the many that had probably been dug back in 1942, and lost and retaken several times) until dark, but could come out at dusk. With their hearts pounding, in short dashes, they ran back to the quarry and safety. "If you make it back to the quarry, you live to see another day," the girls would say.[149]

They soon learned that when they made a kill the Germans were likely to retaliate with mortars, in which case you could only lie flat and pray you survived. Once, Zhenya and her partner (that day for some reason, she was not with Katya) were on night duty in the trench and escaped an even more serious threat. A German patrol looking for a "squealer" – a prisoner who could provide intelligence – came very close to their trench and would have captured them or slashed their throats if they had spotted them. Zhenya had fallen asleep but her partner was fully alert. The girls shot two of the group and threw a hand grenade at the rest. More Soviet soldiers arrived and repulsed the attack.[150]

The months passed with no change: the same strange, debilitating life in the catacombs, where water was so scarce; the same millet or barley porridge; rust-coloured herring; frozen, unpalatable bread.[151] One time they met up in the catacombs with Zhenya Grunskaya, Galya Koldeyeva's best friend from school in Krasnodar.[152] Zhenya had just arrived after being seconded as a nurse to the regimental headquarters. She asked to be transferred to the sniper platoon, who had no medical orderly, and stayed with them until she was killed. The girls got filled in on all the news from Krasnodar by Zhenya. She had even attended the trial of Nazis and those of their local accomplices who had committed atrocities in Krasnodar and the Krasnodar region. It was attended by a number of writers, including Alexey Tolstoy.[153] When one of the girls asked if it was true they had hanged the collaborators, Zhenya said, "Oh, girls, the things that went on! They brought them to the square in front of the military commandant's office and stood each of them in front of a noose. They were looking at the ground and shaking feverishly. Then there were speeches, all demanding they should be hanged. Alexey Tolstoy was one of the speakers."[154]

In the catacombs they established their own routine. There was a "great hall" in which, following the removal of the limestone, there was a raised area, like a stage, where they held indoctrination meetings and amateur concerts. An accordionist would play and they would organise dances. How Katya and Zhenya loved to dance! Zhenya was the more outgoing, though Katya was far from timid. When the girls were walking through the catacombs, boys would try to chat them up. It was usually

Zhenya who responded, in a humorous, friendly, though never coquettish, manner.[155] If a boy was really keen on a girl, he'd spare some of his precious water or bread: boys used to put a frozen piece on the parapet in the girl's trench.[156]

For International Women's Day on 8 March they brought out a wall newspaper and arranged a concert. A couple of days later someone called out to Katya, "Peredera, your sister's here!" A soldier she knew had brought her sister, Nina, through the dark gallery. It was a miracle. They had not been exchanging letters, and all they knew about each other they heard through their mother. Nina's unit was in fact just fifty kilometres away, and she heard about Katya's whereabouts by chance from a wounded soldier at their field hospital. She got herself a pass, hitched a lift for part of the way and walked the rest. In the hour they were able to spend together they talked, shared the heel of a loaf of bread Nina had with her, and Katya's lunch of millet porridge and herring, before Nina set off back the same way. They would not see each other again until after the war was over.

The girl snipers had already spent a month in the catacombs without washing. In the catacombs they would use precious drops of water to rinse their faces, although they longed to drink it. "Why wash? It's dark, isn't it?" Zhenya Makeyeva, ever the optimist, would laugh at Katya. Zhenya, of course, was in the same boat. Some of the soldiers knew where water could be found dripping in the caves and would collect it in a shallow bowl; occasionally they would share it with the girls, especially the pretty ones. "Quick, Katya, the boys have brought some water!" Zhenya would call, dangling a flask with water splashing at the bottom of it: a few sips to drink and a handful to wash with. Nevertheless, the girls had given up hope of being able to wash properly.

Something had to be done, and their new commander, Captain Seryogin, a teacher from Moscow, a strapping young man almost two metres tall who had grown a black moustache to make himself look more distinguished, informed their sergeant, Rozalia Reznichenko, that he would permit them to organise a trip to Kolonka to get washed. To get washed! It was beyond their wildest dreams!

Lyuba Visnitskaya and Valya Pustobrikova went out to reconnoitre the ruined village and, incredibly, found a house on the outskirts that had survived unscathed and had an old lady living in it.[157] She was kind and gladly agreed to help. The next morning the barber did his best to bring their hair back under control, and after lunch they set off.[158] They crouched down and dashed in short bursts over open ground. The front was only a kilometre away. "Auntie" Fenya made them a bathroom in her warm home and filled two wooden barrels with water, warming one with hot stones from the stove. Their bath, with real soap and clean underwear issued by Sergeant Reznichenko, was something they never forgot.[159] "Perhaps this will not be the last time we meet," the old lady said when they parted.[160] Alas, they were never able to wash in the village again. The next time they returned, the old lady was dead and, instead of a face, her white headscarf framed a hideous mess where it had been gnawed by rats.[161]

The men around them were forever suffering from a dearth of tobacco, while the girls hankered after sweet things. The only sweet thing they got, however, and that only rarely, was sugar. Sergeant Reznichenko issued it just twice a month, and the girls dipped their bread in it and gobbled it up immediately.[162] They were generally very hungry in the catacombs, which made all the more memorable a New Year's gift they received from Krasnodar.

The deputy platoon commander and Sergeant Reznichenko were invited to H.Q. to receive two parcels from the Krasnodar district committee of the Young Communist League. Throughout the war, gift parcels of this kind were sent to the front in large numbers from across the U.S.S.R. The initiative was widely promoted in newspapers and on the radio, and people in the rear sacrificed their last pennies, donating money for the war effort and sending clothes and food to the soldiers. "We put mittens, socks, cigarettes and warm clothes in the parcels. We even sent parcels of potatoes. I sacrificed my brand new felt boots and wrote a note: 'For a young nurse, so she does not catch cold,'" Anisia Komaneva from Siberia recalled.[163] *Peasant Woman* – a popular Soviet women's magazine where articles on high-achieving women in agriculture and girls on the front line alternated with patterns, recipes and poems – wrote, "Every collective farm worker sends warm clothes to the army with love: her contribution to victory."[164] In the rear, food was issued on the basis of ration coupons, but people sent bread rusks, sweets, and even roast chickens or meat, to the front. In a cold climate, that was a practical possibility. Cured bacon fat was the most prized gift of all, it was delicious and essential, as they always lacked fat in their diet. These parcels were a wonderful morale-booster for soldiers at the front, as were letters written to them by girls they had never met. Many bachelors returned from the front to marry girls they knew only through correspondence.

The parcels the girl snipers received at H.Q. contained white bread, two rings of homemade sausage, knitted socks and mittens, undercollars, handkerchiefs and also, completely unbelievably, sweet homemade biscuits, face powder and perfume! The new year was still far off, but they all had a biscuit to try, and the bottle of perfume was passed from hand to hand.[165] Shortly afterwards, the girls found a battered tin of "fascist" Nivea cream in a German trench. They couldn't believe their luck![166] Katya Peredera and many of the others had never used face cream before. They made the jar last for a month, all of them rubbing in just a tiny bit at a time.

Katya also remembered that new year for the fact that she wished a happy one to the Germans she had recently been shooting at. An enquiry came round to see whether anyone had learned German, and Katya immediately said yes. She had studied it at school and come top of the class. Even in the lower grades she had peered over her older sisters' shoulders when they were reading, and had memorised words. She wasn't good at speaking it, but was certainly capable of reading a leaflet into a megaphone. The girls were indignant at the arrogance of the Germans, who dropped propaganda leaflets and shouted, "Surrender, you all *kaput*!" The Russians gave as good as they got. Katya quickly forgot the text she had had to read out, but it was along the lines of, "*Kaput* yourselves! Surrender!" And "Happy New Year!"[167]

The new year of 1944 started dreadfully for Katya Peredera's platoon. An attempted offensive on 10 January failed. Height 33.3 changed hands three times and when, on the third day of fighting, the Germans brought tanks into the battle, the advance came to a halt.[168] [169] The sniper platoon, joining the attack alongside the infantry, lost six of its members: Anya Pechyonkina and Nina Krivulyak, both from Kropotkin, were killed and Galya Koldeyeva, Klava Kaleganova, Valya Pustobrikova and Shura Khomenko were seriously wounded.[170] The rest were still in the catacombs, greatly saddened by the deaths and injuries of their comrades. The place felt empty. They just wanted to attack, to get away from their claustrophobic, sinister quarters once and for all, to drink as much water as they wanted, to be properly fed. And to avenge their dead friends.

The Young Communist League organiser assured them that an offensive was imminent. During her talks she told them about the situation at the fronts, the military operations of the Allies, and the deeds of Soviet heroes. She told them the tale of Lyudmila Pavlichenko, and read them an article about Natasha Kovshova and Masha Polivanova, and Katya remembered their names.

The decree awarding them the title of Hero of the Soviet Union had been published only on 14 February 1943, six months after their deaths. It appeared thanks to the efforts of Klavdia Nikolaeva, an old Bolshevik and the wife of Yemelian Yaroslavsky, the main Soviet propagandist. Klavdia Nikolaeva had "adopted" the division in which Natasha and Masha fought, and on a visit in late 1942 was told the story of the heroic deaths of these two girl snipers.

The girls had been fighting since 1941 in 3 Moscow Communist Division, where they had enlisted as volunteers. Natasha came from a family of revolutionaries. A fanatical member of the Young Communist League, she did not think twice about volunteering for the front. Masha, a simple country girl and, according to those who knew her, not very educated, admired Natasha and followed her in all things, including going to the front.

The girls repeatedly tried to volunteer at the army enlistment office, and were accepted in July 1941 when, recognised as being among the best Osoaviakhim sharpshooters, they were selected for training at sniper school. Nina Aralovets, Natasha Kovshova's mother, saw her daughter off to the front on 16 October, a day when the Germans had advanced very close to Moscow. Their column left that same afternoon.[171] It included two other girls who were soon to become a sniper pair at the front: Nina Solovey and Ziba Ganieva. Nina joined the volunteer battalion along with 300 boys and girls from her aircraft factory. Nina and her friend, Katya Budanova, were active members of their factory's ski team, and also of a flying club. She wanted not only to build planes but also to fly them (Katya, as an experienced pilot, was enlisted at the beginning of the war in a fighter regiment. She was killed in summer 1943). Nina became a nurse, because that was the only profession the call-up committee would agree to enlist her in. Fearless, energetic, and with great physical stamina, she was an ideal volunteer. She mastered the art of sniping after arriving at the front. Ziba Ganieva was a beauty, "slim as a wraith and with the face of Nefertiti", and she had been studying ballet at drama college. In autumn 1941 she was sent to the front as a nurse.[172]

Their brigade was on the North-Western Front and participated in the offensive of November–December 1941 that forced the Germans back from Moscow. Natasha Kovshova and Masha Polivanova gained a reputation as skilled snipers, Natasha being seen as brave to the point of recklessness. She was a particularly accurate markswoman, able to hit an enemy soldier in the head at 300 metres. Her comrades were greatly impressed by the corpse of a German Natasha had killed, which they were able to inspect after their unit took a village. The bullet had hit him precisely on the bridge of his nose.[173]

Fighting continued for six months in the same district near Demyansk, where troops of the North-Western Front succeeded for the first time in the war in encircling six German divisions, although they were unable to force the Germans to surrender. By May 1942, the encirclement failed, and the troops made repeated attempts to close the ring again in the face of German counter-attacks. Bouts of fighting alternated with periods of respite, and during these lulls the two girls spent weeks doing the real work of a sniper, "hunting the enemy", which took place far behind the front line. In the summer Natasha wrote to her mother that they were living in a shelter with a sign reading "Dacha No. 13", among birch trees, as if they were holidaying in the countryside surrounded by an abundance of berries and mushrooms.[174]

Nina Aralovets received her daughter's last letter on 13 August. Natasha wrote, "We have made a major move, about 115 kilometres, and are now attacking in a different place and with another army. It is very swampy here and we are in mud up to our knees." Responding to her mother, who was embarrassed that Natasha was sending her money, she added, "As it's possible for you to buy something, and something so delicious too, it's better if you have the money rather than me. I won't need it till after the war, and then I'd like to buy a really nice dress!"[175]

Natasha Kovshova and Masha Polivanova died on 14 August near the village of Sutoki in Novgorod Province. It is not known exactly what happened. The girls and a male sniper, Novikov, were covering a group of riflemen holding back German counter-attacks. At some point, all three of them found themselves wounded and on their own: either the riflemen had retreated and they had not had time to do so themselves, or all the men had been killed. Novikov was shot in the stomach and the Germans took him for dead. That night he crawled back to the Soviet lines and told them that when the Germans approached the girls had blown up themselves and several of the enemy with a grenade. One of the girls' friends, Nurse Sonya Naidyonova, wrote to tell their families what had happened.[176]

Natasha and Masha's fellow hunters, Ziba Ganieva and Nina Solovey, had been put out of action even before this. Ziba was carried, seriously wounded, from the battlefield by three comrades. She left hospital disabled and, realising there could be no return to drama school, became an academic (though this did not prevent her from securing a role on one occasion in a movie).[177]

Nina Solovey, recovering from severe wounds, declared her willingness to return to the front. She was sent to the Women's Sniper School in Podolsk. On arrival she was instructed to prepare the next cohort of female snipers for the front, of which she had first-hand knowledge, and then go with them into combat as their commander.

Chapter 6

"Klava, I beg you, don't take up smoking there!"

In mid-March 1944, the day finally came when the second cohort was ready to be sent to the front. Some of the top brass delivered speeches to the departing corporals – the rank to which they had all been promoted – who now stood in dress uniform in perfect ranks like real soldiers, and in addition Commissar Nikiforova spoke, as always from the heart, words they were long to remember.

A couple of days after this official farewell, Anya Mulatova's company was lined up with their full complement of equipment: new sniper rifles slung over their shoulders, kitbags, entrenching tools, and a cartridge pouch on their belts. Gas masks were issued later, at the front, but very soon discarded and their convenient containers used for all sorts of more useful things. (The soldiers joked that when the sergeant asked,

"What does a gas mask consist of?" he was answered, "A packet of tobacco, a chunk of bread, spare leg wrappings . . .")[178]

They marched in rank to the station, past the grey wooden huts in which almost all the residents of Podolsk then lived, before being loaded on to a troop train in total darkness – the whole operation was being carried out under conditions of strict secrecy. The officer from the sniper school who had been accompanying them handed a package to the commandant of the train. The girls were bundled into a goods wagon and were soon on their way. They fuelled up the iron stove with bits of wood that someone had left for them in the wagon, warmed themselves, and fell asleep in the bunks.[179]

They travelled for several days, and were fed the standard army fare – it was time to get used to it – millet porridge and dried bread rusks. Some of the girls, however, shared some very rare treats with their friends: American sausage, corned beef, and an unfamiliar kind of hard biscuit. Those who had come top in the final tests at the school were awarded special rations of US products that had begun to arrive under the Lend-Lease Act. Klava Panteleyeva split her "American present" 50/50 with her sniper partner, Marusya Chigvintseva. If Klava had been a Communist Party member, she would have been presented with a specially engraved rifle, but even so she was very pleased with the gift, the recognition of her excellence and, of course, the delicacies.[180]

Klava, who was not a tall girl, had a round, sweet, serious face and beautiful grey eyes, and had volunteered for the army the moment she turned seventeen. She went to the military-training-for-all classes at a gas mask factory in Orekhovo-Zuyevo, where she worked from the age of fifteen in order to get the worker's ration card of 700 grams of bread per day.

Klava and other girls were told in the factory's Young Communist League committee about the sniper school in Podolsk, which was selecting its second cohort, and asked whether they wanted to volunteer. Many, including Klava, did. They agreed to send her there when she said she would shortly be eighteen.

Her mother was not at home when Klava left. Like all the women around them, she had gone into the countryside to exchange clothes for bread. Her father knew he could not stop Klava, the youngest of eleven children in a working-class family, from going to war, even though she was only seventeen. His parting words to her were, "Klava, I beg you, don't take up smoking there!" Later, Klava recognised he had not only been referring to smoking: in those days it was considered a terrible disgrace to lose your virginity before you were married, but that was too shameful to mention.

Some time later, her mother came to visit Klava at the sniper school. Her most valuable gift to her daughter was Psalm 90, "A Living Refuge", written out by hand.[181] This prayer was believed to afford powerful protection. Klava's father was an old communist. He had joined the Party while serving in the imperial army in 1914, but her mother remained deeply religious and all their children were baptised. Young Communist League member Klava believed in God, and saw nothing incongruous in that. That is how she had been raised, by her father with his faith in communism, and by her mother with her faith in Christ. In Klava's heart the two allegiances co-existed in perfect harmony. Throughout the war, Klava carried a piece of paper with a prayer in her breast pocket, and believed that Psalm 90 saved her life on at least three occasions. During the conflict, such prayers, copied by a mother's hand, or small icons, were carried in their breast pockets by many communists and Young Communist League members: after twenty-five years of communism, the Orthodox faith and its related traditions were alive and well.

Klava, the youngest in the company, applied herself very diligently to her studies, but her shooting was decidedly indifferent. She kept missing the target, and was even threatened with expulsion. At this, Barantseva, the section commander, took matters in hand and decided to give her individual lessons, with the result that Klava became one of the best at shooting, both while standing and lying prone on the ground.

Klava remembered her American present later. There had also been sausage and cheese, biscuits and chocolate. She and Masha shared it, just as they shared everything at sniper school. While they were there, Marusya fell ill and Klava went to visit her. Her friend came out to her bearing a very, very small piece of white bread, something given only to patients. How long it was since Klava had last seen that. She tried to refuse, of course, but Marusya was having none of it.

Not everyone in the second cohort went to the front immediately. As with the other units that had been trained previously, some were kept behind to become squad commanders, and the best markswomen were sent to be trained in the instructors' company so they could be deployed to the front three months later as sergeants. Klava Loginova was very upset, because this meant she was parted from her sniper partner, Valya Volokhova. It had never occurred to them that they might not go to the front together. Klava's feelings were shared by most of the girls in the instructors' company, the best sharpshooters of the second cohort. It was the spring of 1944, the war situation had changed radically, and victory seemed within striking distance. What if they missed out on dealing the death blow to the Germans?

On the pages of *Peasant Woman*, celebrity sniper Lyudmila Pavlichenko called on women on the collective farms to work harder. "Every day we hear of new victories of the Red Army against the German occupiers. Our troops have raised the Siege of Leningrad, destroyed the enemy's armies at Stalingrad and, rapidly advancing, the Red Army has liberated Nalchik, Stavropol, Pyatigorsk, Armavir, Krasnodar, Kursk, Rostov-on-Don, Voroshilovgrad, many other towns and thousands of villages . . . The enemy has been severely wounded and is bleeding heavily, but is not yet finished."[182]

Pavlichenko suggested that women working in agriculture in place of their menfolk should keep the same sort of tally of their victories against the enemy as the soldiers were doing – by counting up the work targets they met during the spring sowing. Nineteen forty-four must be the year in which the Germans were totally driven off Soviet territory. Already the Caucasus had been liberated and an offensive was under way in Crimea, the Siege of Leningrad had been lifted, parts of Byelorussia had been freed and two thirds of the occupied territories had been cleared of Germans. Any day now, the Allies would be opening a second front. The mood across the country, despite all the hardships, was now quite different from what it had been a year before.

There were, of course, some who were in no great hurry to put their lives at risk: not every trainee sniper in the second cohort longed to be sent into battle. There was a parting of the ways for two friends in Anya Mulatova's company, both Ritas. Rita Moskva was placed in the instructors' company along with Klava Loginova. Rita Barkova, however, as tall as Rita Moskva, a beautiful girl with a beautiful voice who always led the singing in their company, was retained at the school. All the girls in her platoon knew and, of course, gossipped among themselves, about the fact that Rita Barkova was now the mistress of one of the important generals involved with the school, who would turn up for the shooting practice and reviews. "All rather sordid," Anya thought to herself.[183]

The girls were still very young, and it never crossed the minds of most of them that in this war they would have to "fight on two fronts"; that they would be the object of continual attentions from men, often obnoxious; that when they arrived at the front, some platoons could expect humiliating "parades" (they were told to stand in a line so that, as they would learn later, the staff officers could inspect them and select the prettiest ones to work at staff headquarters, so that the officers would be advantageously positioned to start an affair). The girls would have been in less of a hurry to get to the front if they had known that some of them would be raped not by Germans but by their own side – many would decide the lesser evil was to embark on an intimate relationship with one of the commanders so as to be shielded from all the others.

Masha Maximova was disturbed by hints in the letters she received from her fiancé, Vanya. In almost every letter he repeated that the front was no place for her, or, indeed, any other girl. "You cannot imagine how bad and downright unpleasant you would find it here," he wrote; any more than that would have been erased by the censor. Masha was not stupid and had seen quite enough in her poor, working-class district of Kaluga to have a fair idea of what he was talking about. She simply did not believe the women who came from the front to the school to tell the trainees how great it was there, and so was not at all upset when she heard she would be staying behind as a squad leader for the next, third, cohort.[184]

By the third year of the war, however, a majority of the girls had not only patriotic motives but also personal scores to settle with the Germans. Some had lived in occupied territory and seen the enemy at close quarters; some had had to leave their families behind; others had lost people close to them; while some, like Lida Bakieva, had had no letters from their husbands at the front for an ominously long time.

Lida, a slim, athletic girl with dark skin and black hair, went to the front from Alma-Ata in Kazakhstan. In 1944, she was just nineteen years old. At seventeen she had married a kind, cheery orphan, a cook only a couple of years older than herself. His name was Satai Bakiev but his friends called him Volodya. Lida was able to live only a few months with her husband before war broke out and he was immediately conscripted. Would she have gone to the front if Volodya had not preceded her? Of course. Lida, an energetic Young Communist League member, could not picture herself refusing to come to the aid of her country in its titanic struggle. She was particularly pleased, though, that after sniper school she was sent to the Second Byelorussian Front, the very combat theatre from which she had received her first, and last, letter from Volodya. It had been sent long ago, but then . . . nothing. Perhaps he was wounded, and she would find him in a hospital? If he had been killed, she would make the Germans pay for it and bring victory closer.

Commissar Yekaterina Nikiforova escorted the first cohort to the front, but sent the second on their way only with words of encouragement.

Former trainees often recalled the consideration this calm, firm woman had shown them; they remembered the talks she had given them, about being a sniper, about war, politics, life, and about Zoya.

The story of an unknown girl, who told her German interrogators her name was Tanya, was related to Pyotr Lidov, a reporter, by a peasant in a liberated village in Volokolamsk District in Moscow Province. He lost no time in writing about her. "Tanya" was captured in the village of Petrishchevo and tortured. The Germans demanded that she should betray the other members of her group of saboteurs and her leaders. The partisan was stripped and lashed, paraded about for several hours barefoot and in only her underwear in the biting frost. Her nails were pulled out, but she admitted nothing and betrayed nobody. Lidov wrote that when the girl was being led to the gallows, she urged the assembled villagers to fight, and shouted at the Germans, "No matter how many of us you hang, you can't hang us all!" After Lidov's report was published, those words resounded throughout the U.S.S.R.

"Tanya" was the first Soviet girl saint, an iconic figure whom the ideologists urged other girls to emulate. Listening to Young Communist League political meetings taking an oath in the presence of their comrades to be as dauntless as "Tanya", young girls devoted to their Motherland and the ideals of communism measured themselves against this blood-curdling role model, and wondered whether they would be brave enough to withstand torture and not betray their comrades; whether, like Tanya, they would be capable of threatening the Germans as they faced the gallows. It was a question which kept them awake at night, tainted their lives, and to which there could be no answer.

It was soon discovered that Tanya's real name was Zoya Kosmodemianskaya and that she was just eighteen years old. Lidov wrote a more detailed article, accompanied by photographs of Zoya's execution, which had been found on a dead German soldier. All the newspapers wrote about her, and penned editorials calling for Zoya to be avenged. Everybody knew what she looked like, because all the press printed a pre-war portrait photograph, always the same one, which had been chosen by Zoya's mother, a schoolteacher. In reality the story was more complicated, with any elements that contradicted the propaganda story omitted.

Zoya was an anxious, romantic, very vulnerable girl, a teenager who had spent a month in a clinic for nervous illnesses after a conflict with her classmates. She was a fanatical Young Communist League member and, at the outbreak of war, felt an overwhelming desire to go and fight the Germans. Her wish was granted on 31 October 1941 when, with a number of other volunteers, she was enlisted in a sabotage and reconnaissance group. They were given just a couple of days' training and then, on 4 November, deployed in the vicinity of Volokolamsk, near Moscow. There they laid mines on the roads and gathered intelligence, but their main mission was something different. On 17 November, Order No. 428 was issued by Supreme Command Headquarters, instructing the army to deprive the German army "of the ability to find accommodation in villages or towns, to drive the German invaders out of all centres of population into the cold of the open countryside, to smoke them out of all premises and warm places of shelter and force them to freeze to death in the open". To achieve this, the army was to "burn and destroy all centres of population for a distance of 40–60 kilometres behind the German front lines and for a distance of 20–30 kilometres to the right and left of roads". The total inhumanity of this order is extraordinary.

Winter that year was exceptionally severe, with frosts of about minus 40 degrees. The villages near the front were by now inhabited only by old men, women, and children who had seen soldiers, first Soviet and then German, take all their stores of food, requisition their horses, slaughter their cows and eat their chickens, not leaving them even seeds to sow the following spring. They were now also, at the beginning of this fearsome winter, to be deprived of their homes.

Without the slightest qualms about the reasonableness of the order, the members of Zoya's group, armed with bottles of inflammable liquid and pistols, made a start on 27 November 1941 by burning down three

1. Girl snipers – *The Young Communist League Central Committee conducted seventy-three youth mobilisation campaigns. Of the 800,000 young people they sent to the armed forces, 400,000 were girls.*

2. Lyudmila Pavlichenko meets Eleanor Roosevelt, late 1942 – *Mrs Roosevelt asked Lyudmila how she, a woman, could bring herself to shoot at Germans after seeing their faces in her sights? Pavlichenko replied tersely, "I have seen with my own eyes my husband and child killed. I was next to them."*

3. Lyudmila Pavlichenko and Vladimir Pchelintsev in the U.S.A., 1942.

4. *(left)* Klava Loginova as a teenager with her nephew.

5. *(above)* Vera Barakina (right) with her mother and sister, before the war – *After dinner at the sniper school, Vera Barakina, who was constantly hungry, would always collect every last scrap of bread from the table.*

6. Kalya P. (right) with her mother and sister, 1938 – *Kalya Petrova was one of the many "involuntary volunteers" who were conscripted in the summer of 1943.*

7. Lida Bakieva with her husband Satai Bakiev, 1941 – *Lida lived for only a few months with her husband before war broke out and he was immediately conscripted; she would never see him again.*

8. *(right)* The hanging of Tanya/Zoya Kosmodemianskaya – *A partisan captured by the Germans, Zoya was said to have shouted "No matter how many of us you hang, you can't hang us all!" as she was led to the gallows. She would become a Soviet saint.*

9. *(left)* Anya Mulatova with Tasya Pegeshova. 1943, the Central Women's School of Sniper Training, Podolsk
- Anya's partner Tasya helped her overcome her initial squeamishness at the sight of blood. Within months Anya would happily bayonet a bloated German corpse "to let the gas out".

10. *(above)* Klava Panteleeva during her training

11. Taya Kiselyova's platoon with the teachers at the School of Sniper Training, 1944
– The strict commanders, when seeing the new snipers off to the front, could not conceal their affection and concern for "their girls".

12. School of Sniper Training. Taya Kiselyova and her would-be comrades in arms with their instructors – *Once they learned to shoot more or less well, ordinary rifles were replaced by sniper ones.*

13. Taya Kiselyova, Muza Bulatova, Bella Morozova and their party administrator, 1944 – *"A Red Army soldier is a warrior in the world's most powerful and well-disciplined army,"* the political instructors and Party administrators were responsible for morale and political indoctrination.

14. *(above)* Taya Kiselyova with partner while training in Podolsk. *The snipers' relationship with their partners was utterly crucial. They trained together as a pair, sat next to each other in the canteen and slept next to one another on bunks.*

15. *(right)* Klava Loginova (left) with partner Valya Volokhova at the shooting range in Silikatnaya, 1944 – *Soon their ways would part and they would not meet again until after the war.*

16. *(left)* Nina Lobkovskaya at the front of her platoon – *She started in 1943 at the Kalinin Front and over the course of the following two years was promoted to the rank of an officer, and appointed to command a platoon of female snipers.*

17. Masha Polivanova (centre), Natasha Kovshova (right) and their friend Tatiana –
Masha and Natasha died exemplary, heroic deaths, which inspired Katya Peredera.

18. Katya Pederera in the Army.
Katya's response when asked by a preacher to repent for the sins that she must have accumulated during her long life: "What sins do I have? I have never stolen anything. I have never killed anyone."

19. Zhenya Makeeva – *Katya was shot as she tried to bandage the dying Zhenya. It was "as if someone had hit me very hard on the legs with a stick", she remembered.*

20. Roza Shanina, Lida Vdovina and Sasha Ekimova, 1944 - *Ilya Ehrenburg wrote of Roza Shanina, "Let the Russian mother rejoice who gave birth to, brought up and gave this glorious, noble daughter to the Motherland!*

21. Roza Shanina, Alexander Stanovov and Dusya Krasnoborova, 1944 – *Stanovov, like others, had initially laughed at the chatty, animated girls: what kind of soldiers were they? But before long the front newspaper sent him to write an article about them.*

22. Snipers' platoon with Roza Shanina, Kalya Petrova, Sasha Yekimova, Lida Vdovina - *Roza would write: "I'm used to having Sasha and Kalya around and feel lost when they are not there . . . Sasha, Kalya and I are 'The Runaway Troika'. How will I live without them when the war is over and we all go off in different directions?"*

23. Kaleriya Petrova - *Roza was often dissatisfied with her comrades. The exception was Kalya Petrova who was "the only brave one".*

houses in the village of Petrishchevo. Their instructions were to completely gut ten villages within a week. One member of the group decided not to wait at the agreed rendezvous for his companions and returned safely, but a second was captured. Zoya, finding herself alone, decided to go back to the village and continue the arson. By now, however, both the Germans and the local people, who were not in favour of the Supreme Command's decision to destroy their houses, were on the lookout. When Zoya attempted the following evening to set fire to a barn belonging to a peasant called Sviridov, he summoned the Germans, who captured the partisan and tortured her at length. The two peasants whose homes she had burned down were eager to join in the torture. Even the next day, as Zoya was being led to her execution with a sign round her neck proclaiming "Arsonist of homes", Smirnova, one of these women, beat her legs with a stick and shouted, "Who were you harming? You burned my house down and did nothing to the Germans!" After the village was liberated, both victims of the sabotage and Sviridov were shot. Vasiliy Klubkov, the only member of Zoya's group to have got back alive, was also shot. Before that he had been beaten into confessing that he had betrayed Zoya. The intention was to include this detail in the propaganda account of her death, but in the event it was not used, the authors having changed their minds.

One of the witnesses gave this description of Zoya Kosmodemianskaya's execution:

They led her to the gallows, pinioning her arms. She walked steadily with her head held high, silent and proud. They brought her to the gallows where there were a lot of Germans and villagers. She was led there and they ordered people to move back, to make the circle round the gallows bigger, and started photographing her. They put a bag of [the incendiary] bottles near her. She shouted, "Citizens! Do not stand there! Do not watch! You need to help us to fight! This is my death. This is my achievement!" One officer punched her and others shouted at her. Then she said, "Comrades, victory will be ours. German soldiers, surrender before it is too late." She said all this while she was being photographed. Then they put a box there. Without any command she got up on the box herself. A German came and started putting the noose on her. She shouted at that time: "No matter how many of us you hang, you can't hang us all. There are 170 million of us. For me, my comrades will take revenge on you." She said that when she already had the noose round her neck. She was going to say something more but at this moment they took the box from under her feet and she was left hanging. She took hold of the rope but a German hit her hands. After that, everybody went away.

Kosmodemianskaya's body was left hanging on the gallows for about a month, and was repeatedly desecrated by German soldiers passing through the village. At New Year 1942, drunk Germans tore the clothes off the corpse and further defiled it, stabbing it and cutting off the breasts. The next day the Germans gave the order to remove the gallows, and the body was buried by local people outside the village. It rested there only temporarily, and was later reburied in the Novodevichy Cemetery in Moscow.

Chapter 7

"That was somebody's father, and I have killed him!"

The wounded soldier brought in during the night to the regimental doctor's dugout was no longer in need of help. The body in its blood-soaked greatcoat was left at the entrance until morning. When Anya Mulatova came out of a neighbouring dugout during the night for a pee, she saw it, already rigid, the bloody coat frozen stiff. Anya, who had had a horror of blood ever since she was little, felt sick.[185]

In the morning, when the millet porridge was being served for breakfast, she found she could not eat it. As soon as she put a spoonful in her mouth she imagined it was full of warm blood. The same thing happened the following day and the next. Anya's partner, Tasya Pegeshova, took matters into her own hands and told the doctor, who soon found a cure.[186] He rolled a cigarette and told Anya, who had never smoked before and never did afterwards, to take a deep drag. The strong tobacco made her cough terribly and she "evacuated through every orifice". The tobacco trumped her aversion to food, and a year later Anya had no problem bayoneting a bloated German corpse "to let the gas out".[187]

It seems you can get used to anything, even to corpses in varying states of decomposition, which at first seem completely hideous. In those March days of 1944, somewhere near Anya in Byelorussia, Zoya Alexandrova, a young nurse, took advantage of a lull in the fighting to move a little away from the front and into the woods. She found herself in a place where there had been a battle long before. All around, powdered with snow, were the frozen corpses of Soviet soldiers. They did not disturb her in the least, and indeed few things could have prevented her at that moment from relieving herself. "I would have done it even if there had been shrapnel flying everywhere," she recalled many years later. She took off her quilted jacket and other clothing, exposing her body, which, as if covered in pepper, was "burning from the bites of innumerable lice".[188] She did not try to squash them but just scraped them off her clothes with her nails and threw them into the snow. At that moment, nothing in the world seemed more urgent.

The dead soldiers that lay around Zoya had been here since since the first, failed, offensive here in the winter. Klava Panteleeva's platoon arrived at the 3rd Byelorussian Front at a time when the opposing armies were occupying stable defensive positions. This is when snipers become indispensable. Their work constantly undermines the enemy's nerves, creating a relentless tension.

★

March was coming to an end, but the snow was still on the ground in Smolensk Province. Slowly moving in the direction of Byelorussia, Klava Panteleyeva and her comrades saw snow-covered woods and snowdrifts through the train windows. When the platoon got off the train, a long way from the front as it transpired, and was loaded on to a truck, a terrible blizzard started. There was so much snow! The truck was no match for it and for most of the way they had to push it.[189] How long did they "ride" like that? A day? Two? Endlessly, it seemed to Klava.

They finally reached their regiment, by now close to the front line, and were allocated dugouts, a new form of accommodation they found distinctly unpleasant. The dugouts were dark and damp, dank, in fact. The girls did not lose heart, but lit a fire, lay down on their "bunks", which consisted of two long pieces of wood with sticks nailed across them and fir branches laid on top. That night they slept the sleep of the just.

Two days later, with the snowstorm subsiding, it was time to familiar-ise themselves with the German front line. They were issued white camouflage suits, and bandages to wrap round their rifles so they did not show black against the snow. They were given breakfast early in the morning: bread and porridge, and an open sandwich with a slice of American sausage for lunch.[190] "Not over-generous," the girls decided, but it was only recently that this American lend-lease sausage had appeared. How many people were to remember it ruefully in the hungry post-war years! Before that, anyone who could not get their lunch from the field kitchen had to make do with bread, dried rusks, a frozen food bar you had to gnaw at, or nothing.

The German positions, it was explained to Klava and her companions (one squad of twelve snipers), were only 300 metres or so away. They would have to crawl to their trenches on their bellies, but where exactly were they? Everything was deep in snow. Nadya Loginova crawled by mistake in the direction of the Germans, on to no-man's-land, which was mined. What should they do? They were afraid to shout, scared of everything on this first day. Someone did, nevertheless, call loudly,

"Nadya! Nadya! This way!" Nadya came back and they all finally made it to their snow-covered trench.[191]

Something similar happened in another sniper platoon, but ended tragically. Two pairs, Serafima Vasina and Nadya Selyanina, Lena Milko and Valya Shchelkanova, were ordered, immediately after arriving at the front, to monitor the forward position of the German defences. They stood in the trench all day, peering through the sights of their rifles and, when darkness fell, headed back home. Serafima recalled, we "were so tired we lost our sense of direction and headed in completely the wrong direction, straight towards the fascist trenches".[192] Why there was no one more senior to guide them is unclear. Where was the platoon commander? Many girl snipers recall it was uncommon to see a platoon commander on the front line.

Serafima remembers, "We were walking quietly, not speaking, and suddenly there was a terrible explosion under Valya Shchelkanova's feet." She had stepped on a mine. Flares hung in the air above their heads and the Germans opened fire with mortars. The girls bound up what was left of Valya's leg and "pressed ourselves to the ground, not knowing whether there were more mines nearby". The wounded Valya was groaning and the others urged her to keep quiet in order not to reveal their position, which would be fatal. She fell silent, having evidently lost consciousness. The girls lay there terrified, not daring to crawl back. Suddenly they heard a voice, "Okay, lassies, we've come to take you home." Several reconnaissance soldiers had come to the rescue. They took Valya and carried her very quietly back. The rest followed in their footsteps. When Valya came to, she begged them to shoot her. She did not want to live without a leg. Then she lost consciousness again.

That first day, as the girls in Klava Panteleyeva's platoon later regretfully recalled, "we could easily have killed a dozen Germans."[193] After several days of snow there were drifts everywhere, and the Germans, completely unafraid, were calmly clearing snow in broad daylight. But shooting a person for the first time is not as easy as shooting at a target on the firing range. Standing at one arm's length from each another, Klava and Marusya only observed the Germans through their sights. Neither could bring themselves to pull the trigger.

Zina Gavrilova and Tanya Fyodorova, however, opened their tally that first day. These girls were older: Zina had come to the school from a partisan group, and Tanya was the platoon's Young Communist League organiser. They had not been scared. They related how "Zina's German" had come out in just his underpants that morning to wash. After Zina's shot killed him, he lay there all day in full view of everyone. The Germans waited until after dark to remove his body.

That evening, when everyone was exchanging their experiences in the dugout, Klava and Marusya had nothing to say. They cursed themselves: "What cowards! What did we come to the front for anyway?" Why had others opened their tally and they had failed to? The next time they were taken back to the trench from which they always operated, they knew they were not just there to wait and observe. You see one, you shoot him! The first German Klava got in her sights was a soldier clearing the snow away from a machine-gun point. She saw an embrasure in the German parapet and a machine-gun mount, and then the German rose up into sight to clear away snow. Klava fired and he fell on to the parapet. He was immediately pulled back down by the legs. That day Marusya too opened her tally, as did many others. The Germans stopped clearing snow during the day, as did the Soviet soldiers. In any case, it soon melted.

The liberation of Byelorussia was hastened by the work of a huge army of partisans. By 1944, 143,000 people were said to be fighting in numerous companies (although, as this is a Soviet estimate, it may be inflated). Half the territory of Byelorussia was under partisan control. They blew up tens of thousands of railway tracks, causing major disruption to German lines of transportation. Without waiting for the arrival of the regular Red Army they liberated villages and hamlets and dozens of district centres.

Women and children fought alongside the men. In addition to women from the surrounding villages (many of whom had no other option), the partisans included women who were Young Communist League or Party workers in Byelorussia. Hundreds of Young Communist League girls were parachuted in as radio operators to help the partisans. Many were dropped off-target or suffered injuries and fell into the hands of the Germans. Almost none of them had any training in parachute jumping, which did nothing to improve the success rate. Twenty-year-old Klava Romashova was one of the luckier ones.

When, in autumn 1942, she was parachuted into Bryansk Province, all she knew was how to fold a parachute. She was helped to jump from the plane by the simple expedient of a shove in the back, and her main parachute opened automatically. It occurred to her later that if anything had gone wrong with it, she would have died because nobody had told her how to operate the emergency parachute. She drifted – weighed down by an assault rifle, three magazines for it, a walkie-talkie radio and power source, and a greatcoat – towards bonfires lit by the partisans, but before she could descend on to her target, her parachute snagged on a pine tree. Cutting through the risers, Klava climbed down and crawled to one side, blissfully unaware what an easy target the parachute hanging in the tree above would have made her for any Germans in the area. Fortunately, she was greeted only by the partisans, who saw her parachute and began calling, "Radio operator! Radio operator!"

Klava remained silent, fearing that these might be Byelorussian collaborators working for the Germans, but in the end one of them tripped over her and shouted, "Here she is!" The twenty-year-old was offered "partisan grapes", a bunch of frozen rowanberries. This berry, normally unbearably bitter-tasting, becomes quite palatable after it has been frosted. A few hours later, Klava made contact with Moscow for the first time.

Talking about it many decades later, Klava Romashova who, before the war, had been a Young Communist League secretary in Perm, was surprised how brave she and her comrades had been when they were young. When asked at the end of their radio operator's course whether any of them would like to stay on to work as instructors instead of flying behind enemy lines, they all turned the offer down, except for one girl whose name, Klava remembered, was Bolshakova.

At first, everything in the partisan company was very strange to a city girl like herself: the people, the food, the living conditions.[194] On top of the still-warm ashes of a big bonfire they would spread fir branches, and erect tents on them in which they could sleep warmly even during that particularly cold winter. Out on a mission with the commander, she spent one night in a peasant hut and contracted typhoid fever. She was still very weak when the Germans launched an operation against the partisans and they had to move elsewhere. They put her on a horse (for the first and last time in her life), and she felt it was a miracle she managed to stay in the saddle. Her trials did not end there. The Germans drove the partisans back to a marsh and they only managed to escape with the help of local villagers who guided them. They put their feet in the villagers' footprints, each of whom was testing the way with a stick. At the end of that crossing, Klava suffered concussion that left her deaf for a time, and although she got some of her hearing back later, she was no longer able to work as a radio operator. In 1944, after the partisans merged with regular army units and began advancing with them, she was sent to the rear.

In mid-March 1944, a Soviet offensive on the Vitebsk–Orsha line was called off. The army was saving its strength for a major operation, subsequently named "Bagration". For the time being, both sides were occupying defensive positions, which meant the snipers were much in demand. The day after they arrived in the village of Krasnoye, near Orsha, their platoon commander, Senior Lieutenant Rakityansky, took the twelve girls in Anya Mulatova's squad out to familiarise them with the front line of defence. Their commander, a short, skinny lad with typically Jewish features, seemed very mature, although, at twenty-two or twenty-three, he was only a few years older than they were themselves. At their first meeting, when Rakityansky came from the regiment to collect them from the school, this already seasoned senior lieutenant seemed to them a battle-scarred front-line fighter. There was a huge gap between an officer and them, mere corporals. Rakityansky treated his subordinates confidently, politely but firmly.[195] He was not a sniper and had gone to the front immediately after infantry college, but he taught them a lot.

On their first day at the front, the girls got up long before dawn. The sky was still starry, and all around was a "solemn stillness", as if the enemy must be very far away. The snow crunched; the path meandered down into a hollow, then up again. In a dell Rakityansky suddenly whispered, "We need to take this next stretch at the double, crouching down. It is exposed to fire." They ran across, and continued along communication trenches that were about one and a half metres deep. Rakityansky brought them to the observation post of the commander of the infantry company on whose territory their platoon would be working.[196]

His dugout was solidly constructed, with four layers of logs in the roof and a tarpaulin serving as a door. Though it was cosy and had a stove heating it, they did not stay there long.[197] After checking the passwords with the company commander, Rakityansky took the girls on to the embrasures in the trenches. This was where they would be "hunting" from. Anya's partner, Tasya Pegeshova, wanted to get a better view of the German positions than she could through the embrasure and stuck her head above the parapet. Rakityansky was alert and immediately tugged her greatcoat to get her head down. He reminded her that the enemy was observing them too.[198]

Anya stood at an embrasure a few metres from Tasya so they would not need to shout to each other, and peered through the scope. Everything looked different, not at all as it had at the school. Immediately before them was no-man's-land, then, about 200 metres further on, the first line of the German defences: several rows of barbed-wire entanglements with

"Bruno Spirals"* between them. Beyond that was the dark edge of a forest, a slight haze just above the ground, and nothing else.

They peered out until their eyes hurt, or until they had to take a walk along the trench to warm up. It was still very cold. They had not been able to dry their boots, damp from yesterday, and these froze stiff. Their index fingers, pressed all the time on the trigger, grew numb with cold.[199] They stood there till dusk without a making a kill and, exhausted, frozen and hungry, went back to their dugout. Sitting themselves down with the other girls around the stove, they took off their boots and white camouflage suits and laid them out to dry for the next shift, who would be on duty again tomorrow. They took off their greatcoats, ate their dinner and, without undressing, collapsed on to their bunks. When one of the girls began monotonously snoring, Anya, warming up, felt herself also rapidly drifting off into sleep.

Anya and Tasya opened their tallies the next day they went hunting – simultaneously and from a considerable distance. No sooner had they started watching at dawn than they saw two German soldiers in the distance carrying a box or a large jar with handles. At first the soldiers were far away, just two black dots, and the girls decided to wait. The Germans disappeared into a communication trench and Anya concluded that the moment had passed. Then, however, the pair reappeared out of a hollow, walking fully upright. They were now about 600 metres away and within range. Anya and Tasya fired at the same time, and both Germans fell as if they had been scythed down. Tasya had a clean kill with "her fascist", but Anya's was writhing in pain on the ground. They needed now to move to a different embrasure, because they had been taught that you could only shoot once from a particular spot if you did not want to be hunted down yourself.[200]

Anya realised later that the first time she shot a German had been

* The Bruno Spiral was concertinaed barbed wire, an anti-personnel obstacle in the form of a cylindrical spiral 70–130 centimetres in diametre and 25 metres long. It consisted of several intersecting strands of barbed or ordinary wire stretched on stakes.

relatively easy, because of the distance. "As if it was just target practice," she recalled. She was feeling on top of the world at having made a start. Killing people at a distance is easier on your conscience; shooting at 200 metres, a sniper can clearly see their victim's face in the telescopic sight. Just two months later, Anya had to shoot a German at five metres, and afterwards was tormented by the thought of him, and even dreamed about him.

For those of Anya's classmates from sniper school who had a clear sight of the face of their first German, killing or wounding that person was deeply upsetting. Firing a "good shot" at a human being was not, the sniper suddenly realised, anything like the hundreds of other shots they had fired during training. This human figure, this head or chest, was not a target but someone just as alive as you were yourself. Soviet propaganda, which dehumanised the invaders, repeatedly emphasising the terrible crimes they'd committed against the Russia people, was highly effective. It played a hugely important part in defeating the Germans, and it called on Russians to kill and kill again. Even if you killed only a single German, you would bring victory closer and save the lives of Soviet people. Ilya Ehrenburg's devastating, passionate articles told soldiers repeatedly that the quickest way to victory, to liberate their native land and rescue its people, was to physically destroy the enemy, and the more the better.

Tonya Makhlyagina, a slim, fair-haired, pretty girl from the Urals, looked as if she was the sister of her sniper partner, Tosya Bratishcheva, except that Tosya was dark. They were similar in character too, both cheery optimists. Neither was immediately able to open their tally, and both were upset. Other girls already had, but they were afraid to pull the trigger and, in the evenings, after a day's stalking, they cursed themselves. Finally, success! Tonya Makhlyagina shot a German who appeared above the parapet and she saw him fall. Her delight took her breath away. She had hit the target! But she was immediately crushed by a terrible thought:

"That was somebody's father, and I have killed him!"[201] She had noticed the German had a moustache and was middle-aged. Tonya, an orphan who had been brought up by her grandmother, suddenly realised that her shot might have just orphaned other children. Yes, he was the enemy, but he had not fired first: she had. He should still be alive, she thought, and burst into tears.[202]

Spring had finally arrived. On the Second Byelorussian Front the snow was melting, and revealing terrible sights. After battles, whole fields of the dead lay unburied, mostly Russians because, while the Germans made an effort to bury their soldiers, the Russians did not care as much about the fate of their corpses. More and more "cemeteries" of unburied bodies appeared. One night in March 1944, Sniper Lida Bakieva was working her way through just such a field, entirely alone.

That night Lida had been unable to sleep for thinking about what might have become of her husband, Volodya. He had been fighting on this front, but for a long time now she had had no news of him. Lida's heart rebelled against this crushed, obedient waiting. She was used to being active. In a fit of desperation, she went out of the dugout and made for a field where there had recently been a battle. She walked among the dead Russian and German soldiers, looking into the faces of the Russians, somehow sure she was about to find her husband. It was beginning to freeze. In the moonlight, the faces of the dead seemed alive. She walked on and on, turning over those who were lying face downwards.[203]

Lida Bakieva never remarried, and for many years searched for news of her husband, who vanished without trace on the Second Byelorussian Front and who, for her, was forever just twenty years old. She never did find out what happened to him.

When it is not just someone you read about in a newspaper who has died at the hands of the enemy, or even just someone you knew, but a person who is near and dear to you, your hand will not tremble as you squeeze the trigger: you want revenge. At the front, the first death of a comrade from a German bullet or shrapnel fragment was just as shocking as it would be in the civilian world and, after it, shooting Germans suddenly became easy.

Many girl snipers were killed in their first days at the front, before they had learnt the need for caution. Anya Mulatova witnessed the death of a friend while they were still at Orsha. Tanya Moshkina was killed soon after they arrived, but Anya had not been there to see it. Masha Vasiliskova, though, was killed in front of her. That day, Anya was not with Tasya. She was having her period, so was exempted from hunting. The trench Commander Rakityansky was leading several of them along had been dug in zigzags, and as the German positions were on higher ground, they evidently had sight of the far side of some of the zigzags. Rakityansky was in front of them and, as the girls were negotiating one of the trench's sharp bends, Anya heard a crack and saw Masha fall. "Oh my God, why has Masha fallen down?" she wondered, not yet realising what had happened. Klava Lavrentieva was immediately behind Masha, and the next bullet hit her in the shoulder. Anya was next in line. She immediately fell to the ground and crawled towards her wounded comrades. Blood was spurting from Masha's neck, but she was still conscious and asked for water. They bandaged her up somehow and pulled her away, but she soon died.[204] This was Anya's first encounter with an enemy sniper who, just like her, had spotted "heads" bobbing along a trench through his telescopic sight.

They gave Masha a proper funeral, unlike all the other snipers in Anya's platoon who were killed subsequently. They made her a real coffin, decorated it with bandage gauze, and made artificial paper flowers. The funeral was photographed, and all the girls cried and cried. Friends who died later were mourned with considerably less ceremony. Later on they were seldom in a position to give their dead comrades a proper funeral, and in any case death gradually ceased to make a big impression on them.

★

It was spring, the snow melted, the trees came into leaf and the first flowers appeared. The front was not moving, and Klava Panteleyeva's platoon developed its own routine, replacing the infantry in the trenches and hunting while it was light, sleeping at night. It was just the same that day. There was no sign of movement from the Germans, and Klava and Marusya left their rifles in the embrasures and took it in turns to observe. You could not watch all the time because your eyes would get too tired. "My turn now," Marusya said. She went to her rifle and must have moved it so that the lens reflected the sun. It was just what a German sniper was waiting for. A shot rang out and Marusya fell. She died instantly, and Klava screamed and wailed terribly. The soldiers around her woke up and ran to her, begging her to keep quiet because the Germans were only 200 metres away. "Quiet, quiet, or they'll open up with mortar fire!" Klava just could not calm down. She stayed with Marusya's corpse until evening. When finally night fell, the soldiers helped her carry her friend's body on a groundsheet. Klava wanted to change Marusya's clothes, but she was buried in her blood-stained uniform, the grim spectacle relieved only by the first spring flowers, which they picked for her. Later Klava was given a new partner, Marusya Gulyakina, a Muscovite who had worked before the war as a domestic servant. Marusya was older than Klava, already a woman. She had a kind, pockmarked face and treated Klava like a younger sister, braiding her plaits (many of the girls had grown their hair long again at the front) with ribbons made from bandage gauze. But soon she too was killed.[205]

"Nowhere do you need close friendship and comradely relations more than in war. Even a soldier's mess tin is designed to hold two servings of soup. A greatcoat can cover two of you, and a cape-groundsheet also has room for two. If you are lying wounded, a friend can drag you to shelter, bring you food and drink. A friend in war means survival." These sentiments, which Vasiliy Selin, a mortar gunner, recorded in his memoirs, will probably be recognised by anybody who has survived combat.[206]

And if this friend on whom they rely so profoundly is killed, the surviving partner grieves for them for a lifetime. In psychology this is called "survivor guilt": why my friend but not me? The girls in a sniper pair ate together, slept on one of their greatcoats while covering themselves with the other's, went on missions together, shared secrets and fears, and dreamed together about the future. If one was killed, the other felt as if they would never be the same person again. "Marusya was killed, and today I am still living for her," Klava Panteleyeva reminisced many, many years later.[207]

Masha Shvarts, the partner of Kalya Petrova, died at the very beginning of their time at the front. She was half-Jewish, a pretty young woman with black hair and dark eyes, a little older than Kalya and very clever – a good friend to talk to. Kalya respected and imitated her.

On the day Masha died it was very cold, and the girls took turns to run and warm up in the dugout. Masha went off but did not return, and a soldier came and told Kalya she had been killed. She was shot by a sniper on a stretch where a trench had yet to be dug, meaning that you had to run across it on the surface. Kalya had crossed that terrain a few times herself that same day, but it was Masha who had been killed. At night, her body was brought back to the platoon on a drag and Kalya and her friends buried her.[208]

Kalya was not found another partner and, in any case, they shortly began an offensive, where, because snipers took part in them as ordinary soldiers, they did not need to be paired up. On her own now, Kalya became friendly with Roza Shanina and Sasha Yekimova, and they became known as "the troika". "Our battle troika", Roza called them in her diary. Roza was uneducated and rather coarse, and Sasha was a bit full of herself, so Kalya was never as close to them as she had been to Masha, but she greatly respected their bravery.

Chapter 8

"Your daughter died for the Motherland. It has not been possible to bury her"

On 8 April 1944, the Fourth Ukrainian Front began the assault on Crimea from the direction of Syvash and Perekop. The 46 Guards Night Bomber Regiment, the only one in the Soviet Air Force composed entirely of women, bombed the Germans in Kerch. On 9 April, just two days before the city was liberated, the regiment lost a young pilot, Pana Prokopieva, and her navigator. That night her partner had been the regiment's chief navigator, Zhenya Rudneva. Zhenya was highly experienced and, while for Pana this was only her tenth flight, for Zhenya it was her 645th. Rudneva, always demanding of herself and others, considered it her duty to take to the skies with all the novice pilots.

More than familiar after two years with losing their friends, the girls of Zhenya's regiment mourned her probably more sorrowfully than anyone they had lost before. For the night bombers' guards regiment, this loss was one of the most painful in the entire war. They had been in awe of Zhenya, a dreamer who knew an endless number of folk tales, a punctilious navigator, and a loyal, fearless friend.

Prokopieva's aircraft failed to return from bombing in the vicinity of the village of Bulganak near Kerch. When Kerch was liberated, they searched in vain for Zhenya and Pana, and after three months the regiment's commissar, Yevdokia Rachkevich, wrote to Pana's parents, "Your daughter died for the Motherland. It has not been possible to bury her. She was incinerated together with Zhenya Rudneva and their ashes were carried away by the wind."[209]

That was not actually true. The plane crashed in the centre of Kerch, and the girls were found and buried by the townspeople. Her soldiers' boots had been preserved on Pana's charred body, which was assumed to be that of a man and buried in a mass grave. Zhenya's body was thrown clear of the plane, so it was less burned. The local people buried her in the city park, writing on the plaque, "Here lies an unknown airwoman." The members of her regiment learned this only in 1966, when the graves were found by Commissar Rachkevich.

570 Infantry Regiment left the Adzhimushkai quarries on 10 March 1944. Zina Galifastova wrote to her mother in Armavir, Krasnodar Region,

> Yesterday the army went on the offensive. We girls marched with our regiment. There was intense fighting. The Germans resisted desperately. Sometimes you have to lie on the ground and cannot lift your head. You know your friends are running behind you and alongside. We broke through very strong German fortifications and burst into Kerch. Now, dear Mother, we are driving these fiends back to Sevastopol. I am happy to tell you that in this battle none of my sniper friends were killed or even injured. Our sniper platoon has been given a truck. Now we will not be pursuing the Fritzes on foot but in our own transport.[210]

227 Infantry Division was part of the second formation of the Maritime Army. The first, in which Lyudmila Pavlichenko served, had been almost entirely captured or killed in Sevastopol in 1942. The division, and with it the sniper platoon, began the attack on Kerch during the night of 10 April: by morning the city was liberated. The Soviet soldiers found themselves in a deserted realm of devastation. A population of 100,000 had been reduced to only thirty souls or so. Many had been killed; others the Germans had expelled. Nothing remained of the large, verdant pre-war city. One of the liberators wrote in a letter, "A few impressions: night, the crossing, and we are standing on the soil of Crimea. Everywhere is broken, mangled equipment, tanks, guns, transport. This is Kerch, the gateway to Crimea. Or rather, this is what used to be Kerch. Heaps of rubble, traces of those bastards with swastikas."[211] The time had come to liberate

Crimea, and the Soviets made plenty of resources available for the task. Although the peninsula was no longer of great strategic importance, given the huge advances being made elsewhere, the loss of Crimea would represent a great symbolic blow for the Germans, and one likely to substantially undermine their morale.

On 11 April, the Maritime Army broke through the fortifications of Turetsky Val on the Isthmus of Perekop and approached the Ak-Monay stone quarries, where the Germans had built a further line of fortifications. The next day, Feodosia fell. Galya Koldeyeva, returning from hospital after being wounded in the throat, caught up with the snipers there. She brought Nurse Zhenya Grunskaya a newspaper containing the letter she had written to her School No. 36. "When the war is over," Zhenya wrote, "I will come and sit down again at my desk and catch up on all the lessons I've missed. Girls, I wish you every success in your studies and hope you become skilled professionals."[212]

Zina Galifastova wrote home, "Soon you will be hearing that Crimea has been completely liberated!"[213] After Feodosia, the Maritime Army liberated the town of Stary Krym and continued to advance towards Sevastopol. There was rain in the mountains and the roads were reduced to mud, which meant that they frequently had to get out and push their truck.

The German 17 Army retreated towards Sevastopol, from where it was to be evacuated by sea. Although Hitler confirmed his order that the Crimea was to be held and rejected all evacuation proposals, a plan to evacuate troops from Sevastopol did exist. The final version, signed off in April 1944, was codenamed "Adler". It was proposed over 6–7 days to withdraw troops from all sectors of the peninsula to the fortified district of Sevastopol, where transport ships would evacuate them. In Sevastopol itself they built a series of fortifications with anti-tank ditches to delay the pursuing armour. The German command on the peninsula believed they could hold out in Sevastopol for three weeks and save 17 Army.

For the sniper platoon, the truck they had been assigned was undoubtedly a godsend: from 12 to 16 April the Independent Maritime Army just pursued the German and Romanian units that were fleeing in panic to Sevastopol. As the Soviets approached the Sevastopol fortified district, German resistance stiffened, and on 16 April the pursuit ended. The Maritime Army came to a standstill on the near approaches to Sevastopol. An assault on the city was imminent.

On 12 April, Hitler issued a lunatic order to defend Sevastopol to the last man. This was subsequently watered down: the troops were ordered to hold out there for 8–10 weeks. On 24 April the evacuation was completely stopped. The fortified area contained 55,000 German troops who now had no choice but to die there or surrender.

On 18 April, after heavy fighting, the Maritime Army took Balaklava, a small town on the outskirts of Sevastopol. Now the only obstacle to the city was the Sapun Ridge, which was protected by unbroken minefields of anti-tank and anti-personnel mines, trenches up to two metres deep, and triple, quadruple and quintuple barbed-wire entanglements. Every 25–30 metres along the trenches there were machine-gun emplacements, and every 150–200 metres there were pillboxes and bunkers. When combined with the line of hills the engineering works made the boundary all but impregnable.

"Before I knew it, there it was, the Sapun Ridge," Ivan Shpak, one of those who took part in the assault recalled. "They certainly had put in all sorts of stuff there, bunkers, pillboxes, trenches, foxholes."[214] For several days before the assault on the ridge, the snipers went about their business, stalking Germans on the fortified line. They picked off gunners and observers, officers and ordinary soldiers. Nina Kovalenko managed to shoot a German sniper who had been causing a lot of trouble.[215] At night they would fire randomly at bursts of fire from the machine-gun nests, just to make sure the Germans felt as if they were under continual pressure.[216] All around them the ground was cratered and the smoke of gunpowder hung over the hills.

They broke through the German defences on 7 May. A powerful artillery barrage lasted an hour and a half, and tanks fired directly at the German fortifications, "flushing out of their burrows" some at least of the mountain range's defenders. Maria Ivashchenko took part in the assault on the Sapun Ridge with an artillery regiment where she was serving as a signaller. She recalled, "The assault was terrifying. The Germans had dug in very thoroughly, and the Sapun Ridge was by then completely bare with never a tree or a twig for shelter. The infantry started going in to attack, but the German positions, which you would have thought had been completely flattened by the shelling and bombing, suddenly came to life and brought a hail of bullets and mortars down on the heads of our young lads."[217] The infantrymen whom Ivashchenko's unit was supporting were mercilessly wiped out by this fire, and she felt tremendously sorry for the soldiers, especially the very young local boys who had just been conscripted and given only a few days' training.

The poet Eduard Asadov, seriously wounded at Sevastopol and blinded at the age of nineteen, wrote about those days that, in the hell of Sevastopol, ill-fortune struck, his "lucky star" deserted him.

And in that battle, when the earth was burning
And Sevastopol vanished in the haze,
You could not make me out amidst the churning
To hold at bay the tricks misfortune plays.[218]

Early in the morning of 7 May the girls' sniper platoon got mixed up with advancing soldiers. "Mortars and shrapnel were whistling through the air," Nina Kovalenko recalls.[219] A former student of Krasnodar Pedagogical Institute, in the war Nina became the commander of a squad of girl snipers. Katya Peredera, reflecting later on the disaster, wondered why all the girls immediately lost sight of each other as they moved forward. She found herself alone with Zhenya Makeyeva and surrounded by infantrymen. When they saw the girls, the soldiers began shouting to them to go back. There was only sparse undergrowth around, which provided no cover from the Germans who were shooting from above.[220]

"Where the hell are you going!" someone shouted. "Take cover!" They could see themselves that they needed to get down and wait for the firing to tail off. The Soviet soldiers around them were no longer advancing: "They were all rolling downhill," Katya remembered.

The girls saw a shallow artillery shell crater where they could hide. Katya left her rifle up at the edge of the crater and it was immediately blown to bits.

Zhenya was wounded as she was crawling in. "She faded immediately," but managed to ask Katya, "Bandage me!" The bullet had hit her heart, but she held out for a couple of minutes. Katya was wounded too before she had time to get properly into the crater. "My legs were sticking out." Needless to say, a German sniper, using dumdum bullets (which were designed to explode inside the body of the victim – the girls used this ammunition themselves), aimed at them. Katya felt a terrible blow, "as if someone had hit me very hard on the legs with a stick". Her leg, with half the boot ripped off, was a terrible mess. She took a bandage pack with the intention of bandaging Zhenya. Overcoming a deadening sense of weakness, she opened the package, only to see that it was too late to help her. Zhenya Grunskaya, their platoon's nurse, should have been somewhere nearby, but Katya realised there was no time to wait for help. She needed to get back down the hill before she lost too much blood or she too would die, unless the German sniper finished her off first.

She started crawling, twice losing consciousness on the way, but managed to get down by herself. She was put on a stretcher and taken to shelter. "Where's Zhenya?" someone asked, and Katya told them she was dead.

Later, as she was moved from one hospital to another, and after the war, Katya was always thinking about Zhenya. What had become of her body? Had somebody buried her? Would anyone remember where? Would there be a grave for her mother to visit? She learned later that

Zhenya had been buried in a mass grave on Sapun Ridge, and another of her comrades-in-arms was also there, Nurse Zhenya Grunskaya, who died in the same battle.

The dumdum bullet had shattered Katya's heel and she had to spend a year in hospital. In August 1944, having been in two hospitals already, she was sent to a third. Things were not going particularly well: her leg was not healing properly and she faced further operations. The hospital food was awful, there were no painkillers, but there were other people there suffering far more than she was. Katya decided that, after the war, she would study to become a doctor. She wanted to help people. She was very homesick and missed her mother, and then in August, moving to the next hospital, after many days in a hospital train which sometimes moved along quietly but had now been standing for hours at a station, she suddenly realised she was close to home.

"Goodness, this is Kavkazskaya!" she exclaimed, waking up one morning at a station and looking out the window. The station building was not in good shape, but Katya recognised it immediately. This was where she lived. "Oh, Kavkazskaya! My mother lives here!"[221] she cried, and one of the walking wounded called some of the local women to her window. A lot of them met trains with the wounded in the hope of finding their sons or husbands. "Tell me the address and we'll fetch her," someone volunteered. Katya gave them the address (her mother lived two or three kilometres from the station), and two women ran off as fast as their legs could carry them. Unfortunately, her mother was not at home, but these total strangers rushed on to find her where a neighbour thought she might be. Katya had asked for her mother to bring sauerkraut, bacon fat and flowers, the things she had most missed at the front and now in the hospitals. She peered out of the window and waited and waited. The train might move at any moment. Would her mother really not get here in time? In the end, she did, completely out of breath. She brought sauerkraut, such boiled potatoes as she had left, a good piece of bacon fat and some flowers: morning glory, zinnias of all shades from red to yellow, the first asters and little blue thumbelinas. Katya loved these simple flowers, and later planted morning glory and asters, "plain country garden flowers", in her own garden too.

Her mother was able to spend a couple of hours with her before the train moved on, but its destination, and Katya's new hospital, were not too much further away. Her mother often visited her, bringing Katya meatballs, pancakes and radishes to supplement the plain hospital food. Her sister came to see her too, not Nina, who was demobilised only after the end of the war, but Valya, who had just been released from prison. She had run away from a military unit where although she was employed as a civilian she was subject to the army's regulations: jail was her punishment for desertion.

Katya's sniper platoon moved on, pursuing the Germans. In the fighting at Sevastopol they had lost another two snipers, Lisa Vasilenko and Lilia Vilks. The others went on to liberate Romania, Hungary and Czechoslovakia. On 1 February 1945, Galya Koldeyeva was killed in Zvolen in Slovakia. She was just nineteen years old.[222] [223]

Chapter 9

"The girls behave with exceptional modesty and discipline"

"The female snipers who arrived have killed eight Germans," a report about 1138 Infantry Regiment records on 7 April 1944.[224] Roza Shanina and her comrades had only recently arrived at the front. The army to which the snipers were sent was occupying defensive positions in Byelorussia. Although a decision had already been taken to advance at this sector, the offensive was not due to start until June, by which time everyone at the front was familiar with the work of the girl snipers, especially Roza Shanina.

Senior Reserve Sergeant Zhudin later described the girls turning up in the regiment, and how he took them to the front line to show them where there were most Germans.[225] He best remembered Roza, the most dynamic of them. In less than a month, on 1 May, the front-line newspapers *Red Army Pravda* and *Destroy the Enemy* were writing about Roza. She featured also in the leaflets of front-line units, under such headlines as, "Follow the example of Roza Shanina!" or "One cartridge, one fascist!" At the end of May, Sergeant Zhudin and Roza were both awarded the Order of Glory. By this time she had over twenty kills to her name.

Shanina told the press about her first German: "Finally, in the evening a German showed in the trench. I estimated the distance to the target was not over 400 metres. A suitable distance. When the Fritz, keeping his head down, went towards the woods, I fired, but from the way he fell, I knew I had not killed him. For about an hour the fascist lay in the mud, not daring to move. Then he started crawling. I fired again, and this time did not miss."[226]

Alexander Stanovov, a photographer for *Destroy the Enemy*, got to know this sniper platoon as soon as they reached the front, and heard about their first successes during the deadlock between Vitebsk and Orsha. At first, he too laughed with the soldiers at these "cheerful chatterboxes". What sort of soldiers would they ever make? Soon, however, he was photographing them for his newspaper: Roza, Kalya Petrova, Sima Anashkina, Lida Vdovina, Dusya Krasnoborova and Sasha Yekimova. This group was even included in an Informbyuro press announcement on 19 May, and Roza was mentioned separately as having "exterminated fifteen fascists".[227] When Stanovov appeared where the platoon was quartered, Roza, "a tall, slender girl with smiling eyes", refused to be photographed. She finally agreed, providing all her friends were in the photo too.[228]

While talking to her he learned that Roza was from the north, and had worked before the war as a teacher at the Beryozka kindergarten in Arkhangelsk. After the start of the offensive Stanovov lost track of her and her friends, and only heard about them from others who had met up with the girls at the front line and from what he read in the newspapers. Forty years later he was in Arkhangelsk and went looking for the Beryozka kindergarten. It had a large portrait of Roza, which Stanovov recognised as a picture he had snapped so many years ago.

Sniper Vdovina, a very pretty, petite girl with a doll-like face, was nicknamed "the old woman" in her platoon, no doubt because her fair hair could be taken for white. People living near the White Sea, where she was from, often have this kind of look. Lida lived in Arkhangelsk and arrived at the front at the same time as Roza. She fell short of Shanina's tally, but was also quite a sharpshooter and was written about in the newspapers, as was Sasha Yekimova. "In the fighting for Vitebsk, Lida Vdovina exterminated eight fascists."

Like Kalya Petrova, Lida's war began with a tragedy. A signaller crawled to her trench to report, "I've come to collect your friend, Nina. She has been killed."[229] Lida followed him until they reached the spot where her partner, Nina Posazhnikova from Dzhambul in Kazakhstan, had been. Lida saw "only her boots and the barrel of her rifle, the rest of her was covered with earth." Lida "took her rifle and I went back to my position. Pain and sorrow overwhelmed me, and were not healed by time." In the battles for Vitebsk, Lida would avenge Nina, but her first German was payback for her brother, Viktor, killed in 1941.[230]

By summer 1944, the front-line newspapers, and even the national press, were writing about many other girls from that second cohort. They published letters from commanders thanking the Central Women's Sniper Training School for their specialists. Commander Spivak of the sniper section of 125 Krasnoselskaya Infantry Division wrote to the school, "I have been sent ten girl snipers. I was entrusted with them as I am myself an experienced sniper in this war, and am passing on to them my experience of combat. They work very successfully and their tally of vengeance grows by the day. Bogomolova has put paid to 14 Hitlerites, Adoratskikh – 11, Shvetsova – 14, Morozova –12, Bulatova has 10, Tupekova – 5, Nevolina – 5, Karenysheva[231] – 6, Kiselyova – 4, and

Veryovkina – 9. These snipers have forced the enemy to crawl. The girls behave with exceptional modesty and discipline."[232]

That is more than could be said of some of their commanders.

Shortly after Taya Kiselyova's platoon reached the front, their battalion commander started taking a great interest in Zina Karenysheva. Zina declined his offer of intimacy and did not respond to threats. In the end, seizing an opportunity, the battalion commander locked himself in with her on the first floor of a building and raped her. That was not the end of it: the rapist would not let Zina out and kept her imprisoned there for two days. Finally she called to her friends, and they helped her climb down on sheets knotted together. Should they seek justice against a senior officer? It was just too dangerous and few dared. The rapist could shoot you on the front line and that would be the last anyone heard of you. In any case, they thought it better to keep the disgrace to themselves.

Taya Kiselyova herself rejected the advances of a captain who was the chief of staff. He promised to festoon her tunic with medals, but otherwise . . . He even threatened to whip her. When Taya flatly refused to sleep with him, the captain tore up an application for an award in front of her. It was very hurtful, but she decided that, having taken his revenge on her in that manner, the chief of staff would leave her alone. He was incapable of anything more serious.

The 31 Army political reports mention the arrival of 129 girl snipers conscripted by the Young Communist League Central Committee. They were split into five groups and assigned to various divisions. The snipers were given "appropriate guidance by workers of the Young Communist League branch of the Army's Political Department", and approval was also given to "a special list of themes for talks and reports in working with the girls". For example, in addition to the standard programme, they heard presentations on the topic of "Girl Heroes of the Soviet Union". Meetings were organised for them with leading snipers, they were "inducted into military life", and regular reports were forwarded on their achievements. Care was also taken over their living conditions. The report mentions that the girls' platoons were each accommodated in their own dugout, with two-tier bunks, with a desk in each dugout "suitable for writing, reading newspapers and books, playing dominoes and draughts". There was to be a drying room near the dugout.

Noting the "exceptionally good condition of the rifles", the report's author moves on to "shortcomings in working with the girl snipers". The main, and often the only, problem he noted was sexual harassment by officers. "In 331 Infantry Division there have been instances of a number of senior commanders at headquarters attempting to summon girls to their dugout at night. The divisional command placed Captains Moiseyenko and Borovsky under house arrest for five days, with deductions from their pay for such behaviour."

The political reports contain no information about complaints against a regimental commander of 31 Army who blighted the life of probably more than one girl. Was it hushed up? Did no one dare to complain? Anya Mulatova would never have dreamt, as a corporal, of complaining about the misconduct of a lieutenant colonel.

One evening the adjutant of the regimental commander, Lieutenant Colonel Golubev, came into the snipers' dugout (which, in the interests of discipline, had a sentry posted at its entrance to keep men out). "Which of you is Sniper Mulatova? You are required." The top brass lived in a different world, with which people like Corporal Mulatova had no contact. Until now they had taken no interest in Anya, and her first reaction was alarm: "What have I done?" It soon transpired, however, that the regimental commander was in a very amicable mood.[233]

"Ah, reporting for duty," he commented. "With a smirk," Anya noted when she came into the dugout. "Well, come in, since that's the case." The bald, middle-aged lieutenant colonel invited her to sit down, and in came the adjutant with a teapot and some biscuits, "a great temptation" and delicacy at the front. Golubev had no sweets to go with the tea, but did have sugar lumps, which are delicious if you sip your tea through them. So there they were, drinking tea, the commander asking about this and that, how well they had studied the German line of defence, the soldier's newsletter Anya was editing with Lida Anderman, their sniper record books . . .

Then everything suddenly took an unwelcome turn. Perching himself on a broad bunk next to the log Anya was sitting on, her regimental commander abruptly, without so much as a by-your-leave, grabbed her and pushed her back on the bench. He lost no time in starting to unfasten her trousers (which were buttoned down both sides on women's uniforms). Reluctant to scream – she was worried the ageing sentry at the top of the stairs would find out what was going on – Anya fought the lieutenant colonel off for a while. She was strong and healthy, and as fast as Golubev was unbuttoning her trousers on one side, she pushed him back and refastened the buttons on the other. She finally managed to get free and gave the rapist a hefty kick. Regimental Commander Golubev fell off his bunk on to the floor and Anya rushed to the door, still doing up her trousers. There were three or four steps to go up before she could escape the dugout. She stumbled and fell, but managed to shoulder the door open.

"On your way, my dear, on your way," the sentry said. Anya thought Golubev would hardly come chasing after her, so did not run but walked away, sobbing, back to her quarters. She had never even kissed a boy, and suddenly this!

In the dugout she said nothing to the girls about what had happened. What a disgrace! She took her greatcoat off the nail, lay down on her bed of fir branches, put her head on her knapsack, and pulled the greatcoat over her head, sobbing to herself.

She was surprised that none of the other girls came over to her, and that they were whispering, "Anya's been over *there*!" It turned out she was not the first of them to have experienced the commander's advances, but nobody talked about it. She supposed that if she told them what had actually happened it would only make matters worse, because nobody would believe her.

The next day Anya was very worried, expecting trouble from the authorities, but nothing happened. Soon after that the offensive began and their platoon joined up with a different unit, the 123 Infantry Regiment led by Vasiliy Slavnov, an excellent officer and a gentleman.

The new Soviet weapon which, perhaps in honour of the heroine of a popular song, was given a girl's gentle diminutive name, terrified the Germans.

> From behind us we heard a sudden grinding, a rumble, and over our heads and up on to the hill in front of us there passed a flight of flaming arrows. Up on the heights everything was covered with fire, smoke and dust. Amid the chaos, candles of fire flared up from individual explosions. We heard a terrible roar. When everything had settled and we heard the command, "Forward!", we took the height almost without resistance. The "Katyushas" had blown everything away. Up on the heights, when we reached them, we saw the ground all churned up. There was almost no trace left of the trenches where the Germans had been. There were a lot of corpses of enemy soldiers, and any surviving Germans looked terrified. They had no idea what had hit them, and never recovered from that Katyusha salvo.[234]

In June 1944, it was Klava Panteleyeva's turn to hear the Katyusha for the first time. What power! "It made the tunic on your back flutter," she recalled.[235] Multiple rocket launchers were cutting-edge technology for the time. They delivered explosives to a target area more quickly than conventional artillery but with reduced accuracy, and they required a longer time to reload. That day the sniper platoon had been taken to the front early in the morning. The artillery barrage designed to soften up the German defences began. Finally, the division went on the attack. It felt to Klava as if they had been static, defending Orsha for almost the whole summer. Around them "the army was advancing on all fronts," but all they were doing was demonstrating "amazingly effective defence".

Further advance and the liberation of Byelorussia would be possible only if the "Byelorussian balcony", a German eastward salient, could be cut off. If not, the fronts advancing to the north and south of it would be vulnerable on their flanks. The balcony consisted of two towns the Germans had designated as fortress cities: Vitebsk and Orsha. An offensive in May failed, as did the one in the winter of 1943–44, and the operation to liberate Byelorussia, given the name "Operation Bagration", began only at the end of June.

The attack opened with a reconnaissance in force early in the morning of 22 June 1944. As noted in the Soviet reports, in the course of this probing, the Soviet side managed in many places to drive a wedge into the German defences and capture their forward trenches. But on the first day Klava Panteleyeva's division did not manage to move forward at all.

The soldiers advanced, and Klava and her comrades found themselves doing a job they would be called upon to perform numerous times in the future. Even though they had not been trained as nurses, because they were female, it was considered that this was their job. They were sent in to bandage and evacuate the wounded, and though they did not always particularly like it, they generally put up with it.

On that day Klava found herself tending an officer who had been carrying a very heavy case. The girls had been on their feet since four in the morning, had had nothing to eat, and were disinclined to observe niceties. Dragging some bloke back by herself was unreasonable enough, but now he was also demanding that she should haul along this case of his! Although only a corporal, Klava told the officer in no uncertain terms to abandon it. What had he got in it anyway? Gunfire, explosions all around. "Dump that case will you? It's too heavy for me." The officer was having none of it. "Certainly not! If you don't want to carry it, dump me!"[236]

Twenty years after the war, Klava found out what was in it. The officer recognised her at a veterans' reunion, rushed over to thank her for dragging him to safety under fire, and told her the case had contained his violin, from which he had never been parted throughout the war.

On the stretch of the front where Klava's division was fighting, the German resistance was so strong that by the evening there was almost no one left on the Russian side, while the Germans were still in their trenches. The commanders gathered together everyone capable of holding a rifle: the drivers, the cooks and the penpushers. They posted everyone in the trenches to repel a possible German counter-attack during the night.

When the girl snipers were ordered to stand in the trench that night, Klava was puzzled. It was dark. What were they supposed to be doing? A middle-aged cart driver posted next to her explained that they had very few people left and it was up to them to defend the line until morning. There were wounded out in no-man's-land that they had been unable to evacuate during the battle. Standing in pitch darkness, she heard their cries. It was said that the Germans were bayoneting them.

The girls "were all ears". Until that night they had known they were protected from the Germans not only by their fellow soldiers, but also by minefields and barbed wire on which tin cans were hung, to rattle if anything was afoot. Now there was none of that and if the Germans were stealing up silently no one would know. The snipers' platoon commander was an Armenian lieutenant and was with them in the trench throughout the night. He went constantly from one girl to the next. There were so few of them and they were far apart. They had plenty of cartridges, and the snipers kept firing tracer bullets into the darkness at random. There was little practical benefit to this, but the tracer bullets lit the ground for a split second, as well as demonstrating to the enemy that the Russian soldiers were alert and had no shortage of ammunition.

At last the terrifying night was over. In the morning they were sent Byelorussians, recruited right there in the recently liberated villages around them. In truth they were fairly useless, but they were at least rein-forcements of a sort. Again there was a preliminary artillery bombardment, but when they attacked they found the German trenches deserted. The Germans had taken a beating too, and quietly withdrawn during the night. Now they would be pursued all the way to the River Dnieper. Operation Bagration was gaining momentum.

The operation involved making two converging strikes, from Vitebsk and from Bobruysk, towards Minsk. The plan was then, over the next 40–50 days, to occupy the whole of Byelorussia and Lithuania, as well as to reach the coast of the Baltic Sea, and the borders with East Prussia and Poland. Four fronts were involved in the operation on the Soviet side: the First, Second and Third Byelorussian Fronts and the First Baltic Front: in all, over 2 million, about one third of all the troops on the Eastern Front. The Soviet forces had significant superiority over the Germans in terms both of numbers and of armaments. Although the German Army Group "Centre" knew of the impending Soviet offensive, their general staff agreed with Hitler that the main thrust of the attacks should be expected in Western Ukraine and refused to send any significant reserves.

On 25 June Vitebsk was surrounded and the German 53 Corps, when it tried to break out of the encirclement the next day, was annihilated. On 28 June, troops of the Second Byelorussian Front advanced 50–80 kilometres, crossing the Dnieper and occupying the city of Mogilev.

Klava Panteleyeva's infantry regiment caught up with the Germans only at the River Dnieper. This mighty river has its source in Novgorod Province and is not particularly wide in the region of Orsha: less than 150 metres. As they were climbing in short bursts up a hill planted with rye, Klava noticed a shed on the other side. At the foot of the hill the rye was high and dense and afforded good cover for the advancing soldiers, but at the top it was quite sparse. When they took up their positions at the top of the hill, someone shouted that there was a sharp-shooter firing a machine gun on the other side of the river. At that very moment, Klava saw Alexey Kitaev, the regiment's young chief of staff, fall next to her.[237] Somebody crawled over to him and Klava was also going to go up but then saw the chief of staff's face was already blue and that he was beyond help. "That bright band on his cap!" flashed through her mind. The German sniper on the other side was targeting officers first.

The commander of the regiment Klava's platoon was advancing with – Yerdyukov, a thirty-year-old moustachioed Odessan – ordered the girl snipers to take out the German machine-gunner.[238] They looked and finally spotted him, and when several of the twelve girls fired simultaneously, the other side of the river fell quiet and the troops were able to cross.

Snipers were ferried across after the soldiers in an overloaded inflatable boat that capsized close to the other shore. This was lucky for Klava, who could not swim. "Girls, let us save your rifles!" the soldiers shouted, but the girls had already raised the precious weapons above their heads to ensure they stayed dry. They themselves were, of course, soaked.

Soldiers helped the girls to the shore and then the snipers were ordered to evacuate the wounded, which was easier said than done. Klava crawled over to one man who had a stomach wound and saw "his intestines spilled out of his body like rising dough." She had no idea what to do. "I'll get you a doctor," she told him. It was very hot and he was turning black in front of her. She crawled over to another wounded man. Many years later, she heard Zina Gavrilova say at a reunion, "I crawled to one wounded man. His intestines had spilled everywhere. He grabbed my arm and went rigid. I didn't think I would be able to pull my hand free."[239] The other injured soldier Klava tried to help died too.

On the shore they saw their regimental commander punching a soldier in a German uniform. He was begging for mercy – in Russian. The girls realised he must be in the anti-Soviet Vlasov army. Its soldiers, civilians recruited from occupied Soviet territories and from amongst Soviet P.O.W.s, were regarded as traitors and were much hated by the Red Army. They were almost always shot on the spot rather than taken prisoner. Klava's commander killed the Vlasov soldier.[240]

After the fighting their regiment was terribly thinned. Klava's unit also suffered losses: Tanya Fyodorova and Irina Grachyova were wounded.

Klava's partner, Marusya Gulyakina, was wounded for a second time. Klava was concussed and could hardly hear. Her tunic was peppered with holes and she had numerous cuts but did not go to the medics. "What can they do for me? They're surrounded by wounded people who have lost arms and legs. They don't need me making a fuss."[241] She marched on with her regiment and recovered as time went by.

After Operation Bagration, 125 Guards Bomber Regiment was awarded the further honorary title of "Borisov" for its part in the liberation of Borisov. 3 Air Army provided support for the Third Byelorussian Front. The Vilnius operation started. Once Lithuania was cleared of German troops, the front was to advance on the enemy's territory, East Prussia.

On 4 July 1944, nine twin-engined Pe-2 bombers took off from Bolbasovo airfield near Orsha to bomb the railway station. Eight of them returned. While the regiment was wondering what had become of Lena Malyutina and her crew, the seriously wounded pilot had already been taken to a field hospital far from Bolbasovo.

"Hurry! Pilot with a stomach wound!" someone shouted as they ran into the operating room. It was an ordinary village hut, where surgeon Ivan Fyodorov operated on a table put together from planks. The girl had been flown in that afternoon on a little Po-2. She was unconscious and in a very bad way. She was carried through a courtyard strewn with straw, where dozens of wounded, sitting or lying, were waiting their turn in the open air. The surgeon looked at the wound and told them to prepare for an operation.[242]

Lena Malyutina had notched up thousands of flying hours as a civil aviator before the war. A Leningrader, born in 1917, she decided as a teenager that she was going to fly. Lena graduated from the Bataysk flying school, and for several years ferried the mail, medicines and patients around Tatarstan in regions where roads were almost non-existent. Later she was transferred to work as a flying instructor in Magnitogorsk because the U.S.S.R. needed pilots, and professionals were needed to train them.

She was still working in Magnitogorsk when the war broke out. In 1943 she was sent to a flying school at Yoshkar-Ola, a city in the Republic of Mari-El in the Urals. Here Lena Malyutina was retrained to fly the Pe-2 bomber. At flying school she met many girls she knew, professional pilots like herself from civil aviation, or flying club instructors whose experience was now needed at the front. They all had thousands of flying hours, and they were still young, none of them over thirty.

In the evenings, tired out by the day's work, they would sit on their bunks in the barracks in just their white men's underwear, singing, joking and chatting. Lena thought that in those white shirts they looked like the saints. It was summer underwear. The moment the girls were issued with the warm, flannel men's winter underwear of a vest and underpants, they bartered it for honey. A kilo of honey cost 400 rubles, the same as a set of underwear. It was not as if they were starving, but the girls always craved sweet things. Later, at the front, they would raid their emergency rations for condensed milk.

They were to fight in the women's heavy bomber regiment formed by the legendary Marina Raskova, which by this time was known as the 125 Guards Regiment. Raskova was dead now, but for these young pilots she remained their idol and role model. When the newcomers arrived in the regiment in March 1944, Lena again saw many familiar faces, mostly of her schoolmates from Bataysk.

That summer, just before Operation Bagration began, they relocated to Bolbasovo, an excellent airfield built by the Germans near Orsha. They were used to flying from grass airfields, and were amazed by the concrete runways and solidly built hangars. All around, however, was terrible devastation. Here in Byelorussia, in Soviet territory recaptured from the Germans, Lena saw the dreadful damage caused by the war. Many villages had been burned to the ground. In the spring of 1944, teams of women harnessed themselves to ploughs to till the soil. In other places they ploughed with cows, but there were none left here.

At Bolbasovo Lena met Sasha, a pilot she had worked with in the instructor team at Magnitogorsk. Sasha flew a Po-2, and the next day Lena heard he had been killed. She did not even have time to ask where he was buried. She had other things on her mind, because her regiment was going into combat. The mission was always the same: to bomb the enemy's troops and hardware. With bombs weighing 100, 250 or 500 kilograms, the Pe-2 dive bomber was a no less formidable and advanced weapon than the Katyusha missile system. Navigator Lyudmila Popova recalled how in the early stages of Operation Bagration she saw a photograph taken with a camera mounted on her plane of the bombing of Orsha. "It was terrifying. Railway wagons were up in the air . . . When we were deployed near Orsha we went to take a look at our work. Everything was completely wrecked."[243] The crews of these mighty aircraft also had to fear for their lives. Nine of the huge Pe-2s on the way to a destination were a magnet for enemy fighters and anti-aircraft guns. "From the front line all the way to our target we were under constant anti-aircraft fire," Popova recalled.

On 4 July it was raining in the morning and the cloud cover was low. It seemed unlikely they would be flying. The crews were sitting under the planes. In the afternoon they suddenly saw the white flare for them to take off: the weather had marginally improved.

They flew in a formation of two nines, with Lena Malyutina in the second under the command of Major Nadezhda Fedutenko, a highly experienced pilot who had returned to her unit after recovering from a head wound inflicted at Stalingrad. They approached the railway station at an altitude of 800 metres owing to the low cloud. (Normally they would have bombed from a height of one and a half to two kilometres.) The target was hidden by clouds just as Lena's flight reached it and they had to circle round for a second approach. This was dangerous because the anti-aircraft guns now had a bead on them. They again approached the target and found "a whole fireworks display" coming up towards them from below.[244] The navigator dropped the bombs and, with its load released, the plane bounced upwards. Lena always felt that freed of its bombs the aircraft exulted like a human being. The pilots exulted too – their mission had been accomplished and the main thing now was to return safely to base. As soon as they flew away from the target, however, Lena felt something burning her stomach. "I think I've been wounded," she told her navigator, Lena Yushina. An anti-aircraft gun had hit them.

The formation was flying away but their bomber was lagging behind, slowed by the damage. The navigator urged her to hold on because they were flying over a forest with nowhere to land, but in three minutes' time there should be a fighter airfield they could land at. They certainly would not make it back to their own. The navigator gave Lena smelling salts to sniff to keep her from losing consciousness. After four turns, they made their final approach to the field. When they were down to fifty metres they saw that the runway was not free: a fighter was taking off. With a huge aircraft like the Pe-2 it would have been no easy matter for even a healthy pilot to head up again and go for a second approach, but Lena managed. She remembered landing the bomber gently, bringing it to a halt, turning off the engines, releasing her snap hooks, but then nothing else. She was dragged from the aircraft unconscious.

She came to at a field hospital two kilometres from the front line, on the operating table. Her small intestine was damaged in eleven places and her colon in four. The anaesthetic was a litre of alcohol poured into the abdominal cavity. She recovered from the operation in a corner curtained off in the same hut. For the umpteenth time in her life, having chosen a man's profession, she was the only woman among men, and from beyond the curtain came an endless barrage of swearing and groaning from wounded soldiers.

Lena spent a week in the field hospital, then two more in a hospital in Poland, then a month in an aviation hospital in Moscow. When they tried to send her from there to a sanatorium to recover fully ("Your blood is crap!" the doctor scolded her), Lena decided enough was enough and that she would return to her regiment. Without asking anyone's permission, she went to the Central Airport and found a civilian flight to Lithuania. By September she was back flying with Lena Yushina. Their radio operator and gunner was now a lad. The girl who had been with them on that terrifying sortie wanted never to fly again, got pregnant and was sent to the rear. Before the end of the war, Lena Malyutina completed a further seventy-nine sorties.

Chapter 10

"Hey, was that you who whacked him? Well done, now go and wash yourself!"

There are few things more distressing than the sight of a horse drowning. Anya Mulatova saw a soldier manage to jump to safety, but his horse, evidently injured and unable to cope with the current, sank. It was 28 June and the Third Byelorussian Front had been ordered to cross the River Berezina and advance on Minsk and Maladzyechna. Despite heavy shelling, which caused horrendous casualties, the sniper platoon managed the crossing unscathed. The Berezina is quite wide, but the regiment crossed it on rafts the size of the single room in Anya's house, which were hastily improvised from logs.[245] They were propelled by whatever means was to hand, even shovels. On reaching the far bank the girls poured the water out of their boots and marched on towards Minsk. The retaking of Byelorussia would soon be completed.

The attack went well. On 4 July 1 Guards Tank Corps entered Minsk and, joining up with 2 and 3 Tank Corps, completed the encirclement of a group of over 100,000 Germans to the east of the city. The neighbouring divisions of 49 Army pressed ahead in pursuit of the retreating Germans, but the division to which Anya Mulatova's sniper platoon was attached stayed behind. The woods around Minsk were full of trapped Germans who needed to be captured.

Anya was to remember one day in early July 1944 for the rest of her life. She was not acting as a sniper but as a straightforward foot soldier, and her partner, Tasya, was not with her. The girls were mixed in with riflemen combing the woods. Several divisions discovered huge numbers, 105,000 soldiers, mostly demoralised, of the German 4 Army wandering about in the tree-covered areas east of Minsk in the hope of finding a way out of the "cauldron". On 17 July 57,000 of these soldiers, led by their generals, were paraded through the streets of Minsk. What happened to the others? Some managed to slip out of the encirclement, some remained for ever in the boundless forests of Byelorussia. Anya Mulatova met one who had no intention of surrendering. He was the only enemy soldier she looked straight in the eye, before shooting him at almost point-blank range.

Anya had lost sight of the other girls and ended up with a group of soldiers she did not know. They arrived at an extensive clearing and had to cross to the other side of it. One of the soldiers, who was on horseback, volunteered to check what was on the far side. "Wait here, lads. I'll gallop over there and let you know," he called.[246] He jabbed his horse in the belly with his boots and "it took off as if it had gone mad." It would have been folly to stay in such an open space for long. Suddenly, a shot rang out and the horseman slumped. The horse, unseating its dead or wounded rider, bolted. The others, stunned, just "stood there gaping", at a loss until one of them, a daredevil, surprised them all by running out, zigzagging across the clearing. As he ran, Anya, who was, after all, a sniper, was looking not at him but across to where she thought the shot at the rider had come from. She was just in time to see the flash of a second shot, which hit the second soldier. Just as she thought, it was a German sniper shooting at them. "Look, let me see what I can do," she said to the officer in charge. She decided to approach the German marksman from behind. "Go ahead," said the officer. They were now a group of only three.

It was unbearably hot. Anya went deeper into the woods as fast as she could, estimating how far to run and in which direction. She finally turned and saw the clearing was at an angle to her. She ran to the edge, lay down and crawled with a pistol in her hand through dry grass that scratched her face. When she recalled the episode after the war, she was amazed she had been able to crawl so fast, just like in the films. She reckoned the German must be 30–40 metres away. Crawling most of that distance, she raised herself on her elbows to check how much remained and saw "his ginger head", very close, about ten metres away. The German sniper was lying with his back to her and looking in the opposite direction. Anya jumped up and rushed at him, shouting the first, heavily-accented German words that came to mind (not having learned German at school): "*Khende hokh, shmutsige shvaine!*" The German stood up and water poured off him. He had propped his sniper rifle up on a mound and had the lower half of his body in a hollow full of water, "like in a bath". The heat and lice had evidently really been getting to him, Anya decided later. She took aim and pulled the trigger, but the pistol did not fire. "Idiot, you have to release the safety catch!" flashed through her mind. She released it, aimed at his head and pulled the trigger. The German was only a few metres away, so Anya got sprayed with blood. It never occurred to her she might have taken him prisoner. This German sniper, who had just shot two of her comrades in front of her eyes, seemed far too scary for that.

Anya breathed a sigh of relief, but then heard the bushes rustling as someone approached from behind. "This is the moment I die," she thought, but then saw that a Soviet soldier in camouflage had emerged. No insignia of rank were visible, but from his confident demeanour Anya knew immediately he was an officer. "Hey, was that you who whacked him?" he said approvingly. Anya just nodded. "Well done, now go and wash yourself!" he ordered, confirming Anya's belief that he must certainly be someone quite senior. She rinsed her face in brackish water, wet and rubbed the trousers and tunic that were spattered with the German's blood, and ran to join the lads. They were carrying the body of the impetuous soldier in a groundsheet, and had bandaged up the other, tearing a shirt into strips. They rarely had bandaging packs with them then, "a disgraceful careless attitude", Anya recalled later.[247]

She was shortly afterwards awarded the Order of the Red Star for taking out the German sniper. The commander who had sent her off to get washed was a colonel and put her forward for the award. Anya, though, never forgot the German's face, long and pale, with red stubble. He would have been around thirty years old, middle-aged in Anya's eyes. For the rest of her life she found it painful to recall the episode. Killing someone at close range proved very different from shooting at tiny figures magnified by a telescopic sight.

Anya and her small group continued combing the woods. It was frightening and there seemed to be "a Fritz behind every bush".[248] They were fortunate, however. They soon came upon a group of Germans who had no wish at all to continue fighting. Twelve of them had tented their rifles together and were resting on their grey greatcoats. "Prisoner, prisoner!" they shouted, jumping up when they saw the three Russians. Anya's companions, naturally, set about searching them, going through their coat and trouser pockets, helping themselves to watches and rings. This was standard practice. Watches became a kind of wartime currency. Before the war, and indeed for long after it, comparatively few Russians possessed one. In September 1941, the local committee of Leningrad State University asked the dean of the Geography Faculty to "issue a men's pocket watch for the LSU partisan unit" because none of them owned one.[249] Watches were routinely removed from dead and captured Germans, and soldiers would sometimes show off several wristwatches on their arm. Survivors came back home after the war with looted watches. (This was not just a Soviet peccadillo, there is plenty of testimony that watches were popular as a trophy with Allied troops too.)

Anya could understand the soldiers, but was still ashamed. She always found this kind of "army behaviour" repugnant. She stood aside and comforted herself with the thought that the Germans, of course, treated Russians in exactly the same way. One of the Germans suddenly came over to her, "*Frau, gut, bitte, bitte!*" He handed her a gold watch on a chain.[250] Anya refused, "*Nicht, nicht, nein!*" but the German was adamant, giving her to understand as best he could that the soldiers would in any case take it from him and he would like to give it to her. He must have been afraid of the Russian soldiers, and hoped that this woman might protect him. Anya took his watch and kept it. One of the Russian soldiers led the prisoners to an assembly point. They were "exhausted and very glum". She felt sorry for them, yet, after all, "they were better off being captured than slaughtered." By the summer of 1944 an order had already been issued forbidding the shooting of prisoners.[251] It was not always obeyed, but in the first years of the war it had been very rare to take any prisoners at all. "Thank God these ones are not being done away with," was Anya's reaction, despite the fact that many members of her own family had already been killed in the course of the conflict.

She had shortly before come across an atrocity perpetrated by some of her regiment's reconnaissance team. One dawn as they were on their way to hunt, Anya and Tasya met some scouts they knew returning from a night-time mission with two squealers. Trying to capture a squealer was dangerous and to manage it was a considerable success, therefore Anya was disturbed to see that one of them was half dead and the team were having to drag him back with them. "What's wrong with him?" she asked, and the lads confessed they had got over-enthusiastic and cut off the German's "bits". She heard later he died before they got him back, and that they had been disciplined.

Anya declined to condemn them. How could they be judged after what they had seen in Byelorussia? The enemy they were at last driving from their land was leaving behind a legacy of charred villages, dead bodies, and hatred in people's hearts. Anya viewed the half-dead squealer with mixed feelings of horror at the brutal killing of a man who possibly had done no evil to anyone, but also of justified retribution against the

Germans as a whole. A Young Communist League organiser of her age in a mortar regiment had looked on with similar ambivalence in 1943 at Germans being led to execution by Ukrainian peasant women. "The women were leading some of the Hitlerites down the street. Each had an axe or a pitchfork, a fire iron or a bludgeon in her hands. The women were enraged, screaming and shouting in Ukrainian and I could not understand a word they were saying. They stopped at a pit and began pushing the Hitlerites into it. They threw several Vlasov soldiers down there too. One fascist tried to resist, wailing, "*In meinem Haus drei Kinder!*" The women hurled back at him, "And you think we have puppies, do you? Chuck 'im in!"

Many decades passed, the Young Communist League organiser worked for half a century as a schoolteacher and was awarded the title of Distinguished Teacher of the U.S.S.R. but, remembering how those peasant women had murdered the German prisoners, he still thought no power on earth would have induced him to try to prevent them taking their revenge.[252]

Chapter 11

"I knew nothing about him and I had just killed him"

The instructors' company, sent to the front three months after the snipers of the second cohort, were bedevilled by misfortune. Their troubles began even before they reached the battle lines, though at first everything had gone splendidly. They arrived at 152 Fortified District near Vilno on 2 August, and above them they could see a dogfight unfolding. Klava Loginova's platoon of thirty-three girls was billeted with a reserve regiment in a barn at a paper mill.[253] The commander at first made no attempt to hide his scepticism about their abilities, and the minute they arrived he gave them a test. He set up jars and bottles, ordered them to shoot, and within minutes was proud of his "girlies"; after that he held them up as an example to the rest of the men.

They were informed that they would be transferred from this reserve regiment to the front in a couple of weeks' time, but even so they were taken hunting. Preparing them for combat consisted here, as at school, of marching, digging trenches, shooting, and more shooting. As sniper record books were issued only on active duty, kills while back at head-quarters were recorded on a sheet of paper headed "Official Document". These unique records were signed by the company commander, the sniper platoon commander, and several other people, and registered the first kills of Klava and her companions. For instance: "On this day 2 Sniper Squad operating on the defence perimeter of 1 Company killed: 3 German soldiers, including: 1 by Sergeant Lukicheva, A.F. – 1 . . ."[254] Klava Loginova, as Young Communist League organiser of the sniper section, also signed it.

Tragedy struck during shooting practice on 4 August. Klava and her sniper partner, Katya Makoveyeva, a likeable young girl from Vologda, as unpretentious as Klava, were on duty that day. They tidied the living quarters, brought food from the kitchen, fetched water and stoked the stove. When lunch arrived, one of them had to take it to their comrades on the firing range, where that day the company was being trained to fire machine guns. Klava was about to go, but Katya said she would make the journey instead. Klava never saw her again.

After lunch, the girls, including Katya, were wandering over the meadow picking flowers. God only knows what impelled Nonna Orlova, a rustic, sturdily built Siberian, to lie down behind a machine gun and pull the trigger. There was a burst of fire and four girls were hit. The wounds of two were not fatal, but Rita Moskva was killed instantly and Katya Makoveyeva, severely wounded in the stomach, died some hours later in hospital. It was claimed later that the gun did not have its safety catch engaged, but perhaps Nonna had released it. She and the instructor of the reserve regiment were arrested immediately, and it became known that they had been sent to serve in a penal company. Klava's friends told her Nonna was in a state of shock and shrieking, "Kill me! Shoot me, I don't want to live!"

Klava had no clear memory of that day, and could not even remember who had told her of the disaster or where, as if her mind had rejected the memory. She had only a vague recollection of the funerals of Katya and Rita Moskva.[255]

"Picking flowers? Hardly!" was Anya Mulatova's reaction when she heard this appalling story. She found it a strange suggestion that girls could have found flowers during the war. She had no memory of any at the front at all. She also commented that, as she played at being a machine-gunner, Nonna must have aimed deliberately, turning the gun and pointing it directly at people, because otherwise how could she have hit the target from such a considerable distance?[256]

As fate would have it, her former comrades met up again with Nonna long after the war, in the 1960s, at the first reunion of girls who graduated from the Podolsk sniper school. Nonna Orlova turned up there covered in medals, but the snipers refused to let her in the door and shouted at her to clear off. Neither Klava Loginova nor Anya found that in the least surprising. Why on earth had Orlova gone there? There was much discussion of how Nonna could have come by so many medals after being in a penal company. None of them, though they had also been continuously at the front, had anything like so many. They never heard another word about Nonna Orlova.[257]

Anya Mulatova's reminiscences of Vasiliy Slavnov, the commander of 123 Infantry Regiment, add a certain amount of colour to his own memoirs, which he published in the Soviet era. One night an unknown officer appeared in the snipers' dugout. Nobody had any idea who this man, wearing a quilted jacket and a fur hat with earflaps, could be. They had all had an exhausting day, some were already in bed, and this stranger appeared at the door and began railing at them. "What are you all lying about for? Are you not going to tidy up the place you live in? Where's the *Soldier's Newsletter*? How are you going to know how the Germans are behaving, which stretch of the front is more active?" He concluded his monologue with, "So, you have no shortage of work to do," and departed. It was only the next day that the girls learned who their visitor had been.[258]

Slavnov's own description of the episode is more restrained. "I went in to see the girl snipers. The day was nearly over, they were back from their hunting and tired. I had had no opportunity to visit them up till then. 'We'll soon have been here a week and there's been no sign of the regimental commander,' one of them said reproachfully. 'What do you need him for?' I asked. 'What do you mean? It's his regiment we're working for. And anyway, we want to see what sort of man he is.'" Without revealing his identity, Slavnov made some critical comments: "'You don't have a wall newspaper,' I said to the Young Communist League organiser, Klavdia Chistyakova. 'You haven't nominated anyone for outstanding service. Evidently no one has been good enough!'"[259]

Their commander's interest in their work, if rather stern, was beneficial. Young Communist League Organiser Klava Chistyakova, who in peacetime had been a student in the literature faculty at Yaroslavl Teacher Training College, soon came to see Slavnov with some suggestions. Klava was also the person who maintained order in the dugout. She was the oldest and most serious-minded girl in the platoon, and was well liked and respected. Soon the girls tidied up Slavnov's own quarters, washing the wooden floor and cleaning his window, and put a bunch of wild flowers picked by Klava and Anya Mulatova on his table.[260] The commander found this "simple little bouquet of flowers" very touching, reminding him of "a different, peaceful way of life". When, very soon afterwards, it was time to leave the dugout and go on the offensive, he decided to leave the flowers on the table, "as if I were only leaving them, and the girls, for a short while".[261]

The Third Byelorussian Front was advancing with great speed. At dawn on 6 June, having passed through Minsk during the night, 123 Regiment of 62 Infantry Division reached the River Svislach by the village of Mikhanovichy. The official history of 31 Army dryly records that during the ensuing days 62 Division undertook a forced march of some 500 kilometres – a journey that took two weeks.[262]

The girls in the sniper platoon made the same march, on foot, carrying the same weight as the men, only with a rather heavier rifle because of the telescopic sight. They put behind them dozens of kilometres a day, and sometimes even walked at night. "These gruelling marches took the last of their strength from the fighters. Everybody was abandoning helmets, gas masks, entrenching tools because, covering such distances, even a needle seemed to weigh a ton. It is difficult to find words to convey the sense of exhaustion."[263]

Happily, knapsacks could occasionally go forward on a baggage cart, but would sometimes disappear from it, causing major trouble for their owners. The commander would try to give everyone a brief respite on the march. "He might find a ditch and get us to lie in it with our heads down and our feet up," Klava Panteleyeva recalls.[264] These rest breaks would last no more than half an hour, and then they would be on their feet again. The regimental accordionist would play something rousing to wake and cheer them up.

The regiment Klava's platoon was marching with stopped for the night at an empty house in Lithuania. After all the kilometres they had travelled, they all just collapsed on to the floor, men and women together, and fell asleep. Klava was slow off the mark and, when she went into the house, found there was not a single free spot on the floor. There was no space for her "short of lying on top of someone". She noticed a little trough of a kind used for chopping cabbage in and, huddling up, climbed into it and fell asleep. The minute she moved a leg or an arm out of the trough in her sleep, she would get it shoved back in. Suffering all through the night, Klava saw someone going out to relieve himself at dawn and immediately occupied his place, but no sooner had she fallen asleep than she heard the order, "Rise and shine!" It was time to get back on the march. One time they came upon a bathhouse. They fired it up, and the commander gallantly sent the girls in first. Not realising they had to open the damper, they got carbon monoxide poisoning and, as soon as they emerged, "collapsed on the ground". It took a long while for them to live that down.[265]

"We marched and slept." "We fell asleep on the go." Many of the girl snipers recalled genuinely falling asleep as they were marching. In 1944–5 it became common for soldiers to march like that. They were pursuing the enemy and might cover thirty kilometres in a day. Many of them found they had dozed off for a few seconds. You would be walking along, your feet somehow moving as required but with your mind switched off. The comrades alongside would not let you wander away from the column or get lost. Anya Mulatova almost found herself in deep trouble when she fell asleep after she had been separated from the column.[266]

How she came to go off into the bushes alone she could not afterwards explain, because they were not allowed to do that. Instead of hastening to catch up with the others, she fell asleep on her haunches as she pissed. Moreover, she must have been asleep for a good fifteen minutes because, when she ran back to the road, the whole column had passed and disappeared into the darkness. Before she had time to get really worried, she heard the clatter of a horse's hooves. When word passed along the column that she had been left behind, Mitya Kuznetsov, the adjutant of the regimental commander, had been sent back with orders to find her. Anya was very relieved, but it turned out that Kuznetsov's intentions were not entirely honourable.

"Come on, let's go over there," he urged, trying to put his arms round her and navigate her towards the bushes. Anya pushed him away. A brief, heated exchange ensued, at the end of which Kuznetsov threatened to shoot her. "Come on, or you'll be lying here for the rest of time." Anya was confident he would not dare to shoot her and risk facing a lot of trouble. "Shoot me then, and they'll send you to a penal company," she said calmly, but decided nevertheless it was best not to get on the wrong side of the adjutant and assured him his dreams would come true, only first they should catch up with the regiment. Sitting behind him on the horse, Anya held on firmly to the belt of a young man who had just threatened to kill her. Once they caught up with the others, of course, nothing happened. When Mitya complained to the commander that Anya was refusing to be his mistress, he was advised to try it on with a different Anya, a signaller who was more suited to him. "She was already a woman." Mitya Kuznetsov found love with that Anya, but Anya Mulatova was to face a similar situation when a man called Volodya from the artillery tried to rape her. That was later, though, at Suwałki in Poland.

Regimental Commander Slavnov had a "front-line wife" himself, but Asya Akimova, a machine-gunner, was more than a match for him.[267] They later married, apparently while still at the front, and lived a long life together.

Asya was brought to the regiment by Shura Okuneva, who had been fighting alongside Slavnov since 1941. Shura was in charge of a platoon of machine-gunners, and by the time of her death was a celebrity. A lot was written about her in both the front-line and national press. Mikhail Svetlov, a famous Soviet poet and, during the war, correspondent for the army's *Red Star* newspaper, came specially to interview her and Fyodor Chistyakov, another machine-gunner who was later killed.[268] Shura died in 1943 in the fighting for the village of Potapovka near Yelnya in Byelorussia. She fired at the peephole of an approaching tank and was killed by a shell from the tank.

Asya was a friend of Shura's before the war, and her turning up in 123 Regiment was unusual: Shura just brought her back after going on leave to Moscow.[269] Asya, later Anastasia Slavnova, described in her memoirs how Shura, when she arrived in Moscow, came to visit her in her anti-aircraft battalion. Asya and she enjoyed Moscow together, and Asya came to the station to see her off on the train. They were lost in conversation when the train pulled out, taking Asya with it to the front. She had her Young Communist League membership card and a leave warrant in her bag, so that, luckily, her documents were in order.[270]

Slavnov was angry about this and told Asya to go back to Moscow. Shura assured him that she had been in an anti-aircraft battalion, so was already virtually a machine-gunner. Though he was not convinced that fire-watching duty on a rooftop was relevant, he was impressed by Shura's confidence that she could train Asya to be a machine-gunner within a couple of days and that she would make a good soldier. Asya remained in the regiment as a machine-gunner until March 1944, when she was concussed in battle and suffered multiple injuries to her head, belly and left arm. She was determined to return to her regiment when she got out of hospital, and in August was back. Her state of health ruled out returning to work as a machine-gunner, and when the girl snipers met her she had begun working as a clerk at H.Q. "She is having an affair with the regimental commander," Anya Mulatova was told shortly after Asya's reappearance. "Well, he's a good man," Anya said with a shrug, not in the habit of passing judgement on people.[271]

Crossing the border into Lithuania, they marched on and on, repelling intermittent German counter-attacks. Not infrequently, they overtook their baggage train with the field kitchen and went hungry. Would it arrive in time? Would the cook find them and have food ready? Klava Panteleyeva often looked back nostalgically in those months to the three meals a day they had received at sniper school. If you were still hungry there, you could fill up with bread. She was grateful now to the commanders at the school for training them to eat quickly. That skill proved very useful at the front. And yet they never did learn to squirrel away even as much as a piece of bread; they ate everything they were given immediately.

One time, the cook, bringing them food during an offensive – in a metal vacuum flask strapped to his shoulders – suspected something was wrong but did not realise that the flask had a bullet hole in it and almost everything had leaked out. The girls went hungry, without even a crust of stale bread between them. Soon after that there was another catastrophe. It took the same middle-aged cook so long to crawl up to them under fire that all the food went bad in the July heat. The commander tried it, said it was off, and ordered it poured away. Some of the girls might have been willing to eat the bad porridge, but you could not risk diarrhoea during an attack. Klava's platoon, like many other soldiers, were rescued by Karasenko, their Ukrainian quartermaster, who occasionally caught a piglet running around near a village, or brought a cow that those girls who knew how to could milk, or even sliced the meat off a horse that had been killed. It was almost impossible to chew the horsemeat, which made your gums hurt terribly, especially if the unfortunate horse was old.[272]

That field kitchen flask with its bullet hole, which meant there would be no hot food for them that day, was associated in Anya Mulatova's mind with another painful memory. A halt on their exhausting travels, a long-awaited rest and meal could suddenly turn into something quite different.

After a week's rest at the little Jewish village of Leipalingis (abandoned, its former inhabitants long since exterminated) in Lithuania, 123 Regiment moved on again on 29 July, following a tortuous route along the Lithuanian–Polish border. You had to watch your step in this region of lakes. At Lake Šlavantas they again found themselves caught up in fighting. Slavnov's regiment had halted to rest at the lake, which they thought had the strange name of Salopirogi ("pork fat pie"). Their lunch, a keg of porridge, was to be brought to them by horse. At this halt beside a beautiful stretch of water, the girls wandered off in all directions. Some took their boots off, rolled up their trousers, and paddled without their tunics, just wearing men's undershirts. Anya and Tasya had no sooner gone off into the bushes than they heard a whine they were only too famil-iar with. A shell! The Germans had just been waiting for the Soviet soldiers to crowd on to the isthmus between two lakes before they struck.[273]

"Run for it!" Anya thought, but where to? Nearby they saw someone had excavated little trenches, really big enough only for one person. There was no time to think; a heavy bombardment opened up. Tasya jumped in and Anya followed. They squeezed tightly together. A young cook jumped in on top of Anya, almost on her head. In this situation the three of them waited for the shelling to end. At last everything was quiet again and they could get up and count their numbers. The horse that had brought the food was lying wounded in its harness, blood gushing from a wound. Porridge was oozing out of the damaged flask. The other girls were all there and uninjured, but there was no sign of Young Communist League organiser Klava Chistyakova. They began searching for her, and someone spotted a white shirt in the lake blown up like a bubble: Klava was lying face down in the water, with shrapnel in her heart. They buried her there, by the lake where their "rest had ended so badly".

They did, nevertheless, eat the porridge, although there was shrapnel in it that gave it a metallic taste. Soon the order was given, "Everybody up!" and they had to be on their way again.

While they were in Lithuania, Klava Panteleyeva's regiment received reinforcements, on this occasion Uzbeks who were "pretty rum soldiers". At first the girls in Klava's platoon felt sorry for them. They quite clearly understood very little. They were feeling the cold terribly, knew absolutely nothing about fighting in a war, and many of them were by no means young. The Uzbeks constantly complained, "We cannot march, bum all chafed, kursak [stomach] very sore." At first, the girls even carried their belongings and rifles for them in addition to their own. (Their knapsacks were being transported in a cart.) However, the marches were getting longer and everybody got fed up with the Uzbeks. Eventually, Panchenko, the company commander, suggested to Young Communist League organiser Shpak that it was time to teach them a lesson. They did so in the spirit of the times, and even the girls saw nothing cruel in it. "He lined them up in front of a barn and said he was going to shoot them." The Uzbeks promised to behave themselves in future. "Bum not chafed, kursak not hurting," the girls taunted them.[274]

A complement of Uzbeks was seen as a blow to the combat readiness of any unit. One war veteran who witnessed the impact of such reinforcements, also in Lithuania, recalled how "a three-man NKVD tribunal sentenced two Uzbeks to death for deserting the battlefield. The sentence was read out, and the two of them stood there, already completely detached from this world. They were no longer with us. It was a bad thing to see, but, to be completely honest, the Uzbeks were useless fighters."[275]

As soon as they crossed the border into Lithuania, the situation changed. In the ruined Byelorussian villages, ragged peasants greeted the Soviet soldiers as family and gave them potatoes to eat, if indeed they still had any. In Lithuania the neat farmsteads with their orchards and vegetable gardens were largely deserted. The people were hiding in the woods. Such local people as the soldiers did meet had difficulty concealing their hostility to the Soviets. In Lithuania, which only a few years earlier had "joined the united family of Soviet peoples", a considerable proportion of the population had been happier to see the Germans than the Russians.

At one farmstead, a boy about twelve years old came to the soldiers of Lida Larionova's regiment. He denounced his mother, saying that when the Germans were here she had lived with one of them. He pointed out a barn to them where the Germans had stashed armaments. The soldiers shot his mother and took the boy with them as their regimental mascot.[276]

Girls from Klava Panteleyeva's platoon were once offered fresh milk at a farm their unit was passing through. An elderly husband and wife carried a whole bucket of it to the roadside, still warm, and a metal mug to scoop it with. The girls were afraid it might be poisoned. They had been taught to expect anything in Lithuania, and their commanders were constantly warning them not to consume any of the food or drink offered them. The wife, however, beckoned Klava, nodding to her. She had probably taken a liking to her sweet face. Klava drank a complete mugful and concluded it was safe. Then all the other girls drank it too. Their hosts gestured to them and said something in an amalgam of Lithuanian and Polish, but it was impossible to understand.

Soon Klava's squad lost another sniper in combat, Zina Gavrilova, who was seriously wounded in the knee. The girls carried her on a stretcher they improvised from Zina's overcoat and Zina and Klava's disassembled rifles. Klava did not get her rifle back and was instead left with Zina's, which she carried for the remainder of the war. She was terribly afraid someone might find out: losing a rifle could bring you before a tribunal (the Soviet equivalent of a court martial). Katya Puchkova was also wounded. Marusya Gulyakina did not come back to them after her spell in hospital, so Klava now had no partner. She was certain that she had survived uninjured, apart from her concussion, because she was protected by the prayer "A Living Refuge", which her mother had copied out for her.[277]

Now and again someone would be killed right in front of Klava. At Volkovysk in south-west Byelorussia they spent a night in a one-storey house with two exits. Someone before them had dug trenches in front of it. In the morning, shelling started and everyone ran to take shelter in them. There was nowhere else to hide, with open ground all around. Klava was just too late: there was absolutely no space for her in the trenches. As the Germans began to find their range, the bombardment drew closer. A shell hit the house, and then a blank fell next to Klava. She ran back into the half-ruined house as there was nowhere else to shelter. The air was thick with dust from the collapsing bricks. At that moment a shell slammed directly into the trench where the soldiers were lying and where Klava had just been looking for a place. There had been living people there and now there were none. A few days later, a shell hit the field kitchen Klava had left just moments before. Nothing remained of the horses and barrels from which they had been dishing out lentil soup with stewed meat. Klava spent a great deal of time pondering this. Your comrade died but you lived, a shell hit the place where you had just been sitting. Why? Some believed in fate, some in God, and probably it was all the same thing.

"We lay down and started observing. I spotted a German climbing out of a trench. I shot and he fell. I started trembling all over; I could hear my teeth chattering. I started to cry. When I had been firing at targets there was no problem, but now I was a murderer! I had killed someone I had never met. I knew nothing about him and I had just killed him."[278] This description of how Klava Loginova first killed a German in the summer of 1944 found its way into Svetlana Alexievich's book, *War's Unwomanly Face*, the first and almost the only Soviet book to talk about what it was actually like being a woman in the army in the Second World War.

Shortly after killing this German in Lithuania, Klava and her division reached the River Neman and saw a still-smoking hut burned down by the retreating Germans. Regimental commander Bulavko showed the snipers charred human remains in the hut. "Look, they burned our soldiers alive." The twisted and blackened insignia and black stars that survived almost intact told them that some ten Soviet soldiers and one officer had been burned. When they had taken up defensive positions by the Neman, the girls returned and buried the remains, the soldiers in one grave and the officer in another. After that, Klava recalled, she "really started killing them".[279]

In her appearance and personality, Klava Loginova resembled her mother, a notably kind woman. Would anybody who was not kind have married a widower with eight children, each born less than a year apart? She had a daughter of her own, and another eight children were born in the second marriage, making a total of seventeen (Klava was fifteenth in the family). The older children, who were almost all girls, got married and moved away, and new babies were born. There were never fewer than twelve people at table in their house.

Her mother was endlessly altering clothes to keep them all decently dressed, and she altered clothes for other people too, to earn a little money. She could neither read nor write, never having been to school, but she made sure the children did, even though life was hard and they were all hungry.

When she was still very little, Klava planted rye and potatoes with the rest of the family. They also brought in the harvest together, from the oldest to the youngest. In 1927, when she was just four years old, Klava badly cut her finger with a sickle while she was helping in the fields. Her father worked on the railway. The family had two cows, some sheep, chickens and pigs. In 1921–3, the years of famine, they were all eaten, her mother only refusing to allow the last cow to be slaughtered: "When the children are hungry I'll give them milk and they will stay alive." Then things improved a little, and when her father had to retire in 1929 they took a whole farmyard of animals, cows, horses, chickens and sheep, and went to live with Klava's eldest sister. All they left behind were the pigs. It took them ages to reach the Urals, all the time in a wagon that railway officials had allocated to her father: the animals were on one side, and their family on the other. In the middle was an iron *burzhuyka* stove, whose chimney her father directed through the roof. When the wagon was in a siding the children would run to collect odd bits of wood and rubbish that could be used to light a fire and cook a meal.

Her father, mother and seven of her brothers and sisters settled in a basement room in her sister's house in the town of Satka in Chelyabinsk Province. Klava was taken at the age of nine by one of her brothers to look after his children. Later she stayed with another sister and, after school, helped with her children; they all joined together to plant the vegetable plot. After this Klava moved to Kazakhstan with her sister's family (her husband was in the army), which is where she was when the war broke out.

This short, slender girl with grey eyes, fair hair and a ruddy complexion could cope with almost anything by the time she was seventeen: she could sow seed and reap, sew clothes, chop wood, build a house on her own, and ride a horse bareback. After completing her schooling and legal training at a law college, she worked in Dzhambul in Kazakhstan as a secretary in the prosecutor's office, which meant that she was not liable for conscription. Her whole class, however, went to the enlistment office and she joined them. From childhood she had been accustomed to work tirelessly, without respite, and now, in the war, her job was shooting people: shooting unemotionally, focused, controlling her breathing because, if you are agitated, you are sure to miss. Yudin, their rigorous instructor at sniper school, had told them nervous people were no good as snipers. This job, like all the other jobs in her life, Klava did conscientiously.

Chapter 12

"How will I live without them when the war is over and we all go off in different directions?"

Guarding the Soviet Arctic was the title of a small front-line newspaper brought to Vera Barakina's unit. The situation here at the Karelian Front had been deadlocked since the spring of 1942, when the Russians failed to push the Germans back across the border. The Germans, on the other hand, never succeeded in taking Murmansk. It was a stalemate that lasted until October 1944.

Vera Barakina's own life mirrored the front's immobility. She went out to hunt every second day – a stagnant front line was the ideal situation for using snipers. The commander of 715 Infantry Regiment was delighted to be sent a sniper squad, and the girls were only too happy to be in his regiment. No one misbehaved towards them.

When they first arrived, they had been staying at divisional head-quarters, in a boarding house where they washed their clothes in a swimming pool, but were under constant siege from randy staff officers. The sentries kept the doors locked, but the officers used every trick they could think of to try and beguile them. They had plenty to offer the girls: food, perfume. This could be seductive because the girls, like all the other soldiers, were constantly hungry, fed on "herring and crusts". Only those who wangled themselves a cosy job at headquarters, Vera and her comrades were certain, people who, they supposed, sat trembling with fear, not daring to stick their noses out of the door or see a day's fighting, were guaranteed medals and officers' rations.[280]

On their second day in 715 Regiment, the commander allocated pairs of girls to the battalions and sent them to the front line to shoot. "It was not frightening in the least," Vera remembers. They had been taught everything they needed to know at school: "Take cover and wait!" Shoot at anyone you see, not just officers and observers. The order from their commander was, "If you see a German, shoot the bugger!" By the time they left the front in Karelia, Vera had killed nine Germans. The Germans, and particularly the Finns, had snipers too, of course, but Vera's squad were lucky and none of them were shot in the Arctic. However, two girls died after stepping on a mine when, in spite of strict orders, they strayed off the trail to pick blueberries during a march. They were buried there and then, in a clearing in a pine forest. Such incidents were not uncommon. The chief of staff of a regiment on the Leningrad Front recalled how "a wounded soldier we met had fallen victim to his craving for cranberries."[281]

The girls were looked after reasonably well. They lived four or five to a dugout, were issued warm, new uniforms, and, as spring came to an end, their felt boots were replaced with strong new leather ones. Under their men's underwear they wore panties and bras brought from home. The one major problem they did have was with their periods, because the regulations made no provision for those. The regiment's male nurse, a middle-aged Jew known as Uncle Sasha, would grumble when he saw a girl coming, "I know what you're here for," but did hand out cotton wool. The quartermaster was not unkind, and promptly issued new trousers, leg wrappings and a greatcoat to a girl called Nastya when hers caught fire while they were being heat-treated to kill lice.[282]

The political instructors explained their mission while they were on the defensive, and prepared them for the future offensive. Neither were defensive measures against men neglected. Unlike the German army, which solved the problem by having official brothels, the Red Army left its men to their own devices. One time Vera was alone on duty in the dugout, an officer appeared whose intentions were soon apparent. When Vera turned him down he started threatening her, but Vera, completely unflustered, immediately yelled, "Back off or I throw this grenade in the stove!" For this she was disciplined, but only by being put in the guardhouse for one night. When she was released the next day, the girls showed her the officer's grave: he had been killed in a mortar attack. Vera felt sorry for him.

She did like Senior Lieutenant Anatoly Lyubilkin, who was seven years her senior. He was handsome, had a pleasant personality, was not as obviously out for only one thing as many of his comrades, and wooed her to the best of his ability. Everything he could offer from his officer's rations, he did, including sugar, and biscuits. For Vera, who had once nearly starved to death, as for everyone who had survived the Siege of Leningrad, few things in life were more important than food. "God grant that we stay here till the war is over and don't end up in the thick of the fighting," Vera thought.

Close by, on the shores of the Gulf of Finland, girl snipers from the second cohort attached to 125 Infantry Division were immediately drawn into the fighting. Taya Kiselyova opened her tally in July 1944 at Narva. "Your first one is horrible," she recalls. "It was only targets in the school, which is quite different. Shooting at a person is dreadful." Taya hit a German signals technician out repairing their communications. Before the assault on Narva she managed to take out another three.[283]

Their squad had been fighting since spring. Captain Sagaidak, the regiment's new chief of staff, met them in the summer when they had already won awards and were battle hardened. After the storming of Narva, there were still ten of them. No one had even been wounded.

Sagaidak came to 749 Infantry Regiment from the navy. Unlike the infantrymen, he sported a beard, wore a striped vest, and a cap with a badge that looked like a crab. He also smoked a pipe. After twice crossing the River Narva and capturing the city during summer 1944, almost everyone in his 2 Independent Marine Battalion had either been killed or severely injured and it was first withdrawn and then disbanded. The captain was haunted by the memory of the icebound river dotted with dead and wounded in their black marine jackets. One evening as he waited for his new appointment Sagaidak was stiffening his resolve with "front-line brandy" concocted by a friend from the chemical section from a selection of unimaginable ingredients. They also had a *zakuska* to eat along with it, a "delicious" frozen onion. At this point a lieutenant colonel they did not know appeared out of nowhere, wearing spurs, and informed Sagaidak he was being transferred – horror of horrors! – to an infantry regiment.[284] He was, however, permitted to keep his beard. Sagaidak saw the war through to victory with 749 Infantry Regiment, wearing his striped sailor's vest under his tunic.

After the capture of Narva, the regiment advanced until it came to a ridge of hills heavily fortified by the enemy. They halted to "freshen up" and get ready for an assault. The enemy was firing constantly at their positions. Coming back from the medical unit, where he had a bandage on his arm changed, the Beard, as he was now known to 749 Regiment, heard folk couplets being sung in a dugout towards the rear of the regiment. He had not heard that at the front very often, and never sung by girls, so he dismounted from his horse to investigate. He drew back the blanket that served as the dugout's door, went in, and at first could not believe his eyes. "Whatever next! A large dugout with bunks, and on bunks and benches what looked to me to be twenty young girls." There were "fair-haired, dark-haired, big girls and small", and they were singing and cleaning their weapons. At the sight of an officer they stood up and greeted him. Sagaidak looked at the weapons: five-chambered 7.62 rifles equipped with a telescopic sight! He finally realised who they must be.

He knew that a group of ten girls had been sent from sniper school, but while the regiment was fighting there had been no time to meet them. The sniper pairs had been assigned to battalions, and up there on the hills life for the Germans became far less relaxed. "All their troops were suddenly crouching down and going underground." The girls looked out for spotters, range-finders, and ordinary soldiers, just waiting to glimpse a helmet or the glint of the lenses of a stereo telescope or a pair of binoculars.

Many years after the war, the Beard would forget the names of most of the girls, but two he did remember: "a sniper called Bella and her partner Muza Bulgakova" (in fact, Bulatova), because they had beautiful names and were themselves very pretty. Taya Kiselyova also liked them very much. Bella Morozova was rather haughty, but Muza ("the Muse") was funny and talented. Her mother was an actress, and Muza, who could already do all sorts of tricks, hoped to join a circus after the war. She was a year or two older than the other girls and had a child back home, but told them little about it, or about why she had gone to the war. Later, Taya heard it was her mother who had told her to enlist. Most of all, though, Taya liked the personable and clever Marina Shvetsova, who was several years older than the rest of them.[285]

After breaking through the fortifications outside the city, the attack on Tallinn advanced very rapidly, in an attempt to cut Army Group North off from East Prussia. "We need to hurry before the Germans can board their ships," their Young Communist League organiser explained. Muza Bulatova was killed during that offensive. Always a hothead, she had leapt into a tank which was later hit by a shell. All those inside were burnt alive, and Muza could be identified only from her rifle. "One of your snipers has been burned in a tank," someone told the other girls, who were driving behind in a truck. They were heartbroken. It was the first death in their squad and everybody had loved Muza.

In Tallinn, the girls were given a rest in a school, all of them together in one room. They had a shower and a bath, which seemed unbelievable after so many months on the march when you had to "break the ice in a stream to wash your hair and your private parts".[286] In the evenings they remembered Muza, the would-be circus star, dried their eyes and sang songs.

After several months of fighting, they felt they were real soldiers. When the staff commandant gave instructions that the girl snipers were to wash the headquarters floors, "No way!" was their unequivocal response: that was work for soldiers on fatigue duties. What did this commandant take them for? Sagaidak had to intervene and "apply appropriate sanctions against the mutinous snipers". They were all sent to the guardhouse, but spent their time there agreeably enough. The regiment's female cooks demonstrated sisterly solidarity by serving the miscreants splendid meals.[287] They were not incarcerated for long, because soon the regiment was put on trains and sent to Lithuania in preparation for the offensive on East Prussia.

Kalya Petrova still has a photograph taken that summer of six girls in pretty summer frocks in a flower-filled meadow. It is a good-quality picture, quite unlike those taken at the beginning of the war. Soviet soldiers were by now making good use of captured cameras and film. The friends have floral wreaths on their heads and you would never know the photo had been taken while a war was raging, or that the girls were Soviet snipers who had shot dozens of Germans.

Roza wrote later about this photograph, "There the six of us stand in Lithuanian folk costumes. They were a troika too. Tanya was killed, Lyuda wounded, and [Valya Lazorenko] is alone now."[288]

Going into houses whose owners were hiding from the Red Army in the woods, Kalya and her friends helped themselves to food and clean underwear. They no longer washed those that were dirty but simply threw them away.[289] They also took clothes that could be used for leg wrappings, cutting up strips of whatever came to hand. Their only regret was that they could not take a supply of spares with them to replace those that got wet.

This became an established pattern from then until the end of the war: as they were advancing they took food and clothing from abandoned houses. Finally, in Germany, they would open wardrobes and help themselves to underwear, panties and lisle stockings, five or six pairs of which nicely replaced the leg wrappings in their boots.[290] When Tonya Zakharova changed clothes in this manner for the last time she was out of luck: the clean underwear in the cupboard, tied with ribbons, was much mended. But nonetheless she returned to Moscow in it and wore it for several years after the war, because there was no other underwear to be found, and nothing to make it from.

It was not just underwear, but also dresses and hats that the girls took from deserted Lithuanian houses. Not because they planned to carry them around in a knapsack, where every extra item meant more pain on marches covering many kilometres, and not to send them home, because that could be done only later, but because they wanted, if only for a short time, to change into civilian clothes and feel like a girl. "I succumbed to one weakness: I had an extraordinarily strong desire to put on a dress and have at least some slight resemblance to a woman," wrote Galya Dokutovich, a navigator in the women's night bomber regiment on 19 February 1943 as she rested after a night-time sortie.[291]

The clothes here really were beautiful. There had been no fine dresses for most of these girls before the war, and would be none in their penurious lives after it. All they wanted was to dress up, take a photograph, and send it back home to give everyone a surprise and themselves something to remember. Such a photograph could also be sent to a young man, if you had one to write to. It did not matter that for the rest of the time you were wearing boots and army uniform and had your hair cropped to keep the lice at bay. In that photograph you were a pretty girl in a pretty frock.

Unfortunately Roza Shanina's diary of that summer has not survived. In Lithuania she had a thick notebook she wrote in almost every day, but things left in the baggage train often disappeared and perhaps that is what happened to the notebook.[292] The fact that her later notebooks survived is a miracle. From them we have a detailed account of Roza's life at the front from September 1944 until her death in January 1945.

"I'm used to having Sasha and Kalya around and feel lost when they are not there. I have great respect for them, more than for the other girls. With friends life is more fun. The three of us are from quite different families and have quite different personalities, but something we share is our friendship. It is unshakeable. Kalya is a good person, brave and without a trace of selfishness. I really value that in someone. Sasha is very sensible: she seems to understand everything and has an amazing memory. Sasha, Kalya and I are 'The Runaway Troika'. How will I live without them when the war is over and we all go off in different directions?" she wondered.[293]

On 30 July, the Third Byelorussian Front broke through enemy defences along the River Neman. On 1 August, German troops pulled out of Kaunas, but their resistance was gradually stiffening and the Red Army was able to advance only slowly and with substantial losses. Communications became stretched and there were shortages of ammunition. The enemy launched several counter-attacks, and in mid-August several infantry regiments were surrounded.

Klava Panteleyeva could not remember where exactly her regiment found itself in that situation. It was not a complete encirclement, "more like a horseshoe", with a small opening on their unit's left. She remembered a two-storey house on a farmstead with "a staircase from top to bottom".[294] They were ordered to bind up their mess tins and shovels so nothing would clatter, and were led slowly past the farm. If the Germans had been nearby, though, the local people would certainly have informed on them. There were several women on the staircase of the big house, watching the unit pass by. One of them let fly a barrage of abuse about the Soviets. No one reacted. She was allowed to have her say, although they could easily have shot her.

By 20 August 1944, the advancing Soviet troops were exhausted and just over a week later the Soviet Supreme Command ordered them to adopt a defensive position in the vicinity of Suwałki. The borders of East Prussia, enemy territory, were only a few kilometres away. The German population began fleeing, no longer believing the assurances of Gauleiter Koch that all was going to be well and that the German army would never surrender

East Prussia. For the Third Byelorussian Front, Operation Bagration had come to an end.

The political instructors began preparing the army for entry into enemy territory, recounting atrocities the Germans had perpetrated in the Soviet Union. "Soldiers see signs of the bloody villainies of the Germans every kilometre of their victorious advance," the Political Section of 31 Army reported. Examples were detailed in talks.

> Subdivisions of 1162 Infantry Regiment passed through the village of Vidritsa in Shklov district, Mogilev Region. Five hundred metres from the village at the edge of the forest lay a girl approximately twenty years of age. The Germans had captured this Soviet girl and, because she was in contact with the partisans, inflicted twenty knife wounds and bruises, having first stripped her naked and raped her. Not one house remained standing in the village. The Germans burned the entire village, where there had been 147 homesteads. It now exists only as a place name.[295]

An Official List of Atrocities was read to the units, inciting the soldiers to "rush into battle with even greater fury to wreak vengeance on the fascist fiends".[296]

Klava Panteleyeva well remembers the brief respite accorded her army in late August to early September 1944. She and her comrades finally had time to write, on captured enemy paper, a lot of letters home to their families. Until this point there had been a terrible shortage of paper, and they would ask their relatives to enclose a sheet with their correspondence. Klava would include poetry in her letters, copied from the *Soldier's Newsletter* – not the little one Zina Gavrilova made for their platoon, but the big divisional newsletter, their own front-line newspaper. Poems were always being printed there, and Klava especially liked those by Konstantin Simonov, one of the most popular Soviet poets of the time. These poems would make her parents and sisters cry. Her elder sister, who thought Klava had written the poems, preserved all Klava's letters, and wanted to send her poetry "to someone to publish". When Klava came back from the war and was told about it, she found it very funny. "Come off it, I'm not clever enough to write poetry. I find it hard enough to copy it out!"[297]

After their period of rest and recuperation, Klava's platoon was split into three squads and "dispersed over different units". She found herself in a different unit from Marusya Gulyakina, who had just returned after being wounded. At the time Marusya was killed she was paired with Katya Ulianova, and it was only some time later that Klava learned she was dead. She was very upset, but not as heartbroken as she was over Marusya Chigvintseva. Her "third Marusya", Klava's next partner, was yet another Marusya, but managed to survive until the end of the war. Once it was over, this Marusya, Marusya Kuzmina, married their political instructor Ivanov and gave birth to a boy who, as far as Klava could tell from the photographs, was "the spitting image" of his father.[298]

In August or early September, Slavnov's regiment was also moved back from the front line for rest and reinforcement. Its numbers were considerably thinned. Soon General Glagolev, the commander of 31 Army, came to review them. Learning of his arrival, arrangements were hastily made to line up the soldiers, and Slavnov noticed for the first time that his regiment looked distinctly sloppy: the men were not lined up in order of height and their tunics were sweat-stained and worn. Good enough for going into battle, but the general was not going to like it.

In the event the general made no remarks about their appearance but was surprised by something else. Going over to the soldiers, he asked who they were and where they had fought, and if he saw anyone with no orders or medals, he wanted to know why. Slavnov explained that after the fighting the regiment had received more medals than it had men left. Few of those lined up in front of the general had fought with the regiment before: most were from other units and had been sent to him from hospital. The general gave orders that those who had been wounded were to be given priority for awards.[299]

Shortly afterwards, they were issued new uniforms, had their worn-out weapons replaced, and on 12 September, a warm, sunny day, the award ceremony was held. There was folk singing and dancing and long tables were laid for the soldiers.

A few days later a circus even arrived. But before long the regiment was again in defensive posture, drawn occasionally into skirmishes with groups of "shaggy, hungry, feral German soldiers as vicious as wolves" who were trying to break through the encirclement and make their way west.[300]

Before the offensive on East Prussia, their neighbouring division, in which Kalya Petrova and her comrades served, was withdrawn for a brief rest. On the very first day, they were getting ready for a visit to the bathhouse and the barber when a stray shell hit Tanya Kareva in the toilet. "They've killed her!" one of the girls shouted as she ran back from the scene.[301] It was terribly upsetting and hard to take in. The front line was not that close, so they had supposed that for a time they were safe.

Roza Shanina could not relax. She kept demanding to be sent to the front with some other unit. "I don't want to rest!" She was constantly writing in pencil in a notebook with heavy covers. This uneducated young girl was drawn to learning, to literature, and aspired, when the war was over, to study at university. Her fellow snipers were able to read her front-line diary only many years later in the Soviet magazine Yunost (Youth).

Kalya, on the other hand, saw nothing wrong with taking a break. She had her hair permed by a barber for the second time in her life. The first had been at the station in Moscow before they were sent to the front, when almost the whole section had had the same thing done. Kalya set about putting the house where they had been billeted in order and the other girls joined in. She begged gauze from the medical company and dyed it yellow with acriquine, a drug fairly ineffective for treating malaria but very good at staining everything it came into contact with.

"'The malarials' were all walking around bright yellow" Kalya recalled. It was just what was needed for dyeing the curtains.[302]

The girls' platoon had bonded well after months at the front. If anyone got hold of food they would share it with the others. If boys tried piling into the snipers' house the girls would giggle but very soon show them the exit. If any men became tiresome, the snipers would not complain to their superiors but turn to their friends for help. United they could conquer.

They felt no particular compunction to obey orders from their commanders while they were resting. Why should they? After all, they were now battle-hardened soldiers, snipers who had taken out a dozen or two Germans, as recorded in their little grey record books. There was in any case very little drill while they were resting. What the commanders really liked was to inspect the girls' shooting skills. This was usually less a test than a demonstration for a particular audience: take a look at the kind of snipers we have! They would line up tin cans for them, throw a bottle in the air, and get them to shoot with all manner of weapons. Kalya vividly remembered an anti-tank gun she wanted to fire out of curiosity. It had such a recoil that her shoulder was bruised for a week afterwards. By this time the reconnaissance scouts had presented most of them with small, ladies' pistols they had captured, and the girls enjoyed firing them. They would come in handy later for those who took part in street-fighting in towns. Easiest of all was firing assault rifles, which they also practised. They were often invited to dances by lads from other units, and a dozen of them would go together and, at some point, demonstrate their sharpshooting.

During that rest period they were awarded their first orders and medals. For shooting five Germans they got a medal "For Merit in Combat", for ten they were given awards such as "The Red Banner", "The Order of the Great Patriotic War" or even the "Order of Lenin". It was around this time that the army held a women's rally, generously supplied with long tables of vodka and canned meat. At the end there was dancing and Kalya, who was not usually keen, even danced a waltz with another girl. She was tempted to change into shoes her uncle, who was a general, had sent from Moscow, but was embarrassed and left them in her knapsack. The shoes soon fell apart anyway and she threw them away.

Chapter 13

"Where's Tosya?" "Dead"

Klava Loginova's third sniper partner was Tosya Lukichyova, no great beauty but an outgoing and cheerful girl. She was killed at Suwałki, at the start of a failed Soviet offensive. The attack got bogged down on the first day, and all night the girl snipers found themselves standing in a trench with a few surviving soldiers. They moved signallers in there too, and even some of the H.Q. staff. In accordance with orders, they all kept firing continuously at the German front line. There were no minefields, no protection from a surprise assault, so nothing could be ruled out. The next day, the Germans were cut off from the rear by another group of Soviet troops. Klava and Tonya found a place in a trench where there had earlier been a machine-gun crew. It was a handily placed firing point, with good visibility. Suddenly a shell exploded right next to them. Klava remembered only being hit by a blast that flung her out of the trench. When she came to, she heard a nurse calling her name. She had been concussed and seemed to be hearing the voice underwater. "Where's Tosya?" she asked immediately, and was told Tosya was dead. After a week in hospital, Klava returned to her unit. She felt it "wasn't right" to take time off sick at a moment like this.

Klava was soon to lose a fourth partner, Tosya Tinigina, but before that she experienced the most important moment in her life as a soldier: a duel with a German sniper. In Soviet literature, and also in much of the material written in the post-Soviet era but still in the Soviet tradition, tales about the fighting career of almost every sniper come up with a description of a sniper duel – battles that go on for hours, and in which there can be only one winner. They make for rousing reading, but for Klava, who had just turned twenty and neither then nor later would have considered herself particularly heroic, it was just a job. She never referred to the episode as a "sniper duel", and it was only later, when she realised she had been within a whisker of death, that she felt really scared.

The offensive had ground to a halt, and, on one of their first days in a new location, when Klava and Tonya Tinigina were standing in a trench observing, soldiers came from another stretch of the front line in need of help. A German sniper had wounded several people there. Klava and Tonya went with them and were shown the area and trenches from which the officer believed the sniper was firing. By now Klava was an experienced sniper and had not forgotten what she had learned at the school about locating the enemy: a handful of freshly dug earth, a wilted leaf next to others that were green, a bush displaced a couple of centimetres, could all pinpoint a German sniper. Scrutinising the German front line through her telescopic sight, Klava soon spotted an embrasure in the parapet well camouflaged with leaves. On closer inspection she saw a concealed rifle in it. Now it was just a matter of waiting, and that was something she was good at: she already had sixteen Germans on her tally. The leaves twitched and she glimpsed a long face with ginger stubble. She shot a split second before the German. He had seen her too and fired almost simultaneously. He had been looking for her just as she had been looking for him. Klava believed that what saved her was the recoil of her rifle as the shot jerked her to one side. The German sniper's bullet pierced the strap and stock of her rifle. For months afterwards Klava was deaf in one ear, and her hearing never fully recovered.

There was no more shooting from the sniper and Klava was credited with a kill. It took her a long time to stop shaking and calm down that day.[303]

★

"Hey, Tasya, let's set fire to that barn!" Anya suggested. Far away on the German side they could see a grey thatched building. "Let's at least give the Germans a fright!"[304] The enemy was a considerable distance, about 800 metres, away and the snipers were having little luck hitting any soldiers, who were in any case fearful and behaving cautiously.

On 8 October 62 Infantry Division had relieved 16 Guards Division near the Lithuanian town of Kalvarija. Nine days later they went on the offensive. With the assault under way, on 23 October the Soviet Information Office announced, "Troops of the Third Byelorussian Front launched an offensive with the support of massive artillery and air strikes and broke through long-standing, in-depth German defences protecting the borders of East Prussia. They invaded East Prussia to a depth of 30 kilometres along a front 140 kilometres wide." The attack was, however, unsuccessful and as October drew to a close the Third Byelorussian Front went on the defensive.

Anya Mulatova's platoon returned to its front-line routine in the village of Raczki near Suwałki: at dawn the girl snipers would take up their positions at the trench embrasures and lie in wait for enemy soldiers lackadaisical enough to let their guard down for just long enough to make themselves a target. But in the absence of careless Germans, why not set fire to a barn?

Without any further ado the two girls began firing at the thatched roof. Anya loaded an incendiary cartridge – these had a distinctive green casing and she and her friends always had a few with them. She pulled the trigger and the bullet exploded on the roof. It crackled and caught fire, but immediately went out – it must be damp, she thought. Anya immediately loaded another and fired again.

She did not understand what happened next. First she heard a crack and then sand was flying all around her. Something warm flowed over her eyes. "Oh my God, blood!" Anya was terribly afraid of blood. When Tasya saw it she was very shocked too and started crying. But Anya was fine. An explosive bullet fired by a German sniper had ricocheted off the barrel of her rifle and smashed the stock to pieces. A tiny fragment of shrapnel had struck Anya's forehead, leaving a triangular scar to remember it by. She pulled the rifle out of the embrasure, sat down with it on the ground, put her arms round it and "started bawling my head off". The soldiers came running when they heard her: in the afternoon it was mostly "old geezers" on duty, men of forty and over. Young soldiers were posted there at night. What was there to cry about if a bullet had exploded a few centimetres away from your head without wounding you? "Anya, what are you crying for?" they asked solicitously. She explained tearfully that she was upset about her rifle. "That's nothing to worry about, your rifle will soon be as right as rain! Just hand it in to the gunsmith and they'll fix that stock for you! The main thing is that the sight hasn't been damaged!"

And yet Anya was inconsolable, partly because she had almost been killed, partly because she had damaged the thing she treasured most, her rifle, and partly because she had broken the sniper's golden rule: never fire twice from the same position.

The girls in Slavnov's regiment particularly remembered that at Raczki they lived not in dugouts but in the homes of local Polish residents. In the mornings, after eating their porridge and bread and drinking some milk given by the local people, they went hunting, sitting in a trench at their embrasures and looking for German soldiers. The Germans tried to keep their heads down, and could usually only be picked off when they were bringing ammunition or food or something else to the trenches. Later the Germans dug themselves even deeper into the ground and everything became more difficult.

The soldiers in the units defending this stretch got used to the fact that every day young girls went out and came back from hunting, that they sat all day long in a trench, watching, watching, sometimes shooting only once during the day, sometimes not firing at all. "Keep an eye on them so nothing happens," one soldier was ordered by his commander. Everybody knew how dangerous it was to walk around here under fire from the Germans. When Klava Lavrentieva met Anya at reunions after the war, she reminded her about one of the singer Klavdiya Shulzhenko's songs that Anna liked to sing on her way to the hunt. Her favourite at that time was, "Let's light up, front-line Comrade . . ." Shulzhenko was a big Soviet star who, in the first two years of the war, gave some 500 concerts on the Leningrad Front, and that song and others were sung there by men and women alike. They were hoping Shulzhenko would visit them on the Third Byelorussian Front, but for some reason she never came. There was, however, in the regiment a young lad from the reconnaissance squad who could play "Your Blue Shawl" wonderfully on a captured German mouth organ.[305] Anya's voice was not powerful, but pleasant. She had a good ear and, for as long as she could remember, had always been singing. But, of course, once they got down to the communication trenches to go to their embrasures she had to stop.

Time passed, the front did not move, and the snipers settled down to a strange but stable life of being shelled and going hunting. Zoya Yermakova began spending the night with the chief of staff. This came as no surprise to her colleagues: Zoya was older than the rest of them and, Anya noted, even smoked. It was only to be expected. To be fair, Zoya did continue to go hunting with the rest of them. Nadya Veretenova became "friendly" with the head of the chemical section, mending his undercollars, and whether there was anything more to it than that, no one could really tell. For Anya and Tasya and most of their friends, who were as yet inexperienced in such matters, it seemed strange and somehow shameful. A couple of times at the front they were all checked by a gynaecologist, and Anya was worried to see a minus sign in one of the columns of her medical record. "What, am I sick or something?" she asked the nurse, and only guessed later why some of the girls had pluses.[306]

Genuine, powerful romances also blossomed during that time, emotional ties that could last a lifetime. Party Administrator Yury Ivanov, who had access to the quarters of the girls' platoon, came to give them talks and lectures, and read Lermontov's *Masquerade* to them. The outcome was that he fell seriously in love with Valya Kondakova. Marriage seemed to be in prospect, and Valya later admitted to the girls that they "almost did it". But then Yury was seriously wounded in the jaw. He was taken away and Valya wrote to his parents that she was not sure he would survive. He did pull through, but after being discharged from hospital did not write to Valya or reply to her letters again. Only thirty years later at a reunion of their division did it become apparent that he had never forgiven her for that letter to his mother.

Anya and Tasya liked to joke with Sergeants Vanya Zakopaiko and Pyotr Fyodorov, who manned a 45-mm cannon. "Girls, come on in!" they were forever urging as Anya and Tasya walked by on their way to hunt. One time when they were returning a bombardment began. A shell exploded in their regiment's area, Pyotr was wounded and the girls rushed to help. He was not seriously hurt and asked his friend to lend him his bandage pack. "I don't have it," Vanya said unhelpfully. When Pyotr asked him to go then to their dugout to fetch his one, Vanya magically found it, not wanting to go out under fire.

Many of the girl snipers later recalled the undemanding, friendly attitude towards them of the boys in the regiment's reconnaissance unit. These young lads had no prospect of intimate relations with them (the commanders had a virtual monopoly), and were content to chat and joke, invite them to dance, and offer them treats of sugar or captured enemy chocolate. When they were on German territory, the scouts might also some pretty item or a watch. If they came across a small lady's pistol, they were certain to present it to one of the girls. On one occasion, Anya was even brought a rabbit fur coat, but it disappeared from the baggage cart, along with her knapsack.

There were some impetuous girls who asked to come along with the boys on reconnaissance missions. They were young, headstrong, and it offered them the chance to do something adventurous – and if the mission was successful they might get an award or a medal. In truth the snipers were little use on intelligence-gathering patrols, because at night there was no opportunity for marksmanship, even if there was sometimes a need for it.[307] The scouts took girls along (without telling the officers) as a favour, and to impress them. It often ended badly. Masha Alkhimova, one of the prettier snipers, lost both legs as the result of one such escapade. She was serving in the next unit along from Anya's and Anya knew her from the school. They heard in her platoon what had happened from Masha's partner, Kalinina. The reconnaissance failed to get through the front line silently, stumbling into cans and bottles that the Germans had hung in front of their positions. The Germans opened fire and the patrol turned back. From inexperience, or in a panic, Masha did not follow in the tracks of the scouts, who knew their way through the minefield. She rushed to one side and stepped on a mine. Risking their lives, the scouts dragged her out of the minefield and brought her back.[308] Masha had first one leg amputated, then the other.

After the war Alkhimova did not lose heart, although she had an awful time with her artificial limbs. Anna heard that, thank heavens, one of the girl snipers wrote to Alexey Maresiev, a famous fighter pilot who returned to battle after losing both his legs, and he helped Masha get decent prostheses. She went on to work for the rest of her life at the Bolshoy Theatre, making hats.

Anya and Lida Anderman ended up with one "boyfriend" between the two of them. That was Slava Chigvintsev, the commander of a reconnaissance platoon. He was a lieutenant, a Muscovite, and a lively, cheerful young man. The scouts' dugout was near the girls' one, and Slava would treat Anya and Lida to his chatter and mugs of tea. When Lida was out hunting, Slava would chat with Anya; when Anya was in the trench it was Lida's turn. Slava nicknamed Anya "the Hedgehog" because of her abundance of curls, which stuck out in all directions after she had a haircut. Anya suspected that her "boyfriend" found Lida, an educated girl from Moscow, more interesting and only chatted to her because he had no one else to talk to. They never did find out which of them he liked better, because one day Slava was arrested and, the girls heard, sent off to a penal company.

It turned out that the regiment's commander had been demanding a squealer, to find out what the Germans were planning. Several missions failed, and then Slava was sent with a group. They came under fire from the Germans and, looking after his men, he retreated rather than going ahead. For that he paid a high price, and Anya never saw or heard of him again. After the war she met up with Lida Anderman; they reminisced over their shared boyfriend, and wondered whether Slava made it back from the war.

You could never tell, though, what these young officers might have at the back of their minds. They could seem just to want to be friends, without any ulterior motive, and then suddenly get up to all sorts of nonsense. Two jolly young gunners, both called Volodya, made friends with the girls. "Let's go and listen to Radio Moscow!" one of them suggested to Anya one day. (They had a radio in their dugout.) She agreed, but scolded herself afterwards for being such an idiot. "Couldn't you see where this was leading, dumbcluck?" When she went into the dugout, though, both Volodyas were there. At first they did listen to the radio, sipped tea through sugar and ate bread, but then one Volodya suddenly got up and left and the second immediately set about her! "What are you doing?" Anya shouted indignantly, fighting him off. Volodya grabbed a pistol and started threatening to kill her. She knew, of course, that he was bluffing, and just said, "Well, what are you waiting for? Shoot me!" At that moment someone called Volodya's name, and he looked out of the dugout. Anya quickly grabbed the gun and hid it behind a sheet of plywood coming adrift from the ceiling. When he came back and saw that his pistol had disappeared Volodya was terrified. Losing a service firearm could get you hauled up before a tribunal. "Take me back to my dugout and then I'll tell you where it is," Anya said. It was late and dark and she would have been afraid to go back alone. Volodya, naturally, did as she said, and she told him where the pistol was. When they parted, Gunner Volodya, emboldened once more, called her a rude name.

Soon, however, an officer came on the scene to whom Anya's heart did not prove indifferent. One morning, as she and Tasya were standing in a trench near Raczki, each at their embrasure and about five metres apart, Anya suddenly saw someone striding towards them. She could not tell whether he was an ordinary soldier or an officer because his epaulettes were invisible under a cloak. He had a forage cap on his head. When this "chap" self-importantly demanded, "What are these unauthorised people doing here?" the girls realised he was definitely a commander. Anya always found officers intimidating, and now was really frightened. She wondered what regulation they must have broken. "Who sent you here?" the unknown figure demanded. Plucking up her courage, Anya reported, "We were brought here by our Commander Rakityansky." Rakityansky had, as usual, escorted them to their position early in the morning, showed them the embrasures, and immediately disappeared – he tended not to hang about on the front line longer than necessary. "Right. Before coming here, you should have come in to see me and get permission from the company commander," he cut her off, "or at least the platoon commander." The officer revealed himself to be in charge of a penal company holding this section of the front. Having told them off he departed, vowing to get to the bottom of the situation.

The next time Anya and Tasya saw him, he was coming to check how they were performing. He was now clean-shaven and had a fresh undercollar sewn on to his tunic. He was about twenty-five. "Brave and strong-willed", Anya decided when she got to know him a bit better. In any case, they would hardly put a duffer in charge of a penal unit! Anatoly had widely spaced, grey eyes, a straight nose, and fine fair hair. He looked in on them quite often. The good-looking, witty Tasya, who was more forward than Anya, took the initiative, but it soon became clear that the lieutenant was more taken by Anya. At the very beginning, not attaching much importance to their conversation, Anya inexplicably said she was from Moscow. Anatoly asked where she lived in Moscow, and she named a street she had heard about from evacuees in Simanschina: "Sivtsev Vrazhek", just off the Arbat. After that, Anatoly, who was himself a Muscovite, gave her no respite, always calling her his "Moscow girlfriend". He asked her more and more questions, but there was very little Anya could say with regard to the city. In the end she confessed, and then it was Anatoly who told her about Moscow. He was very knowledgeable and liked singing arias from operas, but at that time all of it, including the opera, went over Anya's head. She did like him, though, and when she invited her and Roza Shalaeva to visit him and his colleagues, tempting them with the promise of tea and biscuits, she agreed. He sent a horse-drawn sleigh for them. It was November, the snow was already lying on the ground, and they were conveyed the four kilometres to the penal company. They enjoyed it greatly, and Anya was pleased that, although Roza Shalaeva was very pretty, Anatoly sat all the time next to her, his "Moscow girlfriend".

Shortly afterwards the offensive began and Anya lost touch with him.[309]

Chapter 14

"I no longer have a heart. I am cold-blooded"

In autumn 1944, Ilya Ehrenburg wrote of Roza Shanina, "Let the Russian mother rejoice who gave birth to, brought up and gave this glorious, noble daughter to the Motherland! Yesterday Sniper Roza Shanina in a single outing exterminated five Nazis. Congratulations on your military achievement, Comrade Shanina! The personal tally of this fearless young woman is now fifty-one dead Hitlerites and three she has personally taken prisoner."[310]

Roza gave the press a brief description of how she had captured the Germans. "One time, after a vicious skirmish, I came across a severely wounded Red Army soldier. I bound up his wound and went on. I had taken only a few steps when a German appeared. I prepared to shoot, but on the spur of the moment decided instead to take him alive. '*Hände hoch!*' I shouted. Imagine my surprise when, instead of two hands, I saw six go up. I brought the three Fritzes back to headquarters."

In her diary Roza gave a far more interesting account of the episode, with her characteristic bluff humour.

I went back to the front line but was not concentrating. I forgot I was somewhere dangerous. Walking over a bridge, I happened to look down into the overgrown ravine and saw a Fritz standing down there, so I yelled, "*Hände hoch!*" Six hands were raised. One was trying to tell me something, but I couldn't understand. The only other words I knew were "Quick! Out!", so I shouted that. They crawled out of the ravine. I confiscated their guns, watches, cream, mirrors and so on. I guarded them for about a kilometre and a half, looked down and saw that one Fritz had only one boot. He had been asking me in the ravine to let him put his boot on.

Towards the end of their march, on the outskirts of a village, the Germans had recovered their wits enough to ask Roza what would happen now: "*Gut* or *kaput?*" "It will be *gut*," she replied, feeling very proud that "in snow camouflage, with a flick knife, some hand grenades and a rifle at the ready, like a bandit queen", she was leading three Germans through a Polish village.

By October 1944, Roza was a celebrity and was seldom seen in her platoon: she tried by hook or by crook to be at the front line. For her fellow snipers her periodic reappearances were generally accompanied by surprises: "One day she might bring back several prisoners, another she might come wounded, then again she might suddenly appear from headquarters bringing warm clothing and felt boots for all the snipers."

"Now Roza Shanina has dozens of dead Germans on her tally," war correspondent Major Miletsky wrote in a long feature about Roza and her comrades (but, mainly about Roza, since that was what had brought him to her regiment). *Rabotnitsa* (Woman Worker), a Soviet women's magazine, portrayed Roza as a folk-tale warrior maiden, wearing a skirt and patterned boots, but also the helmet and armour of an ancient Russian warrior, plus a pair of binoculars and an assault rifle (the illustrators of a women's magazine evidently were not *au fait* with the specification of a sniper's rifle).

Unlike most of her fellow students at the Podolsk snipers' school, Roza had wanted from the very beginning of the war to fight only as a sniper. She wrote to her great friend Pyotr Molchanov, the editor of the army newspaper, "Please pass on 'to whom it may concern' and give me your support. If you knew the passion I have to be with our soldiers right on the front line and to exterminate the Hitlerites! Instead, imagine it, I am in the rear. We have lost another four black and one red.[311] I so much want to avenge them. Do, please, have a word with the right person."

Soon Roza and the soldiers of her unit had the opportunity to take revenge on the enemy on German soil: on 18 October their unit "breached the frontier . . . we are already wandering about on German territory," Roza noted.[312] That offensive stalled, but in October 1944 Soviet troops at last crossed into East Prussia. What a long-awaited day that was!

Leonid Rabichev, a signals officer with 31 Army, recalled: "One of the divisions of our army breached the defensive barriers on the border. Sappers filled in a great ditch, destroyed five lines of barbed wire entanglements, and neutralised another ditch or rampart. That opened a fifteen-metre gap through which a country road led from Poland into East Prussia." The signaller arrived at the smart estate of Gollubien (Rabichev heard from someone that it had served as a hunting lodge for the King of Prussia) in the wake of the infantry and tank crews, who had clearly been "awed" by the German prosperity on display. "Mirrors in gilded frames had been smashed, duvets and pillows ripped open, a painting titled *The Birth of Aphrodite* had the word COCK daubed on it in black paint. In the courtyard the soldiers caught chickens, wrung their necks, plucked and gutted them, and thew them into a huge cauldron."[313]

This was only the prelude to an orgy of destruction on an incredible scale that was unleashed on East Prussia in January 1945 and continued until May. Now everything was different: if at first they had been liberating their own country, and then other countries occupied by the enemy, they now had beneath their feet the land from which the enemy had advanced against them.

Already in 1942 the fanatical Ehrenburg who, in the words of Alexander Werth, wrote "brilliant and eloquent diatribes against the Germans", urged: "We have realised that the Germans are not human. Henceforth the word 'German' loads a gun. We shall not talk. We shall not become indignant. Let us kill! If on one day you have not killed at least one German, your day has been wasted. If you think your neighbour will kill the German for you, you have not understood the threat. If you do not kill the German, the German will kill you."[314] Two years had passed. The Motherland was no longer in peril, but a terrible price had been paid for that. Now, almost every soldier had something personal to avenge. "Hate propaganda" added fuel to the personal scores almost all of them had to settle with the enemy.[315] Now, on the territory of the enemy, not only German soldiers but also German civilians would pay the price for this. The army's commanders would close their eyes to everything until, six months later, the troops were finally brought to heel.

Meanwhile, in October 1944, alongside the combat units crossing the border of East Prussia came reporters from front-line newspapers, artists and photographers. Their task was to create an image of enemy territory for the soldiers, to show them the "repulsive interior of the lair of the German beast".[316] Ex-soldiers recalled how "On the eve of our entering the territory of the Reich, propagandists were sent to incite the troops. Some were very high-ranking. 'A death for a death!!! Blood for blood!!! Forget nothing!!! Forgive nothing!!! We shall be avenged!!!' and so on. Before that Ehrenburg, whose crackling, trenchant articles everybody read, had been giving it his all: 'Daddy, kill the German!'"[317] Hatred and revenge were to motivate the soldiers to advance fearlessly. "I remember how much we needed Ehrenburg's articles. Hatred was what drove us forward, otherwise how could we have kept going?"[318]

The elation the troops experienced when crossing the border was to be intensified by propaganda. Prussia was the den, the hornets' nest, the breeding ground of wild animals and brigands, inhabited by savage dogs, wolves and predators.[319] "Germans are not human beings." Ehrenburg had little trouble persuading Soviet soldiers and civilians of that: what human being would torture prisoners and abuse the civilian population? The propagandists found a receptive audience: in one regiment alone among those which crossed the frontier in October 1944, "158 soldiers had had close relatives tortured and killed, 56 had had their family members deported to Germany, 152 had had their families left homeless, and 293 had had their property looted and their livestock stolen."[320] Even soldiers whose families had not been affected had seen enough while liberating Byelorussia or Ukraine to be ready to take revenge pitilessly.

Returning to his native village in Ukraine after the Germans left, seventeen-year-old Leonid Shmurak helped his father and uncle exhume the remains of murdered Jewish relatives, including little children. After seeing the children's belongings and clothes, the boy went to the enlistment centre. He had no desire to defend the Soviet regime, which had expropriated his family's possessions and sent them into exile. He wanted to take revenge on Germans. The colonel in the centre took one look at his birth certificate and told him to go away and play football. Shmurak said: "I'll play no football. I've come here to kill Germans." Before long he was at the front shooting them, whether or not they had their hands up. "I had a great anger," he recalled decades later. "There was no fear I might be killed or wounded. All that was in my mind was that I must be avenged, that I must see myself killing that German."[321]

Shortly before her death, Anna Sokolova, who arrived at the front with the second cohort of the Central Women's Sniper School and fought in

70 Infantry Division, told a reporter from *Moskovsky Komsomolets* about an encounter with a captured German girl sniper. Scouts had caught her in the woods where she was camouflaged up a tree. She was the same age as Anna and looked similar; both had the same boyish haircut.

Anna Sokolova was ordered to shoot the German girl, and unhesitatingly led her to a ravine. "After all, if I had been in her place she would not have spared me," Sokolova claimed after the war.[322] The German sniper was Sokolova's eleventh kill, but she did not include her in the tally as she had shot her at point-blank range.

The only snag with this story is that there were no women on the front line in the German army, let alone snipers; and there were no women, not even nurses, among the collaborating Vlasov forces. The most likely explanation is that this girl was a figment of Sokolova's imagination and, if so, it is something for the psychologists to consider. Thinking back to the days of her youth, to the war, an elderly woman imagines an enemy girl like herself, and kills her with the same cruelty she expected the enemy to use against herself.[323] Many decades after the war the sniper veteran was still mentally taking revenge on the Germans.

During the first six months of their war, Roza Shanina and her comrades took almost no part in attack operations. First there was a defensive position at Vitebsk, then pursuit of the retreating enemy. They would only face real, fierce fighting when they reached East Prussia. On 3 November, Roza noted, "I came back from the front completely exhausted. I am going to remember this war. Four times the village was taken and retaken: three times I got out right under the noses of the fascists. Fighting the enemy on his own territory is not to be taken lightly."[324]

They had to "gnaw through" the German positions, a veteran of 17 Guards Division recalled. "Our troops took the town, but many of them were killed," Roza noted in her diary. "Only one man from the penal company came back: the rest were all killed."[325] Roza believed she killed at least fifteen Germans in that battle, although that was not recorded in her sniper's book as it occurred during an attack. Fighting off a "Fritz" assault, she shot at the helmets of crawling soldiers from a distance of 200 metres using tracer bullets, and could clearly see in her gunsight the bullets ricocheting off. When they had advanced to 100 metres, the Germans stood up but Roza kept firing. She and her friends ran for it when the Germans were very close. "In a little grove of trees by the forester's house, a small group of Soviet soldiers took on an enemy tank attack in an unequal battle," a participant recalled.[326] "We were heavily outmanned, with ten times the number of enemy troops to our handful of soldiers. We began slowly to retreat to avoid encirclement. Shortly afterwards we received the order to attack."[327]

"We crawled forward and reoccupied the house, driving the Germans out," Roza wrote. [328] Later she returned to the regimental command point where "for the first time I had a chance to eat, and fell asleep." Roza was reluctant to show her face "back home" in the sniper platoon, because the girl snipers were not supposed to be in the first line of an attack and the decision to take them there had, of course, been hers. "That time Sasha Koreneva was killed, and two others, Valya Lazorenko and Anya Kuznetsova, were wounded. The girls would put all the blame on me." Roza was dissatisfied with her comrades. When the Germans counterattacked, "the girls all proved to be cowards and ran away." The exception was Kalya Petrova who "was the only brave one".[329]

Roza wrote about this skirmish, as about all the most significant scrapes she found herself in, to the editor of the front-line newspaper, *Exterminate the Enemy*, Pyotr Molchanov: "The day before yesterday we buried my comrade-in-arms, Sasha Koreneva. Two other girls were wounded: Valya Lazorenko and Zina Shmelyova. Perhaps you remember them."[330] Roza's fearlessness made a big impression on Molchanov, who preserved all her letters. After she was killed, he was given her diary too and did much to perpetuate the memory of this daredevil who always wanted to be in the thick of the action. Valya Lazorenko, a beautiful blonde who loved horses and dreamed of joining the cavalry after the war, returned to the regiment after getting out of hospital. She and Roza were great friends, and they signed an agreement never to use "front-line language or even a single unprintable word": if either of them broke their word, they would forfeit their sugar ration for a fortnight. All the other girls swore unapologetically.[331]

After the incident at Pillkallen, Roza never again took the whole platoon to the front line but went there on her own, returning "home" to rest, eat and change her clothes. More and more often, unable to abide being in the rear and not wanting to rest, she returned to the front on her own initiative.

You should know that throughout my life at the front there has not been an instant when I have not longed to be in battle. I want to be where the fighting is fiercest. I want to be there with the soldiers. I would give anything to go right now with them into the attack. Oh, gods! Why am I so peculiar? I just cannot understand it. I long for battle, for fierce fighting. I will give anything, including my life, if only I can satisfy this quirk. It pains me. I can't sleep soundly.[332]

Her platoon, although not constantly on the front line, was suffering more and more casualties. "I no longer have a heart. I am cold-blooded," Roza commented in her diary, remembering with her friends some girls the Germans had captured.

The incident occurred in Lithuania in the autumn when they were on the defensive. There was heavy fog that morning and, as hunting was impossible, the girls were standing in a trench at a lookout post with some soldiers. The fog enabled the Germans, a reconnaissance group looking for a squealer, to steal up on them. It all happened very quickly: the girls were talking and suddenly, "like a bolt from the blue, the fascists burst into the trench and seized three of our girls. Of course there was a fight," Sima Anashkina recalls.[333] In fact, four were seized, but two managed to get away.

In good visibility the snipers would have had no trouble shooting the Germans as they were dragging their comrades off, but in the thick fog they did not want to risk firing, even though Anya and Lyuba were shouting to them to do just that: they would have preferred to die. Dusya Kekesheva and Dusya Shambarova were lucky: one of the Germans stepped on a mine and in the ensuing commotion Kekesheva was able to run back to their trenches. Dusya Shambarova was wounded and pretended to be dead. The Germans continued running with her two captured friends and she, "covered in blood", crawled back to her own side.[334] Kalya heard later that the doctors extracted fifty-three pieces of shrapnel from her.[335] Nevertheless, shortly after the war, she died from her wounds.

Kalya Petrova's platoon heard about this horrifying incident that same day. Kalya remembered they themselves had not gone out hunting, so they had a rare opportunity to wash their hair in a nearby lake. They had just finished when someone brought news that the Germans had dragged Anya Nesterova and Lyuba Tanailova away. "Dusya Kekesheva saw it all. She managed to get free, but are the other two still alive somewhere? In the hands of those butchers," Roza Shanina wrote later.[336] The fate of girls who fell into the hands of the Germans did not bear thinking about: newspapers, leaflets and the political officers in their talks described the horrible treatment the Germans meted out to Soviet prisoners of war, and in addition Anya and Lyuba were girls, and girl snipers at that. According to the articles in the Soviet press, army girls faced rape and torture if captured by the Germans. As for snipers, they were hated and were likely to be tortured and killed if caught, irrespective of their sex.

"And, despite everything, Nesterova and Tanailova revealed nothing when the Fritzes tortured them. Good for them, even though the Germans called them support staff," Roza recorded on 7 December. She saw photos of the girls ("old ones, from their Red Army record books") in German leaflets dropped on the Soviet positions. It is unclear why Roza believed her comrades had been tortured. After that German leaflet, no more was heard of them. Their platoon assumed the Germans had murdered them after failing to secure any information during the interrogation.

Kalya Petrova would have to wait until twenty-five years after the end of the war to discover that this was not the case. At that time attention suddenly began to be paid to war veterans, and meetings with front-line comrades and veterans became customary. At one of these Kalya spotted Lyuba Tanailova. She had been imprisoned in a German concentration camp but survived until it was liberated by the Americans. Nesterova, though, died there. Upon returning to the U.S.S.R. Tanailova was sent to a Soviet prison camp, a fate that befell so many Soviet servicewomen captured by the Germans.[337] The conditions in these camps were little different from those in their German equivalents. In Camp PFL 0308, where the inmates included women from the liberated territories and women who had been in German captivity, a commission of inspection found that "the soup was cooked from unpeeled and partly rotten potatoes, and accordingly smelt fetid and was extremely unpalatable . . ." There was a water shortage at the camp, so the premises were never washed. Nor was there any washing of the "special cargo", the prisoners. At the time of the inspection they had not been to the bathhouse or had their hair cut for two months. The prisoners were weak, louse-ridden and suffering from skin diseases. Sick prisoners were not admitted to hospital. The "special cargo" had to walk 2–3 kilometres to work in the mines "without warm winter clothing". Dystrophic prisoners were forced to labour alongside all the others.[338]

Some of those who had been in German captivity were saved by having medals or a distinguished combat record before being captured or, more often, by having seen active service – with partisans or the regular army – after escaping from captivity.

Anna Yegorova, the pilot of a ground assault IL-2 aircraft, was shot down near Warsaw. Her gunner and radio operator, Dusya, was killed but, by a miracle, Anna was thrown clear of the burning plane at the last moment. She managed to pull her parachute's ripcord when already close to the ground and survived, but was barely alive when she was captured, having suffered terrible burns and fractures when she hit the ground. Her parachute had opened only partially. She would have died but for a Soviet nurse, Yulia Krashchenko, who stayed by her side on the journey to the camp and in the Stalag III-C P.O.W. camp in Küstrin in Poland, where a captive Soviet doctor treated the wounded pilot. Prisoners of many nationalities, impressed by Anna's courage, gave her presents of pieces of bread and sugar, sewed slippers for her, and even wove her a straw bag decorated with a red star. After Küstrin, Yulia Krashchenko was transferred to the fearful Ravensbrück women's concentration camp, but survived and met up with Anna after the war. At the risk of their lives, the prisoners in Küstrin had hidden Anna's medals and Party membership card. She had been greatly moved by the courage and humanity of these exhausted, louse-ridden, famished people, her fellows in misfortune.

The SMERSH major who processed Anna in a "filtration" centre after her liberation from the Germans could see perfectly well that she could barely stand and that the thin skin which had grown over her extensive burns was cracking and oozing blood, but he did not allow her to sit down. He would not call this pilot released from enemy captivity anything other than a "German sheepdog". Where had she got those medals and the Party membership card from? Why had she surrendered? What mission had the Germans given her? Who was she to get in touch with in the U.S.S.R.? The nightmare went on for ten days. The officers and guards insulted her constantly, she was allowed to go to the toilet only under escort and she received one meal per day.

Anna Yegorova was saved by the fact that former prisoners and doctors from the Küstrin camp, when they learned that she was being interrogated by SMERSH, wrote to that agency and told everything they knew about her, including the physical state she was in when captured and her uncompromising behaviour in the camp. The SMERSH officers informed her that she had passed their "filtration" process and was free to go. She then had great difficulty obtaining a certificate confirming that she was "clean". Needless to say, despite the fact that she could hardly stand, nobody helped her to find transport back to her unit, but that seemed a minor matter. She was soon back in her own regiment.[339]

The only conscientious biographical publication (the rest should be considered as propaganda) about Roza Shanina notes: "In the battles for the Motherland the following snipers perished: Alexandra Koreneva, Alexandra Yekimova, Anna Nesterova, Lyubov Tanailova . . ."[340] The saga of Nesterova and Tanailova was either unknown to the authors, or they decided not to stir up the embers of an inconvenient topic. The historians writing about the Podolsk snipers' school and the platoon in which Roza Shanina fought kept quiet about the fact that Tanailova returned from captivity. It was better for the public not to know her fate after the war. Reporters took no interest in her and, unfortunately, all we know is that, after her stay in a Soviet prison camp and subsequent exile to Kazakhstan, Lyuba Tanailova returned home to Chelyabinsk Province and worked on the same collective farm as she had before the war. About how she fought during the war, what she endured in German captivity and, after the war, in the U.S.S.R., nobody has written a word.

Chapter 15

"Well, what are you here for? To fight or . . . ?"

Somewhere very close to 31 Army, flying from Poland into East Prussia, the pilots and navigators of 46 Night Bomber Regiment bombed the Germans from plywood aircraft. These women pilots, the "Night Witches", were aerial aristocrats held in high esteem by the army's top brass. By late 1944, 46 Regiment boasted a number of Heroes of the Soviet Union and its members were seen to be in a different league from ordinary girls in the army. But they got killed like anyone else.

On the night of 13 December 1944, Scout Silkin was on duty with his colleagues in a trench and saw a burning plane flying above the front line.

Two figures parachuted out and landed in no-man's-land. Shortly afterwards they heard an explosion and a woman crying for help. They crawled towards her across the minefield, which they were familiar with, but before they could reach the wounded pilot, there was a second, more powerful, explosion. The collar of the pilot's flying suit fell on Silkin's face, along with a piece of her body. The plane was burning, lighting up the area, and the Germans were "firing incessantly". The scouts did manage to retrieve the pilot, but she was already dead. They crawled over towards the other.

Navigator Rufina Gasheva began flying with Olga Sanfirova in Kuban. Olga had returned to the regiment there after a "long and painful saga". Back in Engels, while her newly formed regiment was training, as an experienced airwoman she was accompanying a new pilot, Zoya Parfyonova. Their wheels clipped a high-voltage electricity line and they fell to earth. They miraculously survived but the plane was a write-off. Olga, as the person in charge of the flight, was sent before a tribunal and sentenced to ten years' imprisonment. Fortunately, the regimental command appealed to a higher authority and the sentence was revoked.

Sanfirova and Gasheva were shot down for the first time on 1 May 1943, falling on the wrong side of the front line. They were saved by the marshes, through which they made their way back to their regiment for two days. A day after their return, they were up in the skies again.

When hit a second time, they had considerably less luck. For Rufina Gasheva this was her 813th sortie. They dropped their bombs and turned for home, but then Gasheva saw the right wing of their plane was alight. "For a few seconds, we flew on in silence," she recalled. The fire flared up and was moving towards the cabin. Sanfirova tried to hold out until they crossed the front line, but when it was impossible to wait any longer, she ordered Gasheva, "Rufa, quick, get out. Jump!" Gasheva remembered standing with both feet on the wing and then being blown off by the airstream. As she fell, she tugged the ripcord but the parachute did not open. She was "overwhelmed by horror". With all her strength she jerked the cord again. She felt a sudden jolt and "a white dome" opened above her. On the ground, she freed herself from the parachute, ran away from it and started crawling. There was a terrible racket. It seemed to her as if she was being shot at from all directions.[341]

But where was Olga? Perhaps she had been injured during the jump and was lying helpless somewhere. Perhaps the Germans had got her. Suddenly Rufina's hand came upon "something cold and metallic: a mine!" She had landed in a minefield, but needed to move forward. She groped ahead with her hand, and then with a stick she found, as if that might save her. Finally she found herself facing a wall of barbed wire, which she picked her way through very slowly and with great difficulty. When she heard Russian voices, she stood up and called out loudly. The soldiers shouted back, "This way, lassie!" In the trenches the soldiers gave her hot tea. One of them took off his boots and gave her them so she could get to the command point. There she heard what had happened to Olga. "Your friend didn't make it," somebody told her "She hit a mine. She landed in a minefield too, only hers were anti-personnel. The ones you came on were anti-tank, which is how you got through."[342]

At headquarters Rufina was given a glass of spirits and drank it down like water, not feeling anything. She could not sleep. In the morning the pilot's body was brought back and Rufina went out of the dugout to see it. "Nothing stirred in me. It just didn't seem to be Olga," Gasheva recalled. Her friends came, the girls from the regiment, and hugged and comforted Rufina. As they were arriving back at the house where the girls were staying, she jumped out of the vehicle and ran barefoot to her room, sure that Olga was there, alive and well.

After Olga's death, Rufina found the strength to take to the air again. She continued flying until victory was declared, as the navigator of Nadya Popova, a remarkable pilot.

December 1944 was quiet. Anya Mulatova's division was still posted near Suwałki and the girls often went out hunting. They saw almost nothing of the local people. Only the officers who were given leave in the town met up with them. Open conflict was rare since the troops were instructed to behave well towards the Poles. "Soviets and other authorities are not to be set up and Soviet ways of doing things are not to be introduced. There is to be no obstruction of religious observances, and Polish and other churches and prayer houses are not to be touched." They were also ordered to guarantee Polish citizens "protection of their private property and personal property rights".[343]

The soldiers were given instructional talks. "Victory over German fascism will come through the liberation of the peoples of Europe." "A Red Army soldier is a warrior in the world's most powerful and well-disciplined army," the political instructors and Party administrators explained. And, indeed, what they saw around them did not incline the soldiers to hostility towards the Poles: ". . . the people are poor. All around is sand and more sand . . . coniferous forests and then more sand and more impoverished villages," war correspondent Dmitry Dazhin wrote home to his wife.[344] It was an attitude based on a kind of cross-national class solidarity, but even the poor Poles were often far from welcoming their Soviet liberators. ". . . Everything was petty bourgeois, based on smallholdings. In Eastern Poland they were wary of us and semi-hostile, trying to rip off the liberators whenever they could. The women, though, were gratifyingly pretty and flirtatious. They captivated us with their manners, their cooing speech where suddenly everything became comprehensible, and sometimes they themselves were captivated by our gruff, virile strength or a soldier's uniform. Their pale, emaciated suitors just had to grit their teeth and stay in the shade for the time being."[345]

Brought up to believe in the emancipating mission of the Red Army, Soviet soldiers and officers felt insulted by the fact that many Poles seemed far from happy about being rescued by them. Galina Yartseva who, like Taya Kiselyova and her comrades, had fought their way through Estonia, Lithuania, Latvia and Poland and were currently halted "somewhere on the German border", wrote to a friend: ". . . they have fun, make love, live their lives and it's our job to come and liberate them. While they are laughing at the Russians . . . Yes, yes! The bastards . . . I don't believe for a moment in friendship with these Poles and Lithuanians and all the rest of them!"[346] Soviet military censorship registered such sentiments as "the reality of a misunderstanding of the great liberating mission of the Red Army".[347] The Poles, of course, had plenty of reasons to treat the Russians with suspicion, but an ordinary Red Army soldier was not likely to be aware of that.

The political instructors of 31 Army also talked to the soldiers about atrocities committed by the Germans in Suwałki: the executions of Polish civilians (they lumped the Jews in together, not treating them as a separate category: Soviet publications usually remained silent on the subject of the Holocaust) and prisoners of war at the large German concentration camp in Suwałki, where more than 50,000 people were killed.

Vasiliy Slavnov, the commander of 123 Infantry Regiment, saw in the New Year 1945 in Suwałki while being treated there for sinusitis acquired in the swamps of Byelorussia. The lady of the house in which he was billeted laid on a feast that made it seem as if there was no war on. In his memoirs Slavnov says that the local Polish people often came to visit him there "to learn the truth about the Land of the Soviets", and get a better idea of what it was the Russians were bringing them.[348] German propaganda had portrayed the Russians as complete brutes, and people were very keen to be persuaded that this was not the case. With those who were poor he had no trouble in finding a common language.

The Poles very willingly handed over to the Russians *Volksdeutsche** who had not managed to flee and were hiding in the town. The only thing that puzzled the local people, the Russian political reports note, was why the Soviet soldiers were so badly clothed.[349]

*

---

* The term *Volksdeutsche* applied to people of German origin living, for example, in parts of Poland and Czechoslovakia, as long as they were not Jewish.

As 1944 drew to a close the Soviet army was preparing for an offensive that would bring it to Berlin. Boys born in 1926, and even in 1927, were being called up, along with girls born in 1925 and 1926. Yulia Zhukova and her friend Valya Shilova had been born in 1926, and in December 1944 they were on their way to the front with the third cohort of graduates from the Central Women's Sniper School. The girls had gone together to the army enlistment office in their native Uralsk. They had been called up together, studied together, and had hopes of being a pair at the front together. Their mothers negotiated themselves business trips at work (they would never have been allowed into Moscow if they had just turned up), and came to join their daughters for the November celebrations of the anniversary of the Bolshevik revolution, travelling the length of the country from Kazakhstan. In the barracks, while Yulia was getting ready – she and Valya were being granted leave – the other girls swarmed around her mother. It was a miracle, a mother! Someone else's, but, still, a mother. Most of them were only seventeen or eighteen years old. Parted at such an early age from their parents, they were homesick.

Their mothers had brought dresses for Yulia and Valya, and a relative who lived in Moscow lent the girls her own and her neighbour's coats. They went for a walk round Moscow, to Red Square, and how wonderful it was to be strolling around in civilian clothes and not have to salute every officer you met![350] A month later they were issued their uniforms for the front: tunics and trousers, greatcoats, padded trousers and jackets, warm underwear and downy white American stockings. For the first time they were given wine to drink with their dinner, and before the meal there were speeches and music. After dinner, the girls, as was customary, gave their two snitches a talking to and beat them up but, as everyone was in a good mood, not too badly.

Soon they were on their way to the front, in heated goods wagons. It proved a long journey; the train moved slowly and stopped frequently. They would sit for ages, despite the cold, at the open wagon door, looking out at the fields and woods, singing all the songs they had learned at school, one after the other. They sighed nostalgically as they remembered the excellent food at sniper school. Now they were gnawing black bread rusks, sucking at herrings, and boiling something out of a concentrate that might have been soup or might have been porridge. At all the stations they found Russian women waiting for the troop train, pressing food on the girls even though they hadn't enough for themselves – they felt they had to give something to the soldiers, and then, maybe, someone would feed their husband or their son and be kind to them.[351]

In Minsk they were re-formed and the cohort was assigned, some 400 of them, to the various fronts. Yulia and Valya were devastated to learn that they were to be separated, and afterwards Yulia could not imagine why they had not asked to be together. Nevertheless, Yulia had no presentiment in her heart of anything ominous as she said goodbye. She would not learn until after the war that Valya had been killed in March 1945.

In the reserve regiment in Suwałki, a "chubby, rosy-cheeked major" in a solid, good quality white sheepskin jacket "strutted down the line, critically examining" the girls. "Well, what are you here for?" he finally enquired. "To fight . . ." The most foul-mouthed of the girls, Sasha, finished the sentence for him: "or whore?"[352] They all found that offensive, but there was plenty more, and much worse than that, to come. They were not detained for long in the reserve regiment, however, but went on to join 611 Meritorious Infantry Regiment, which had been fighting almost from the outbreak of the war.

Their baptism of fire came in a mortar attack during their very first meal in the new regiment. Scared out of their wits, the girls abandoned their rifles and the mess tins of soup that they had been delighted to see after so many days of unspeakable food. They finished it, cursing the Germans, when it was already stone cold.

Soon after, during their introduction to the front line, the young officer escorting them taught them that they did not need to be afraid of every mortar shell. At first, they did not find him very impressive: he seemed just to be a young boy, although a very gloomy-looking one. But the medals they saw on his chest under his casually unbuttoned greatcoat duly inspired respect, as did the fact that when they all fell down in the snow during shelling the officer stood there and imperturbably waited for them to get up again. They could soon tell for themselves from the sound whether a shell or a mine would land close to them or far away.

They were warned of the need to be careful, as the Germans in the area had also recently acquired a sniper. As too often happened, they only began to be truly cautious after one of the girls was killed by that sniper's bullet. The precision of the wound in her head left no room for doubt about who was responsible.[353]

They were introduced to their new workplace: a long trench, almost as deep as a person's height, with individual gun emplacements and observation points. On the other side of no-man's-land were the Germans, close, and they could see clearly through the sights of their rifles an occasional helmet bobbing along above the parapet. In the evenings they could hear them singing and playing mouth organs.

As she worked on her memoirs, Yulia Zhukova analysed her feelings in those first days at the front. She noted "a degree of excitement and elation, but also uncertainty and expectation of something unusual, and fear". It was not yet fear of the Germans – that would come later – but that she might not cope, might do something stupid, "make myself a laughing stock".[354]

The first kill in nineteen-year-old Yulia's sniper book was recorded before the old year was out. She opened her tally when she and her pair were tired and cold and it was getting dark. It was not a simple matter to shoot someone. There was only one partially exposed section within their view, and the Germans stooped down and ran across it as quickly as they could whenever they had to traverse it. Yulia suddenly saw, however, a German sauntering slowly along, standing completely upright. "He's either just arrived or is reckless," she thought. She took aim and fired. The German "waved his arms about ridiculously and fell sideways". The girls waited for a time to see whether he would get up, but then left, asking a soldier to "keep an eye on that German." He did not get up again. It was reported to the commander and, calling the entire section out on parade, he publicly commended Yulia. For her part, Yulia felt slightly sick all night. She was shivering and "didn't want to think about the dead man".[355]

The New Year of 1945, which was clearly going to be the last year of the war, was celebrated very happily by the girl snipers and the lads from reconnaissance. So, at least, wrote Yulia Zhukova in her memoirs. She makes no mention of an ugly incident which occurred on New Year's Eve in her regiment, although she does write openly about others. Even if she was not directly involved in the episode, she must have known about it.

A report to Ryaposov, the chief of the Political Department of 31 Army, mentions

an incidence of hooliganism in 611 Infantry Regiment of 88 Infantry Division on the part of staff officers working at the regimental headquarters. After the spirits brought by Voyentorg had sold out (calculated at a rate of 200 grams per officer), three drunken officers "burst into a room where a rehearsal of the amateur dramatics club was in progress".[356] Major Sosnin ordered the accordionist to play a waltz and roughly pushed the leader of the club out into the corridor. After that the drunks started dancing.

Member of the Communist Party of the Soviet Union (Bolsheviks) Captain Pozdnyakov, entering the quarters of the sniper company, began coarsely importuning Sniper Dogadkina. When she broke free, Pozdnyakov chased her, ordered her to stand to attention and swore at her obscenely. After that Pozdnyakov entered the snipers' quarters and, standing in the middle of the room, subjected them to a stream of obscenities: "We know why you have been sent here. You are all whores and prostitutes and you have been sent for us to . . ."

A little later SMERSH Representative Shlennikov, who was also very intent on entering the girls' hostel with two companions, knocked to the floor the snipers' company commander Kaftannikov and Sergeant Bitkova who tried to stop him. When Instructor for Work with Young Communists Dovzhenko arrived on the scene, the delinquents, swearing defiantly, left the premises.[357]

Chapter 16

"Aryan flesh"

On 13 January 1945 the offensive against East Prussia was relaunched. 39 Army, and within it 152 Fortified District, which was provided with a company of snipers, attacked Königsberg as part of the Third Byelorussian Front. The fortress city that the Germans had prepared for a long siege held a great importance for them, both strategic and political, as the capital of East Prussia and a major civilian and military port. The advance was slow because the Germans had fortified East Prussia strongly, and they resisted desperately.

Four days later the Soviets moved on the town of Lasdienen. Klava Loginova and her partner, Tosya Tinigina, spent the night dragging crates of shells for grenade-launchers and cartridges to the front line. This was very hard work: they could only move by crawling, dragging the crates weighing 10 kilograms or more behind them. When Klava went back for another crate she heard that Tosya had been wounded and taken to the hospital. Another loss for the platoon.[358]

Soon there were more casualties, more often as a result of carelessness than of combat. Just over half the platoon's members were still operational: five had been lost after the terrible incident with Nonna Orlova and the machine gun (including Nonna); several were killed or wounded at Suwałki; a beautiful gypsy girl, Faya Borisenko, was taken to perform in a band; and Klava Mitina was moved to the headquarters staff. Immediately after the taking of Lasdienen, from which the Germans retreated without a fight, the platoon was transferred from 152 Fortified District to 174 Division in 31 Army. Nina Isaeva, the commander of a platoon from the first cohort of the Central Women's Sniper School, a battle-hardened sniper and officer, came to collect them. She led them through the woods, giving them strict instructions that they must follow in the footsteps of the person in front because there were mines around. Someone, nevertheless, lost their footing.

Klava was at the back, almost the last in the little column. Suddenly there was an explosion ahead and the girls were screaming. That took out four more snipers. Anya Zamyatina was killed and another girl died of her wounds; two survived but did not return to the front.

When they did finally reach 174 Division, having taken their wounded to a field hospital, they were given a warm welcome and even a special sit-down meal. Then they were split up into groups and taken to different regiments. Klava, with her fourth partner, Zina Novozhilova, was allocated to 494 regiment and shown the front line.[359] Klava fought as a member of this regiment through to the end of the war.

Klava Loginova would not meet Commander Nina Isaeva again until twenty years after the war, because shortly after the girls' transfer to 494 Regiment, Isaeva was seriously wounded. She later recalled the circumstances. On her way to the front line, she saw a shiny new pin on the ground. It was pointing at her, which was a bad omen in Russian folklore. She could not resist, however, picked it up and pinned it to her tunic. While hunting she felt what seemed like a blow to her head and lost consciousness. A German sniper's bullet had damaged her eye socket and jaw.[360]

The man who had fallen in love with Nina at the front remained true to her, despite her disfigurement. He was the commander of 174 Division, forty-year-old Colonel Nikita Demin. He left his family for her and she lived a happy life with him.

★

Klava Loginova raised her tally within a couple of days of arriving in her new regiment, firing from a loft somewhere in the Masurian swamps. The Germans counter-attacked and surrounded their unit. The girls fired armour-piercing ammunition at the tanks closing in on the village, trying to hit the fuel tanks. They failed to set any of them on fire, but Klava managed to get a shot into the driver's slot. The tank fired a shell at them and missed, but the blast threw the girls down from the loft.[361] Klava got away with a few bruises but Zina was badly hurt. The encirclement was soon over: they radioed to other units and the Germans were driven back. After that Klava fought with Olga Nikolaeva, her fifth and last partner. 31 Army pressed on towards Königsberg.

In her year and a half at the front, Klava Panteleyeva found herself on the defensive twice. The first time was right at the beginning, at Orsha; the second was in the Baltic states, at Memel. For two months the snipers did what they were trained to do, or at least for as long as they had boots to wear. One night they all, without exception, lost their boots. After moving to a new location, the snipers' section was accommodated in a wooden house next to the regimental command post. Bunks had been constructed for them and, like well-brought-up girls, before going to bed they put their boots in a row by the door. In the morning they were gone. The problem turned out to be their new neighbours, a penal company, who had already exchanged the stolen boots for vodka. The girls were due to go on duty in their trench, but none of them had anything to wear on their feet. Their sergeant cursed. "Where am I supposed to find you so many boots?"

Boots were, nevertheless, found, and Klava heard shortly afterwards that all the soldiers in the penal company had perished during an attempt to break through the defences of Memel. Their bodies lay in no-man's-land, and when the girls were in the trench the terrible stench of decomposing corpses only metres away from them made them feel sick.[362]

Memel fell on 28 January after two days of heavy fighting. The remnants of its defenders retreated along the spit of the Kurische Nehrung to

Königsberg, and the girls, along with the rest of their army, followed in pursuit. By now there were only half a dozen of them left in the section. Klava Monakhova was no more. Her comrades loved her like a big sister, and when she died during a German counter-attack, her friends crawled out on to the battlefield for the next three nights, eventually finding her body and bringing it back for burial.

In those battles Klava Panteleyeva again suffered concussion: one half of her head no longer seemed to belong to her, and her eye was not seeing properly. She did not report to the medical battalion, however, afraid of falling behind her friends, but complained only to her partner Marusya Kuznetsova, with whom she had become firm friends. After Memel they would not hunt again during the war. While 344 Division was clearing the spit of Germans and moving on towards Königsberg, the girls learned to bandage neatly as they attended to the wounded.[363]

Lida Bakieva had no intention of becoming a nurse: she considered that her job in the war was shooting. On 28 January 1945, she crawled out on to no-man's-land. The Germans were about 600 metres away, too far for targeted shooting. Although the girls had permission only to hunt from their trench, Lida decided she needed to get closer. Having chosen her position the evening before, she crept forward fifty metres at dawn and lay down in the snow behind a fallen tree. On top of her padded coat and trousers (inside the coat there was an extra patch of sheepskin to dampen her gun's recoil) she had white camouflage trousers and jacket. Lida had put dried bread and sugar in one pocket and a captured pistol in the other. There would not be time to fire a rifle in every situation, and they always kept a last bullet in the pistol for themselves, in case it came to that.

Bakieva had always tried not to waste her time on soldiers but to go for the plum targets of officers or observers, but recently it had been so difficult to shoot anyone (the Germans were far away and being cautious) that she had no choice. This day, Lida was lucky almost immediately: she saw a German in a peaked cap, an officer. After she shot he sank down and hung on the parapet, before sliding or being pulled back. Immediately, as often happened after a sniper's successful shot, especially if the victim was an officer, the Germans launched a mortar bombardment. It was impossible for her to crawl away, and while mortar shells were exploding all around, Lida became steadily more frightened. Fortunately the Germans did not see her or she would have been in serious trouble. Lida lay in the snow until dusk. When the pressure became unbearable she had to piss in her trousers.[364] Often when they came back from hunting one of them would hand a pair of damp trousers over to whoever was on duty and ask, "Dry these, please!" There was an order in force in 31 Army requiring that girl snipers should be provided with "skirts or a second pair of summer trousers as, when returning to their accommodation after being on the front line, the girls are unable to change padded trousers in need of drying".[365]

In the twilight, numb with cold, her clothing frozen solid with melted snow and urine, she crawled back to their trench. The soldiers swore at her for subjecting them to a German shelling, and she quickly ran back to the girls to finally warm up, have something to eat, and drink some hot tea, or just hot water, but at least with sugar. She was "exultant, elated": today she had added an officer to her score!

A Soviet officer had taken a shine to Frida Tsygankova, Lida Bakieva's sniper partner, and Frida also liked him. Lida, however, haggard and taciturn, with a dark, weather-beaten complexion and short hair, was not pestered by men. People who did not know her had been known to call her "Laddie". So much the better, she decided. That was not what she should be focusing on right now.

Lida Bakieva ended the war with a tally of seventy-eight in her sniper's record book. When asked, she would readily admit that this was an approximation. In a defensive position you could never be completely sure whether a German who fell after you had shot him was dead or only wounded, and during attacks nobody was keeping the score. Roza Shanina explained in her diary, "The way it worked was that you might shoot many times at targets when on the defensive, but it was impossible to tell whether you had a kill or just a wounding."[366] In target practice, she reflected, she always hit the mark from that distance, but now she was shooting mainly at standing or walking figures. As for runners (soldiers who were not walking but running in a stooped position), she shot at them only to give them a fright, because it was difficult to hit them. So in her record book "they would sometimes put no entry at all, or give me the benefit of the doubt, or include something highly questionable."[367] Overall, she thought this averaged out and that the tally in the book was probably close to the truth, albeit excluding kills during offensives. Here the kills were in the dozens, but were never registered. "I helped fight off counter-attacks using perhaps seventy rounds a time. During that attack when I was firing at tanks I put paid to the lot of them."[368] When she was firing from a distance of about 100 metres with tracer bullets, even though the bullets were not penetrating the helmets but ricocheting skywards, she could see she was hitting the target every time, which she thought meant that her rough estimate was pretty accurate.

Lida Bakieva also shot with her sniper's rifle during attacks, sometimes at close range. After the war she would sometimes try to add up how many Germans she had killed or wounded in all. One hundred and fifty, two hundred?

In a year and a half of war, Lida had no end of occupations, in addition to hunting while on the defensive and participating in attacks. In the Baltic states in December 1944 her 32 Siberian Infantry Division got into a mess. The Germans were resisting fiercely and, very much to everyone's surprise, the division found itself in a "cul de sac", surrounded in front and to both sides but with an opening for retreat. The regiment that was supporting Lida's platoon had been decimated by casualties, and when their communications link was broken the only person they could find to repair it was a seventeen-year-old Byelorussian boy, who was scared to death.[369] He had only just arrived at the front, evidently conscripted from recently liberated territory and, after a few days' training, had been thrown into battle. Roza Shanina had people in that situation in mind when she wrote after the fighting at Pillkallen, "But all the 'Slavs' ran away . . ."[370] Seeing how terrified the boy was at the prospect of going out into the open from their bunker, Lida decided to go herself. The Byelorussian twice opened the door, saw shrapnel flying everywhere, and immediately closed it again. Lida pushed him aside, dashed through the door, fell to the ground and started crawling. She had a pistol and a dagger, both captured. She was particularly fond of the versatile dagger, which could be used for slicing bread or sharpening a stake, or instead of a pair of scissors. The cable that had been severed was covered with snow and ice, and Lida slowly edged forward, raising it with her mitten. She crawled as far as a crater, where a shell had severed the wire. Finding the other end, she felt for her dagger but found she had lost it while scrambling over the ground. She gnawed through the insulation with her teeth, fixed the cable and crawled back, only to be reprimanded by the commander: "You haven't got a clue but you want to risk your life!" Lida, however, knew that she understood as much of the technicalities as the boy. She believed a soldier, regardless of gender, should try to learn as many specialities as possible at the front, and did not take kindly to being sent to do "women's work", regarding it as a humiliation. She had been sent to the front as a sniper, not as a cook or a cleaner.

One time, after two and a half days of fighting, the girls' platoon was put up in a shed that did not even have proper walls. Instead there were screens of woven wicker. An icy draught blew through it, but the girls were past caring. They put their rifles to one side, lay down close to each other and, after two sleepless nights, were soon fast asleep. Shortly afterwards Lida, who was the deputy platoon commander, was woken by a courier with orders to report to the deputy political officer. Cursing the officer, she got up. It transpired that this small 45-year-old man was in urgent need of two girls to clean the wooden floor of the house where the officers were staying. "Silly bastard," Lida reflected as she went back to their icy shed. She tried to wake the girls, but they would have slept through cannonfire. She decided to try again a little later, sat down leaning against a wall, and promptly fell asleep herself. Half an hour later the courier was back for her. "Who did you order to wash the floor?" the officer bawled. "Myself," Lida said. "Why have you not done it?" "Because we have been fighting a war on equal terms with everybody else and have had no sleep for two days."[371]

This made the deputy political officer even more cross and he gave her five days in the guardhouse, a sentence to which Lida reacted philosophically. It could hardly be colder than their shed, and she would finally get to catch up on her sleep. When the soldier was taking her to the guardhouse, minus her belt and rifle, they encountered the chief of staff on the road. "Where are you going?" he asked in surprise. After finding out what was up and who had issued the order, he said only, "Forget it. Go back and rest."

She supposed she would have time enough at home after the war to wash floors. On one occasion, because there had been so many casualties in the regiment, Lida had to help hold off a tank attack until reinforcements arrived. The entire platoon was sent – even the staff officers – because there was no one else. Some officer shouted at the girls to fire at the tank peepholes, but Lida doubted the sense of that. She did not entirely believe snipers who boasted in the newspapers that they could hit that slim target. A number of tanks came too close and two snipers, girls a little younger than Lida, took fright, jumped out of the trench and ran for it: a sure recipe for disaster. People shouted to them, "Get down! What are you doing?" but they continued running, until they were mown down by machine-gun fire from the tank. Lida tried not to lose her head and waited. She had a grenade, and she thought she would throw it when the tank was very close. Just then, however, one tank was hit, caught fire and, when the crew started jumping out, Lida went to work. Another tank was hit, and then the rest retreated.

"Yes, it was a cruel time, an iron time," front-line correspondent Vasily Grossman wrote in his diary, after observing a grim scene in an aviation regiment. Human flesh was being removed with a rasp from the propeller of an aircraft that had returned from attacking a convoy of vehicles.[372] A doctor, invited to examine it, pronounced gravely, "Yes, Aryan meat." Everyone fell about.

Many episodes at the front still struck the women snipers as comical decades later. Lida recalled that she and her partner, Anya Shavets, had positioned themselves in a windmill in East Prussia. The girls were observing "a burly Hitlerite" who had climbed out of the trenches. By this time Lida, an experienced sniper, was reluctant to waste her time on ordinary soldiers, but the sight of the German's fat backside as he bent down to collect firewood was getting on the nerves of her partner. Having got this part of his anatomy in her sights, Anya tried to persuade Lida they ought to shoot. She was not convinced, because they would then have to give up a good position and move elsewhere. Finally Anya could contain herself no longer and fired, hitting the German in the rump. Clutching his wounded bum, the victim "quickly hobbled back into his trench".[373]

If you can laugh at the enemy, he will seem less frightening. The wartime newspapers were full of such anecdotes. "An interesting technique," the famous Georgian sniper, Noy Adamiya (who vanished in 1942), confided to a newspaper, "is to wait until a German goes to relieve himself, squats under a bush, then fire. We say he was hoist by his own petard."[374]

After killing your first German, and the sudden unbelievable and horrifying realisation that you, a young girl, only yesterday a pupil at school, have taken a man's life, the world is changed for ever. Having successfully hit a living target, the girls crossed a line, entered a new territory where the most valuable thing in the world, a human life, became the material they worked with, a topic for jokes and games. Ziba Ganieva, who before the war was studying at drama school and in the war was first a nurse and then a sniper, never felt pity for the enemy again after killing her first German. She talked about her job to *Peasant Woman*, relating how one day, after waiting in the melting snow from eleven in the morning until four in the afternoon, she was told by the spotter (a soldier watching through binoculars from an observation post for any signs of danger, or opportunities that might be exploited) that the Germans were beginning to have dinner and "some of the more brazen ones were walking about upright." Looking out from the bushes Ziba saw two Germans, one of whom was carrying a thermos on his back with dinner for his comrades. Ziba fired and "the German with the thermos fell. The other fled, and a third jumped out of an emplacement to help the wounded man. 'I'll give you two more minutes to live,'" Ziba decided. As a sign of magnanimity, she not only did not finish off the wounded man right then, but allowed the soldier who had come to his aid to drag him back to the trench. Though she did then go on to fire at the soldier who was helping the wounded man before he got down into the trench.[375]

"Constant battles, marches, attacks, wounded people, dead people, blood . . ." That was how, many years later, Yulia Zhukova recalled the offensive in East Prussia. Little remained in her memory from those days, just the endless marches, and the fighting when they were "capturing various towns and villages". A nineteen-year-old girl, she remembered only what was most vivid, and for her that tended to be moments of "everyday, not military, life". Like many others, she was astonished by the amazingly high standard of living of the Germans, particularly the excellent farms. They had never imagined villages could be so rich. On a big, empty farmstead, Yulia and her comrades found a great variety of jars in the basement of a brick-built house: pickles and jams preserved for the days ahead. Although they had been warned not to eat anything (because the Germans might have poisoned them), the girls could not resist the temptation and gorged themselves. How unbelievably delicious! The abandoned farm was so clean and sparkling, and its inhabitants had just fled, leaving all this property behind them! Yulia was greatly impressed by the blued and starched linen neatly folded in a cupboard, and mended "as if it was the work of a jeweller". The trunks of the trees growing along the highway were meticulously whitewashed. After what they had seen in Byelorussia, Yulia and her comrades did not find this touching, rather "it provoked a reaction".[376] "Why did the Germans invade us? What did they lack?" the soldiers wondered, confounded and enraged by the sight of Germany's prosperity. Were all these riches not enough for them?

On the outskirts of a town, terribly tired, hungry, tormented by thirst, Yulia and her companions came upon a dairy. There was no water there, but the girls drank their fill of milk and washed in it. There was no bread either, but so what? They made sandwiches of cheese and butter, and marched on.

In a city whose name Yulia would soon forget, they happened on a big, beautiful house. In a great room on the ground floor an old German was sitting in an armchair with his family gathered around him. When Yulia looked into the ballroom the adults were frightened, but a sweet, blue-eyed boy of three or four ran to her and Yulia took him in her arms. That probably saved the family's life. A Soviet officer who came in after her turned ashen-faced, and aimed his pistol at Yulia and the child, but then hesitated for a moment and left, slamming the door behind him. Yulia was told afterwards that his entire family had been wiped out by the Germans.[377]

In the towns of East Prussia – Rastenburg, Löwenberg, Königsberg – Anya Mulatova helped herself to postcards as souvenirs. Some she enclosed in letters home, others she carried with her, like a collection. German postcards were quite unlike the Soviet equivalent.[378] Soviet postcards depicted the transformation of Soviet cities, hydroelectric power stations, athletic sportswomen in front of portraits of Stalin, collective farm workers learning to read. New Year's cards did not exist, so for New Year 1945, front-line soldiers sent German Christmas cards home.[379] German postcards showed pretty children, flowers or kittens. Anya brought her little collection home from the war and would later show it to friends.

There was just so much stuff in these prosperous abandoned homes! You could not fit much in a soldier's knapsack, but after so many hungry years they stuffed themselves with delicacies. Many of the soldiers had never eaten their fill in their lives before. "You would open a larder and just wonder what to take!" Anya recalls.[380] But it was unwise to grab too much: every extra item in a knapsack added to your suffering on the march.

One girl soldier on the advance into East Prussia recalled the extraordinary night they spent in a German castle. There were "so many rooms . . . such grand halls!" The wardrobes were full of clothes, and every girl chose a dress. She particularly liked a yellow one, and a night gown of ethereal beauty, long and as light as a feather. The girl and her friends were terribly tired, it was late already and, wearing their new dresses, they promptly fell asleep. She slept with this magical robe over the dress. In the morning, "We got up, looked again at ourselves in the mirror, then took it all off and put on once more our tunics and trousers. We took nothing with us. On the march even a needle is too heavy. You push a spoon into the top of your boot and you're off."[381]

A few individuals did manage to send parcels, but parcels were, in the main, a privilege reserved for officers. Ordinary soldiers had few rights. The parcels Vera Chuikova and several of her friends sent were opened by the woman who worked at their post office, who helped herself to what she liked and threw the rest away. Vera, of course, knew nothing for certain, it was just what somebody told her, but when she finally got back home she found that the parcel had never arrived.[382] The officers? Oh, yes, they could send parcels, and as for the generals . . . it was said they sent back loot by the wagonload.

Apart from underwear, the girls might take a headscarf, and perhaps a gold watch if the scouts gave them one. One time the lads brought Anya Mulatova a fur coat. They had far more opportunities than the girls to rifle through German homes. At first Anya was minded to refuse: "Where could I put it?" But the rabbit fur was so beautiful, and she so fancied coming home and wearing this soft coat in the winter, that she gave in and accepted. She struggled with it, hauling it along in her knapsack but then, in late April, in the Carpathians, she lost everything that she had been carrying for so long. The girls had put their bags on a cart, but either the driver fell asleep or the horse was frightened and bolted. The cart, along with the horse, fell over a precipice. The horse and driver were killed, and the cart and all their belongings lost. The fur coat was the least of her troubles: along with her knapsack she lost her sniper's record book and, although she was later given a certificate on which they entered her tally, she was never issued a replacement.[383]

"I saw German Fraus for the first time and did not like them," Roza noted.[384] Beautifully dressed, well groomed and coiffured, the German women gave many girls in the Soviet army an inferiority complex. For Soviet men, many of whom had not had a woman for four years (and many of the younger ones were still virgins) raping a blonde German woman was also an act of subjecting to their will a more advanced civilisation, like defecating on the carpet in a beautiful palace. Roza did not pity the women. "Now our guys will take revenge, but I don't give a damn. I am cold-blooded about everything," she wrote in late November 1944 when units of the Third Byelorussian Front first crossed the East Prussian border.

Today, a lot is said and written about the rape and murder of women by Soviet soldiers in East Prussia, but less about the murdering of children, including babies. Some of the Russians were taking revenge on Germans on behalf of their family, or more generally for their country, but some used protestations of sacred hatred as a cover for sheer sadism. War removes restraints. When Hans Kinschermann, a German machine-gunner, told a friend about how at Stalingrad a Corporal Schwarz "shot wounded Russian soldiers in the head", he was told that "people who kill unarmed human beings unquestionably have sadistic proclivities, and war allows them to show these openly under the pretext of defending their compatriots."[385] Many East Prussians would learn the truth of this at first hand during the terrible days of the Russian invasion.

★

Orders were given by the Nazi authorities to evacuate the civilian population from Löwenberg in East Prussia only on 13 February 1945, when the Russians were already very close. The roads were clogged with refugees. Many, like Hedwig Rosenberg and her children, were unable get out of the town and returned home. For a whole night there was artillery fire and people hid in their cellars. At seven in the morning Russians burst into the house. Opening the larder, they emptied out on the ground the preserved food and looted the shoemaker's shop attached to the house. In the terrible uproar the screams of women were heard as they were raped. No one was spared, and if anyone resisted or relatives tried to protect them it only seemed to exacerbate the situation. Entering the German houses in search of hidden soldiers, the Soviet troops, whether or not they found any, were at times likely to open fire on civilians.

In Löwenberg, Anya Mulatova was with a group of soldiers doing a house-to-house search. They checked them from top to bottom. When they came to the first one with a locked door, a soldier began smashing the lock with his rifle butt. The safety catch was dislodged and a round of bullets whistled past Anya. She had no time to be frightened. Having broken the lock, the soldier turned his rifle round and entered the house. In a ground-floor room were several beds on which women and children were sitting or lying. The soldier opened fire with his rifle. Anya closed her eyes. What could she do? No German soldiers were found in the house.[386]

Anya had seen a lot that was bad in her ten months at the front. Her elder brother Vanya had been killed in the battle of the Kursk Bulge; her family barely survived in the rear and the privation caused the death of her infant nephew, but what she saw at Löwenberg was, in her opinion, not just savagery but "monstrous evildoing". In another house the soldiers found an old woman with a baby. They spared the baby, killing only the old woman. As they were leaving, they saw the baby crawling on to its dead grandmother. Anya was overcome and began to cry. "What you on about?" one of the soldiers demanded. "Forgotten what they done to our people? Locked 'em in a barn and set it on fire, didn't they!"

What could she say to that? She herself had seen the charred embers and human bones in Byelorussia, and the half-decomposed body of a small child on a road in Byelorussia "with its little hands and feet in the air". But the atrocious images of East Prussia were to remain forever "an open wound in my heart"; a wound about which, nevertheless, she kept silent for a lifetime.

Chapter 17

"Maybe it's for the best that Roza has died . . ."

"A tall woman, quite gruff. Didn't say much. Really liked the song, 'Oh, Mists of Byelorussia . . .' Every time she started cleaning her rifle, she was sure to start singing that."[387] That was how Lidiya Vdovina remembered "the most madcap of us all". In the 1960s, Kaleria Petrova, "a handsome, well-groomed Muscovite and research worker", also recalled that Roza Shanina was taciturn. "She walked a bit like a sailor, rolling her broad shoulders from side to side. She was well able to stand up for herself: she would be silent, silent, but then if you went too far she would square up, hands on hips, eyes narrowed, and tell you exactly what she thought of you."[388] When she was off-duty, whenever she had some free time, Roza wrote. "I write all day. I'm tired, I will leave it and finish it later. I have been writing letters all the time, and my diary, on my lap, leaning up against a wall, writing, until my back and arm are tired."[389] Roza mentions in the diary that one day she wrote thirty letters. She wrote home a lot, and to her friends in Arkhangelsk; she wrote to men she met at the front, to the editor of a front-line newspaper, to her superiors, all the way up to Stalin himself, demanding to be allowed to fight on the front line. She said to Kalya, "Let me write to your mother and tell her what life is

24. Leningrad Front, February 1944. Group of snipers – T. Gorinkova, T. Kondratieva and A. Bystrova – *"It was not frightening in the least,"* Vera Barakina remembered of *their days hunting in the trenches there; a stagnant front line was the ideal situation for using snipers.*

25. Lida Bakieva (bottom row, right) with her comrades-in-arms - *Lida Bakieva would end the war with a tally of seventy-eight. Killing a German officer left her "exultant, elated".*

26. *(left)* Military censors at work, 1943 – *The letters the girls received at the front were always redacted by the censor. "Half of it was blacked out: they only left homely details," remembered Vera Chuikova.*

27. *(right)* Roza Shanina, Sasha Yekimova and Lida Vdovina. August 1944 *"In the fighting for Vitebsk, Lida Vdovina exterminated eight fascists." This was revenge for the death of her brother, Viktor, and partner, Nina Posazhnikova.*

28. *(left)* The brave Troika – Kaleriya, Roza and Sasha. June 30, 1944 – *On the back Sasha wrote "Dear girls! Looking back at the tough days of the war, do remember our life together and all the hardships that we overcame. You see their smiles when you look at the faces of these girls but if only you knew how much sadness is in the heart of each of them."*

29. "To dear Mummy from Kaleriya. From the left Tamara Alkhimova, Roza Shanina, Masha Komarova, Valya Lazorenko and Lyuba Reshetnikova, 11.9.44, Lithuania" – *Kaleriya is fourth from the left. Roza later wrote about this photograph, "There the six of us standing in Lithuanian folk costumes. They were a troika too but now only Valya is left."*

30. Vicinity of Kerch. Motorboats with landing troops in the Kerch Strait.

31. *(left)* Comrades-in-arms of Katya Peredera, a group of snipers that took part in battles for the Crimea. L. to r.: junior sergeants Raya Zakharova, Lyuba Vinnitskaya, Anya Bessarabova, Zhenya Makeeva, photographed with their commander Nikolai Zainutdinov (One-and-a-Half Ivans). 1944 – *The stern and vigilant One-and-a-Half Ivans was invariably on hand to thwart assignations with handsome young soldiers.*

32. The crossing of the Dnieper, 1943 – *The snipers crossed the river on rafts under heavy fire. Klava's raft eventually capsized but they were already close to the shore by then. Once in the water, the snipers hoisted their rifles above their heads to keep them dry.*

33. L. to r. – Masha Piskunova, Roza Shanina, Sasha Ekimova, Valya Nikolaeva, Dusya Kekesheva, Lithuania, 1944 – Just one of these girls would survive the war.

34. Red Army entering a town in East Prussia, winter 1944–45 – On November 3, Roza noted, *"I came back from the front completely exhausted. I am going to remember this war. Four times the village was taken and retaken: three times I got out right under the noses of the fascists. Fighting the enemy on his own territory is not to be taken lightly."*

35. Red Army entering East Prussia, late 1944 – *"On the eve of our entering the territory of the Reich, propagandists were sent to incite the troops. Some were very high-ranking. 'A death for a death!!! Blood for blood!!! Forget nothing!!! Forgive nothing!!! We shall be avenged!!!'"*

36. Soviet army unit in an East Prussian town, winter 1944–45 – *The invading Soviet troops were amazed by the luxury in which their enemies lived. "You would open a larder and just wonder what to take!"*

37. *(above)* The capture of Königsberg by the Red Army – *Klava Loginova was stunned by the destruction wrought on the city.*

38. *(left)* German soldiers surrender as they approach a Russian trench.

39. *(right)* Vera Kabernyuk, 1944 –
*Daughter of an "Enemy of the People", she
would later celebrate Victory Day by the
walls of the Reichstag.*

40 . *(above)* Anya Mulatova with Anatoly
Sinyakov, May 1945 – *"So many rich
girls are free now, and look what you
have brought back!" Anatoly's father had
exclaimed when they returned home as
man and wife.*

ЛИЦЕВОЙ СЧЕТ			СНАЙПЕРА	
Дата	Количество истреблен. немцев	Подразделение	Подписи	
			Наблюдателя	К-ра роты
май 1944 по нояб.1944	22 фр			*[signature]*

41. Vera Kabernyuk's sniper's book, score page. Фр stands for Fr., i.e. Fritzes – *The
books acted as a record of their respective tallies, but it was always necessarily an
approximate figure.*

43. *(above)* Ziba Ganieva as Zukhra in the film "Tair and Zukhra" (1945) – *She could not return to ballet school after coming back from the front as she had been seriously injured. Instead she became a famous philologist.*

42. *(left)* The photograph of Klava Loginova's sister Tanya that she carried with her all through the war.

44. *(above)* Bella Morozova after coming back from hospital (1945), having lost an eye and with the left side of her face disfigured – *Bella's comrades assumed she had died, but she surprised them all by returning to the front. "There stood a rather thin, fair-haired girl in a sergeant's uniform, with badges for her injuries and the Order of the Patriotic War on her tunic. She smiled strangely, and tried to show only one half of her face."*

like for us and how we fight. And Sasha's mum, too . . ." Of course, she also received a lot of letters, especially after she became famous. "But," she wrote with her characteristic pessimism, "the letter that would make me happy never comes."[390]

Roza's diary, covering just three months, from October 1944 to January 1945 (an earlier diary either has not survived or has just never been published, but it definitely existed), tells us a great deal about her. Soviet and analogous present-day Russian publications create an image of Roza Shanina as a fearless fighter, a staunch communist who unreservedly gave her all to defend her homeland. To modern eyes she looks more like a fanatic. It is not easy to understand Roza's entries, the notes of someone in a hurry who condenses and keeps a lot back and who, because of a lack of education, often cannot fully express an idea. But if you read carefully, you immediately recognise you are dealing with a very complex person. This diary, which evokes conflicting emotions in the reader, reflects the suffering of an always dissatisfied, young, immature, very talented and insecure person.

In her diary, four themes have equal prominence: the war (hunting as a sniper and her passionate desire to be on the front line); her celebrity; her relationships with men; and her relations with her friends. These themes are, of course, interconnected, indeed, intertwined. Roza often mentions her unstable emotional state, confessing to her diary that she has been crying. Sometimes this is for no other reason than that she is feeling melancholy, sometimes because a song has plucked at her heartstrings, sometimes because friends or men have shown disrespect. She also cries when she is prevented from travelling to the front line. "Went to see General Kazaryan and the political director. Sincerely cried when they would not allow me to go to the front . . ."[391] When she was visiting a major in charge of the operational section, she cried when he put on a wonderful record: "I howled. I cried so much, and played that record, 'Hour by Hour the Day Is Passing', ten times over," she writes on a rest day on 9 December.[392] "I've been sitting and crying for the last three hours," she writes on 18 January. "Who needs me? Nobody wants to know how upset I get about things."[393] And, "I sobbed my heart out all the way, because I was so sad. I'm alone at night, only bullets whistling, fires burning."[394]

"An adrenaline junkie," is the assessment of a modern psychologist after reading Roza's diary.[395] It would seem that this girl felt she was fully alive only at moments of great peril. Roza herself calls her condition, her longing to be at the front, "a thirst for fighting". Why she was so drawn to deadly situations she herself could not understand. "Oh, how I want to be on the front line. It's so interesting, and at the same time so dangerous, and yet, for some reason, I'm not afraid," she wrote during the October offensive.[396] Roza, of course, was in the vanguard with the infantry, although that was not where snipers were supposed to be. "The order: take the hill. I did. I was in the front ranks. I didn't at first see, but then, from behind the mountain, 100 metres away, self-propelled artillery appeared with assault forces. I fired at the enemy troops. Eight metres to my left a first lieutenant, captain and soldiers were crushed. My rifle jammed. I sat down, sorted it out and started firing again. Ten metres ahead, a tank was coming straight at me. I felt no fear."[397]

A short time later, unwilling to be far away in the rear with the women's platoon, she wrote, "I want . . . how can I explain it? Some force draws me back there. I'm bored here. Some people are saying I just want to get back to the boys, but I don't have anyone I know there. I want to see real war."

She wrote endless complaints and letters, seeking to be allowed officially to be at the front rather than having to run off there. "I'm so bored! An accordion is playing in the workshop. I feel dreadful. I want to be back there now, attacking! Where the fighting is fiercest, that's all I want. And why the hell not? Oh, how irresponsible the top brass are!"

Roza analysed the battles she fought in afterwards, writing up detailed accounts of her adventures at the front, reliving them. "During those two days, there was no time to take a breather. Dreadful fighting. The

German had filled trenches with infantry and armed them, and they fought us off resolutely. It was complete carnage. How many times ours sent in self-propelled artillery, brought it up to that Prussian estate. One or two made it back, the rest were mown down. I took a ride in one [self-propelled gun] but didn't shoot: you couldn't stick your head out of the hatch without being killed or wounded. It drove through the valley. I crawled out and fired at Fritzes fleeing from the trench."[398]

Being a sniper was not enough for Roza. "By the evening of the 22nd we had kicked them all out and occupied the estate. I went in. The infantry were lying on the ground, afraid to advance. Two death squad scouts were going ahead and I went with them. As a result, the three of us were the first to take the next estate, and the rest of them came in on the attack behind us and started nipping the heels of the fleeing Fritzes. I was firing, like everyone else."[399]

She fought with a passion, like the bravest of men. Some of her stories testify to a cruelty also more expected in a man than in a twenty-year-old girl. "Spotted thirty Fritzes, then ran with the scouts to catch them. A fight. Two Germans killed our captain with their rifle butts, jumped out of the bushes. We caught and shot both of them."[400]

Many of the girls in her platoon doubted Roza's sincerity when she said she just wanted to run off to the front. They assumed there must be a man there she wanted to be with. By this time, many of the girls had moved to other divisions to be with their "front-line husbands", officers who found jobs for them at staff headquarters. There are documents in the archives of a number of armies demanding the return of girl snipers to their posts, and that in future they should be employed only as snipers. "The division commander ordered: 1. That both personnel who had undergone special training and others trained directly in the units should be employed only as snipers."[401]

There was a lot of gossip about Roza, which greatly upset her. The same things were often said about her in the front-line units where she went to fight. She did, of course, turn up in units where there were commanders she already knew: that made matters simpler, but it also led to whispers.

Roza's closest friends were Sasha Yekimova and Kalya Petrova, but she still felt lonely. She remembered friends who had stayed behind in the rear: Agniya Butorina who was a friend from fifth to seventh grade at school; Valya Chernyaeva, a friend at technical college. She greatly admired a friend in the platoon, Valya Lazorenko, and mentioned she was considering the candidacy of two girls in another division whom she thought she would like to be friends with but was not yet completely sure about. She complained that Sasha Yekimova could be heavy going: she had a high opinion of herself and was self-centred. Sasha could suddenly come out with some unpleasant remark and was capable of abandoning comrades in a difficult situation. Roza herself, however, put up with it, remained friends, and describes in her diary some good moments of warm friendship with Sasha. She respected Kalya Petrova's courage, intelligence and reliability, but although Kalya joined in various adventures and escapades of Roza's, she was relatively unemotional, rational and calm, and hence unable to share Roza's more extreme ups and downs. She considered her time at the front an ordeal that just had to be endured. For Roza, hunting Germans gave her the same excitement as it did to some, although not many, men.

Describing her battles, Roza writes about the men who were at her side in moments of high drama. She often reciprocated their feelings, although her own, as a rule, were short-lived. "Nikolai Solomatin and I were running through the woods above the Neman, along the steeply sloping bank, through the bushes. We were in a hurry. Nikolai looked and saw it would be a hard climb up a cliff, took me by the hand and helped me up; we kissed and ran on. That night we were soaking wet, the rain was so heavy we were in a puddle. We spent the night together in a cart. I liked him so much . . ."[402]

Roza mentions Nikolai Solomatin several more times in her diary, but dozens of other men figure in her notes. She even has what looks like a

Don Juan-style list of amours, annotated with numbers that correspond to an obscure code of her own devising. Seventy years have passed since then, however, and it is difficult to read between the lines. Roza is reticent about many things, but it would be difficult not to suppose she had intimate relationships with at least two or three of these men. Roza did not trust her friends, male or female. She mulls over whether their feelings for her are sincere, or do they just need her for now, when women are in short supply, and only as someone to have sex with? "My heart is heavy. I am twenty years old and have no real, close friend. Why? There are boys in abundance, but my heart trusts nobody. I am thinking of Blokhin, and Solomatin. I liked them, but I knew it was only temporary. When they left they never wrote to me, and that says it all."[403] She got into a serious relationship with Nikolai Fyodorov, an officer, but found it burdensome. She first saw him in an attack during one of her unauthorised absences at the front. At that moment Fyodorov evidently conformed to her idea of the ideal man: "He was a big fellow, dirty, covered in mud and clay, and in his long greatcoat looked a real warrior. I admire his bravery, but his manners and education are not up to much."[404] Nikolai had serious intentions, and tried to persuade Roza they should register their marriage "at least formally" to make it easier for them to live together at the front. Roza, however, was already wondering how to split up with him. She knew she was not in love. "Why did I not have the courage to reject him? The circumstances: it was cold and muddy, I had no warm clothing and needed help, which he gave. In short, it was ridiculous. Even now I quite like him, but for the rest of it, I have to force myself. I din into my head the notion that I have great respect for him."[405] A few days later, before moving to a new location, she writes again, "went to spend the night with Nikolai, not because I am sad to be leaving him but because there are some things I need to collect: a waterproof cape, a book and a watch. Now again I have no one. I am on my own."[406]

Next to feature in her diary is "good-looking Nikolai Borovik", who is fighting far away; then Nikolai Sh., whose address she is upset about losing, and many other names. When she again met up with Nikolai Borovik, she found him a disappointment. He looked sloppy, without the strap to draw his greatcoat in at the back, and even when, shortly afterwards, he was seriously wounded in battle, Roza remained hard-hearted. The man she dreamed of was still not at her side. Did Roza even know what he should be like?

Besides, the girls who had a love affair at the front and those who were still living in hope of finding their true love were all tormented by the same question: what would happen after the war? What if, in peacetime, when there would be so many young, pretty, innocent girls, he preferred another girl to you? What if he only needed you for sex? What if he already had a wife he would be returning to? Even if he did seriously intend to share the rest of his life with you, how would you feel about leaving his children fatherless?

Roza would not have been Roza if she had not tried to find answers. The thick diary in its oilcloth cover, which was passed after Roza's death to Pyotr Molchanov, had inserted in it a sheet of paper, a letter never sent to a girl called Masha.

Dear Masha,
I decided to write to you when I heard by chance about your letter to Klavdia Ivanovna. You write that you are passionately in love with Klavdia's husband . . . You ask her to forgive you, not for permitting yourself something impermissible, but for intending in the future to live your life with her husband. You try to excuse yourself by claiming that you cannot raise a child which is shortly to be born, and that you supposedly had not known before whether N.A. already had a wife and children . . .

If it is difficult for you to stop loving someone you happened to meet on the roads of war, how do you expect Klavdia Ivanovna to forget the husband she loves? . . . I am a sniper. I recently visited the rear. On the journey, in the train, I often found people grateful when they saw my medals, but I also heard unpleasant remarks. Why is that? Why do some people raise an eyebrow when they see a girl in an army tunic? It is the fault of people like you, Masha . . .

I often wonder what kind of reception we girls in the army can expect when we come home after the war. How will people look on us? Will they view us with suspicion, even though we have risked our lives and many of us have died fighting for our Motherland? If that happens, it will be the fault of girls who ran off with other people's husbands . . .[407]

Of course, Roza was well aware that girls at the front were often forced into relationships against their will. In their platoon the girls looked out for each other and could see off anyone. However when she was away on one of her escapades, roaming about on the front line and sleeping among men, Roza was unafraid: she was a celebrity, written about in the front-line and national newspapers, and no one was likely to try to make a nuisance of themselves. In the diary she regularly claims that her fame is of absolutely no importance to her, but the entries suggest otherwise.

I have an aura of celebrity. Recently, the army newspaper *Exterminate the Enemy* wrote: "Shanina, who distinguished herself during the enemy's counter-attack, has been awarded the medal 'For Valour'. She is a renowned sniper in our subsection."[408] In the Moscow magazine *Ogonyok* my portrait is on the front page: exterminated fifty-four Germans, captured three, awarded two Orders of Glory. I picture that being read by the whole country, all my friends and acquaintances . . . Recently Ilya Ehrenburg wrote about me in the newspaper of our army, "I thank her fifty-seven times over. She has saved the lives of thousands of Soviet people."[409]

Roza continued to contemplate fame and her own circumstances while she was in hospital: she had suffered a minor wound to her shoulder on

12 December. Both in the hospital, and in the convalescent home she was sent to afterwards, she again wrote and wrote. She wrote about the books she had read during her enforced rest: *Sister Carrie* by Theodore Dreiser and *Bagration* by Sergey Golubov. Both had made a big impression. "Oh, Carrie, Carrie! Oh, the blind dreams of the human heart!" Roza exclaims in her diary. The book about Bagration provoked her to reflect on glory. "What is glory? It is either getting your own skull split in the name of the Motherland, or crushing the skull of someone else. That is what glory is and, so help me God, I'm going for it!"[410]

She watched films, a rare treat at the front, possible only during rest periods: *In Old Chicago*, *Submarine T-9*, and *Wait for Me*, which was from a screenplay by Konstantin Simonov (which Roza disliked).

While she was on leave, Roza endlessly copied poems into her diary, just as many other girls copied poems into a special notebook. The poems were of all kinds; they found them in newspapers and the *Soldier's Newsletter* (and, of course, Simonov was their favourite), but there were also pieces of folklore, song lyrics, and anonymous poems they had heard from someone at the front. Some were sentimental, some bawdy. Roza copied out the parodied version of "My Sweetie-Pie", which alluded ironically to the phenomenon of front-line wives. For Roza and her friends, this was a painful subject.

> I have forgotten you, you write, and ask the reason why,
> But I'm a man, do understand, at war, my sweetie-pie.
> I've got more loves than I can count with expectations high,
> There's one in Omsk and one in Tomsk, like you, my sweetie-pie.
> My lawful, wedded waits for me (she too, I cannot lie).
> My lot is to forget you now . . . alas, my sweetie-pie.[411]

The war provided all the prerequisites for such tales, and Roza and her comrades were still so young. They had no experience of life, and their hearts were yet to be hardened by cruelty and disappointment.

There is another poem, too, with touches that indicate a talented, if uneducated, poet:

> To the song of the bullets and whistling of shells
> I go out once more, perhaps now to die,
> Wearing a greatcoat that once was so new,
> When we stood close together, we two, you and I.[412]

Other poems written in the diary, pretty and sentimental, take the form of a letter from a loved one at the front. Iosif Utkin's front-line lyric poetry touched many hearts. Utkin was a poet and war correspondent. He lost four fingers from his right hand in 1941, at Yelnya near Smolensk, was treated in hospital in Tashkent, and wrote two books of poetry there. In 1942 he was back at the front, and was killed in 1944. Roza copied out one of his poems, which was very popular at the time, about letters from home. It included the lines:

> In the street it is midnight, a candle is burning.
> The stars shine out bright through the haze.
> You write me a letter, a message of yearning,
> Of love in a world that's ablaze.[413]

Another poem, by an anonymous poet, that proved very popular, talked about how:

> As you journey to the field of strife
> In regions bloody through and through,
> Know that over misty fields
> My love is speeding after you.

There are just two more pages before the diary breaks off. Here, at the end, there is again fighting, again men, anguish and emotional turmoil.

217

Roza admits, "My own life is repugnant to me. I am glad to die for the Motherland, and glad that I have that option."[414] In her entries she often mentions tumult and confusion. "Oh, Lord! Will you really not come to my aid to make sense of all this? Everything is such a mess. Oh, God!"[415]

Her diary finishes on that note. In the last entry, made a couple of days before her death, Roza writes, "Another night-time march. It is dark now, soon it will be dawn. I am sitting writing by the campfire. How bad it feels when I have no superior officer. It is good not to be ordered about, but not good when there is no one to tell me what to do. My heart finds no contentment. Who needs me?"[416]

Roza had described Kalya Petrova respectfully, "She is a good person. Completely free of egotism and brave. She has a lot of common sense, gets to the bottom of everything. She's got an amazing memory, but is just a bit lazy."[417] It was Kalya who, after the war, talked to reporters about the "inseparable Runaway Troika", as Roza called herself, Kalya and Sasha Yekimova. Kalya found Sasha interesting, despite her haughtiness, while Roza was "boisterous and kind".[418] After both were killed, Kalya was not devastated, as she had been by the death of Masha Shvarts, but felt terribly lonely.

Roza died at the end of January 1945. On 17 January she sent a letter to editor Pyotr Molchanov right from the middle of battle, scribbling it during a brief respite in a dugout.

Sorry for the long silence. I've had no time at all to write. My life of combat right on the front line. The fighting was intense, but miraculously I have come through it in one piece. I was in the front ranks of the attack. You will have to forgive me for not listening to you. I do not know why myself, but some force lures me here, into the firing line. The Germans have been resisting terribly, especially around an ancient estate. You would have thought everything had been blown sky-high by the bombing and artillery shells, but they still have enough firepower to keep us well back. Never mind. By morning we will have them licked. I am firing at fascists who pop out from buildings or the turrets of tanks and from SP guns.

For the first time, Roza mentions to Molchanov the possibility that she might die. "I may be killed soon. Please send a letter to my mother. You may ask why I should be thinking I am going to die. In the battalion I am in now, of seventy-eight people we have only six left."

Did Roza have a presentiment? If she did, even in this hellish situation she never considered the possibility of going back to her sniper platoon. Though, in fact, that was by no means a safe place to be either. Half the girls in the platoon had been killed or injured during their year at the front. For Roza, though, the danger involved in being a sniper at the front was insufficient.

On 28 January, during a battle about fifty kilometres from Königsberg, the infantry soldiers heard a "heartrending woman's scream". Running towards the cry, they saw Roza Shanina on the ground with her sniper's rifle beside her. She shouted to them, "Lads! Shoot me, quickly!"[419] She was clutching with both hands at her innards, which were spilling out of her shrapnel-slashed abdomen. The soldiers bandaged her up and carried her to the field hospital. Roza's last hours of agony were documented by Nurse Yekaterina Radkina. She was the secretary of the field hospital's Young Communist League organisation and had met the girl sniper previously, when Roza was shot in the shoulder. She had later seen Roza occasionally in the division's political section, and now met her one last time as she lay dying in East Prussia. There had been heavy fighting and, having transferred a group of severely wounded soldiers to the hospital, she had had to wait with them while the field hospital left with the swiftly advancing division. She was keen to catch up with them, but was again ordered to remain with a new, very large group of seriously wounded, among whom she spotted Roza.

As she later wrote to the family, Roza was in a very grave condition and "fully understood the seriousness of her situation . . . and regretted she had not had time to do more". Roza thought of her family, and called for her mother. Radkina was with her to the last and was very impressed by the girl sniper's fortitude: "No groaning, no tears." She was thirsty, but it was impossible for her to drink. She remembered the "cold, delicious water" of the spring in her native village of Bogdanovskoye. "Katya," she said, "give me some cold water from the spring. I'll only rinse out my mouth with it!"[420]

The girls of the sniper platoon were sad and wept when, some time later, they were given the news that Roza had been killed. They wanted to know where her grave was, but before they could find it the front had moved on to Königsberg. Her family were informed of Roza's death by Captain Stikharyov of Army Unit 14041.

In 1945, Roza's younger brother, Marat, was fourteen and he, like many teenagers, was working on a nearby collective farm under military discipline. His two older brothers had already been killed, and he was very proud that his sister Roza was fighting at the front. One time he was given the day off, and when he skied home saw his mother, who seemed suddenly to have become very small and stooped, aged by the new misfortune that had befallen her. Marat was struck by the fact that her eyes, though full of grief, were dry. She had no more tears to weep. His mother stood, holding the death notification and saying over and over again, "Well, that's that. That's that." "What do you mean, Ma?" Marat asked with foreboding. She could only reply, "Roza."[421] Some time later, his mother, a simple Russian peasant woman, said something that turned Marat's world upside down. "Maybe it's for the best that Roza has died. How could she have lived after the war? She shot so many people."[422]

Chapter 18

"We did not want to bury them looking like that"

Soviet armies were advancing in East Prussia. Months of deadlock were over, now the movement became almost non-stop. And after East Prussia Soviet eyes turned to Berlin. Yulia Zhukova remembered a night on the march: "Complete darkness, no moon or stars in the sky. Everybody around was silent and all that could be heard was the shuffling of feet and the laboured breathing of a great mass of people. Sometimes a halt would be declared, and then all the soldiers would literally collapse on to the loose snow. After fifteen or twenty minutes, however, we were again roused, and again marched onwards, dulled by weariness, lack of sleep, lack of food and the damp." After the war, many of the girl snipers would recall how, during these huge advances, they were often asleep on their feet. Yulia Zhukova found that "eventually my consciousness switched off". She fell asleep as she marched, and landed on top of "something big and hard". She shone her torch and found it was the corpse of a German soldier.[423]

In the course of a week 31 Army advanced, with periodical skirmishes, about 100 kilometres and, after taking Heilsberg, they all assumed there would be "at least a short rest". However, they were ordered to continue immediately on to Landsberg. The so-called Heilsberg Triangle, which consisted of three towns some twenty kilometres from each other, was heavily fortified. It was the last obstacle on the way to Königsberg, the capital of East Prussia. After the fall of Heilsberg on 31 January, the Germans launched a powerful counter-attack to the south of Königsberg, and Chernyakhovsky, the commander of the Third Byelorussian Front, was forced to delay the advance of his army's assault force. Despite a lack of troops, Chernyakhovsky approved a plan to capture Landsberg, delegating the task to Berestov, commander of 331 Division.

In Landsberg, Yulia Zhukova recalled, the soldiers finally had a brief respite. Finding schnapps in the houses, they used their free time in their usual manner. One of the officers tactfully suggested that the girls might want to find somewhere to lie low in order not to be molested by men who had had far too much to drink. They took his advice and all moved to a pleasant little farm just outside the town. They had a bite to eat and "settled in very comfortably".

They spread duvets on the floor and went to bed. Yulia did not know how long they slept. Fortunately, someone had to get up to go to the toilet. "Girls, Germans!" she shrieked, waking the others. They looked out to see German troops moving in an unbroken chain towards the town. Seizing their rifles, the girls "rushed back to the city", under fire both from the enemy and their own side who, in the confusion, were also firing at them. On the highway one of the girls was wounded by a burst of machine-gun fire and was miraculously saved when they were able to stop a wagon which came careering along. Her comrades would other-wise never have been able to carry her to safety. Suddenly, Yulia found she was on her own. She could not imagine how she had become separated from the others, but later heard her companions had been stopped on the highway by an officer and ordered to take up a defensive position in the ditch. One of the snipers, Dusya Filippova, had not managed to escape from the farm in time. When they later went back the girls found her mutilated body showing signs of torture.[424]

It turned out that their neighbour to the left, 50 Army, had lagged ten kilometres behind the division, and 5 Tank Army of the Second Byelorussian Front had been slow to take the town of Mehlsack, and was still some distance away. This gave the Germans the opportunity to attack the division from the north, east, south-east and west, and their assault was not long in coming: Landsberg was the last major junction of roads and railways connecting the Germans' southern group with Königsberg, and they were eager to retake it.

174 Division, which had occupied positions a few kilometres from Landsberg, was given a hard time. When the Germans advanced on them

on the first day and shells were exploding all around, the girl snipers were ordered to shoot first at commanding officers. Klava Loginova and Olga Nikolaeva knew that well enough, but soon began "shooting everyone in sight". Klava believed she "exterminated eight straight away". Later the regiment had to retreat back into the town.[425]

Yulia Zhukova described the several days she and her comrades spent in encirclement as a bloodbath. Everybody who was "capable of holding a gun: the medics, quartermasters, soldiers from the housekeeping platoon, even the wounded, concussed and sick" was in the trenches. The regiment was joined later by the artillery, after they had run out of shells. Their supplies of food were finished, and at night they crawled out into the fields, which had become a no-man's-land, to collect frozen potatoes.

The girls were by now experienced soldiers, but the morale of many of the new recruits was perilously low. One time, Yulia was crawling across a field when she heard someone to one side calling for help. She crept over and saw "a very young soldier" of Asiatic appearance. She dragged him back to the trench, finding this diminutive infantryman surprisingly heavy. Other soldiers helped pull the wounded boy into the trenches. He suddenly opened his eyes, felt himself all over, and exclaimed joyfully, "I all okay!" It turned out he was not injured at all, just scared witless. Yulia "could have throttled him".[426]

They were allowed to go to dry their clothes in Landsberg, where they could also warm up and get some sleep. When it was the turn of Yulia and her friends, the young girl, sitting on the floor in a well-heated house, wrote a desperate letter to her aunt: her unit was surrounded and she was very scared because she did not want to die at the age of nineteen. She did not die, and the letter miraculously survived and was eventually received by her Aunt Nastya who, for years afterwards, would gather her neighbours and read it aloud to them. They would "all sob and wail", which really annoyed Yulia. One day she stole the letter and burned it.[427]

On 7 February, units of the Second Byelorussian Front broke through to the encircled group at Landsberg. What rejoicing! "We embraced, we laughed and cried, and tossed our deliverers in the air!" Of the 400 people in Yulia's defence sector, only ten remained unscathed: the rest were dead or injured, concussed or ill. After standing there on the defensive for several more days, Yulia and her friends were ordered to remain in Landsberg and tend the wounded.

31 Army moved on, advancing on Königsberg, but Yulia never fired another shot at the front. The same was not true of Klava Loginova, who was to fire her sniper's rifle quite a few times more, even as late as May 1945.

Sasha Yekimova and Volodya Yemelianenko had informed the commander in early January that they wanted to get married. At the front this statement, although it had no official validity, was known as "formalising a relationship". Their marriage was solemnised at the Katyusha unit and all Sasha's friends, except Roza, were there. When she came "home" on 8 January to the women's platoon, Roza was scandalised: "I don't recognise the place! My friends Sasha and Tosya have both got married!"[428] Sasha, when she had free time, often went to see Volodya. At the end of February, however, the Katyusha missile troops were moved further away. Volodya finally managed to come and see Sasha on 8 March, International Women's Day. He found only her grave: she had been killed a few days earlier and her friends had been unable to contact him.

That day, Kalya Petrova, who was Sasha's partner, was ill and Dusya Kekesheva went out hunting with her instead. Dusya was pregnant and due to be sent back to the rear at any time. In publications about Sasha she is said to have been sniping that day in no-man's-land, but this was not the case: Sasha and Dusya were in the trench as usual. When they failed to return, a search party went out in the evening and discovered their corpses. They had been killed during a German raid, apparently at dawn just as they arrived. In order not to make a noise, the Germans had cut their throats, "so deeply that their heads were barely still attached".[429] Dusya's body lay in the trench, and Sasha was found in a ditch nearby:

she had evidently tried to escape but been caught. Kalya and her friends brought the bodies to their dugout and bandaged Sasha's and Dusya's heads in place. "We did not want to bury them looking like that." They slept soundly that night in the dugout next to their friends' corpses, having long since ceased to be afraid of human remains. The following day, Sasha and Dusya were buried with military honours, with a volley fired in the air, and in coffins. The other girls' sadness was heightened by the fact that it was clear that the war would soon be over.

Volodya Yemelianenko was given Sasha's possessions. Kalya told him the details. He stood for a time by the grave, wiping tears from his eyes, and went back to his unit. Shortly afterwards, Kalya heard that Volodya had been wounded, was in a field hospital, and wanted her to visit him. She went and stayed talking to him for an hour. He seemed to her not to be too severely wounded, but the next day or the day after she heard he had died. Volodya's friends gave Kalya his diary and letters, evidently feeling that, after Sasha's death, she was the person closest to him at the front. In his diary Volodya had written all about Sasha: how he had seen her for the first time, how they got to know each other, how anxious he had been that she might not share his feelings. Kalya took great care of the diary, and brought it back home with her at the end of the war.[430]

Tamara Rogalskaya learned after the war that many of the girls in the third cohort of the Women's Sniper School never got the chance to fire at the enemy. She considered that she had been luckier. This young Leningrader, who found herself in early spring 1945 hunting in a half-ruined grain elevator near the town of Elbing, knew for certain that she wanted to shoot Germans.[431] That was precisely why she had gone to the army enlistment centre, and why she had graduated from the Central Women's Sniper School with top marks.

The time had come to take revenge on the Germans for many things: for the two years she had spent under siege in Leningrad, when all that saved her from starvation were the rations she was issued for working at a military factory; for the destruction and depopulation of her city where, as a member of a Young Communist brigade, she had had to go round apartments searching for children whose parents had died. The children would be collected and sent to an orphanage, carried on stretchers if they were not able to walk themselves. She wanted revenge for the members of her family who had died, for her brother who had been killed in action in 1944. Tamara was just eighteen when, in 1944, she enrolled on a snipers' course in Leningrad. "Will you volunteer for the women's sniper school?" they asked her at the recruitment centre. "Too right, I will!" she replied.

The Germans had turned the industrial city of Elbing into a powerful stronghold that blocked approaches to the Bay of Danzig. Pillboxes were set up in houses, trenches dug in the streets, and fortifications were also built on the approaches to the city. It seemed that Elbing was ready for a hard-fought defence – the kind of environment in which snipers thrived.

In March 1945 a young German infantryman, Karl-Heinz Schmeelke, sitting in a trench full of mud somewhere near the Balga castle in East Prussia, wrote in his diary, "No one dares to look out of their burrow during the day: the Russian snipers will pick off anyone who risks it."[432]

By this time the Red Army had tens of thousands of snipers, including a significant proportion of women. During the fighting in East Prussia, sniper fire played a major role in further undermining the morale of an already demoralised enemy.

Girls of the Women's Sniper School's third cohort reinforced 184 Infantry Regiment of 56 Division in February. In very early March, Tamara and her partner Klava Pakhomkina first went hunting from the grain elevator in a small town somewhere between Elbing and Danzig. They were escorted to their positions by none other than Nina Petrova.[433] This middle-aged woman was still working as a sniper, and by the end of her career would have trained hundreds of others.[434] However Petrova did not regard these already highly-trained girls as pupils: her task was only to familiarise them with conditions on the front line.[435]

In the regiment, Petrova, a thin, very athletic woman, was known as "Mother". Her biographer describes her as a caring, emotional person. Tamara Rogalskaya had no sense that she possessed strong feelings, perhaps because she spent little time with Petrova. She recalled Petrova as a stricter, more strong-willed and disciplined person than the women commanders at the school in Podolsk, and Petrova was only a sergeant. The girls heard that she would shortly be going to collect her third Order of Glory: first class, the highest level.

There was a sheep pen in front of the elevator. (The girls remembered a splendid dinner of buckwheat with lamb.) Beyond that was some kind of a lake or pond, Tamara did not remember. Further on, some 600 or 700 metres away, were the Germans. The Russian snipers reached the elevator in dashes across open ground, following Petrova. When the sheep saw them, they started running about "as if they were signalling to the Germans".

Petrova positioned them by large windows and went on to see to others. It was dark in their building and the Germans, lit up by the sun, were a perfect target. As often happened with girls when they first arrived at the front, Tamara forgot all about danger and leaned out of the window almost to her waist in order to get a better view of the enemy. Suddenly she heard a strange sound: "thwack, thwack". Bullets! She immediately fell back and, remembering that bullets could penetrate a metre and a half of brick, crawled behind sacks of grain and sat leaning against them. Instantly, "like a madwoman", Petrova ran through the entire elevator building shouting, "Who got fired at?" Scared witless, Tamara just sat there and "could not catch my breath". After her baptism of fire, she and Klava observed the Germans all day without opening fire, obeying Petrova's orders.

Then the hunt began, both from the elevator and out of a trench they were taken to by scouts who knew ways through the defences of barbed or electrified wire. Tamara opened her tally by shooting from the elevator. When she fired, she not only saw the German had fallen, but some sixth sense told her she had killed him. Her hands began to shake, then her whole body. Shooting someone for the first time felt "odd, different". "You carry on, I can't do any more," she told Klava. The only emotion she felt after killing her second German, however, was satisfaction.

Soon after that the offensive began, with huge treks of 50–60 kilometres. First they were told they would be attacking Berlin, but then they were diverted towards Swinemünde on the coast. During the advance Tamara heard that Nina Petrova had been killed.

On 14 March 1945, Petrova had been awarded the Order of Glory in person by General Fedyuninsky, commander of 2 Assault Army. As he was signing the lists of awards he noticed what he thought must be a mistake: Sergeant Nina Petrova, sniper, who was to receive the Order of Glory, First Class, appeared to be fifty-two years old. Summoning his chief of staff, he questioned him about Sergeant Petrova and decided he would like to meet her. Petrova appeared in padded trousers that had worn through at the knees, having nothing else to change into. When she declined a glass of vodka, he joined her for coffee and asked her about her life and career at the front. Sniper Petrova's tally was over 100. As they parted, Fedyuninsky, who was not noted for sentimentality (telephonist N. Nikulin remembered one of his conversations over the phone during a combat operation: "Fucking Ada! Go forward, will you! If you don't, I'll have you shot! Bloody hell!"), embraced and kissed Sergeant Petrova. In addition to her medal (she was only the second woman to become a Full Cavalier of the Order of Glory), she received a watch with an inscription from Fedyuninsky, and a new sniper rifle.[436] Petrova died shortly before the victory in May 1945, trapped in a truck that fell off a bridge. By that time she was already a grandmother, but sadly she never got to see her little granddaughter.

125 Division was advancing on the main axis, the principal route to the German capital. "To Berlin! " the commanders had announced. The situation had been so near to hopeless so many times earlier in the war

that it was hard to believe now that they were so close to defeating the Germans. How they wanted to survive until the end of the conflict, to see victory, and to come back home.

Of the ten girl snipers sent to 125 Division in March 1943, only five were left in March 1945. After the war Taya Kiselyova remembered Marina Shvetsova with gratitude. Marina was a sniper a couple of years older than her, pretty, intelligent, and invariably cool-headed. Marina, "a lovely woman", gave great support to Taya and the rest of them on a tiny bridge-head on the far side of the Neisse in March 1945 during the two most terrible nights and two most terrible days of her war, and perhaps of her lifetime.

The Oder is quite narrow where the Neisse flows into it. The infantry regiment, which had been reinforced with a squad of snipers, crossed it during the night on ice, which, in February, was precariously thin. The Germans detected their presence, although not immediately, and opened fire with machine guns. The regiment had no machine guns of its own, but the commanders were ordered to defend the position. There were Germans on both sides of them, but no order to retreat was given. "Stalin has given orders to hold this position," the commander told them. "The advance on Berlin is under way and we have to tie up German forces here." The regiment was effectively encircled for two days. ("What, Stalin is giving orders to a single regiment?" Taya wondered in perplexity.) During their first night there, on the west bank of the Neisse, they heard the cries of the wounded nearby as the Germans finished them off: a company had retreated and its casualties had been left behind. As was often the practice, women from the company had been left to tend the injured, a nurse and a sniper. They also screamed that night, horribly, as they were tortured. One of them, Taya later learned, had been pregnant. The girl snipers were surprised that one of the victims still had her watch on her wrist: her tormentors had no need of loot.

If Taya had had any doubts about the wisdom of an agreement she had concluded with her comrades immediately after arriving at the front ("If anything happens, you must shoot me rather than let me be captured alive"), she now had none. It was better, far better, to die, she decided, after what she was told by a soldier who had seen the bodies of those girls.

The snipers spent two days together with the soldiers in a large barn on the edge of a village. They had plentiful stocks of food, brought from the deserted local houses whose cellars were full of provisions. The next day, retreating German tanks went by. The girls' commander, who was lying with a small group of them in a ditch on the edge of the village, noticed that the tanks were being followed by a car, containing, perhaps, a V.I.P. When they opened fire and disabled it, a general jumped out and managed to escape. The car was left behind, and they were all greatly interested to examine its former owner's possessions and photographs. None of them knew German, however, so his letters went unread.

On the third day of the operation a pontoon bridge was built, and although it was under incessant German artillery fire, their neighbouring units were able to cross and ferry over artillery pieces too heavy for the ice.[437] The girls' regiment was withdrawn for respite, and given reinforcements to enable them to continue.

They faced more battles and more losses. During the attack on Breslau, Chief of Staff Captain Sagaidak signed an order proposing an award for sniper Bella Morozova. She was put forward for the Order of the Patriotic War posthumously, as were the company's Head of Reconnaissance Kaifman, Battalion Commander Trofimov and Cypher Clerk Sverdlov.[438] "Bella is dead," the girls were told. It seemed that a German sniper had wounded the battalion commander, and when Bella ran to help, she had been shot in the face.[439]

Bella Morozova did, nevertheless, receive her award in person, having survived her terrible injury. Captain Sagaidak recalled, "Very much to my surprise, when we were already in Czechoslovakia, somewhere near Waldenburg, I met Bella in one of the companies, alive and with her posthumous award."[440] Sagaidak himself had seen Bella's personal file crossed out with two slashing red lines, yet here she was, alive. "There stood a rather thin, fair-haired girl in a sergeant's uniform, with badges for her injuries and the Order of the Patriotic War on her tunic. She smiled strangely, and tried to show only one half of her face." The bullet had penetrated her temple, passed through the nasal cavity, and taken out her eye. Bella was only nineteen, and told her friends that when she saw her face after the bandages were removed she just wanted to die. Nevertheless, she found the courage not only to go on living, but to insist on being sent back to work at the headquarters of her own regiment. Scout Gennadiy Kuritsyn, a boy the girls had been fighting alongside for a year in the same regiment and who had long been in love with Bella, did not change his mind because of her disfigurement. They went on to have a family and live a long life together: one of the few front romances with a happy ending.

Chapter 19

"Oh, Mum, how they are hurting us here!"

"Vera, you're drenched in blood!" her friend exclaimed in horror. Vera Barakina looked down and saw that her greatcoat was in shreds below the waist and soaked in blood. Her boots were full of blood too. She felt dizzy.

In the course of several months on the Karelian Front, a static engagement on former Finnish territory, Vera had experienced no major battles or severe bombardments.[441] The battles began for her only in January, on the Third Ukrainian Front when she was in Hungary. She believed that, in the advance to the Danube, she had "taken out" at least twenty people. The infantry regiment with which the snipers were advancing suffered heavily: by the time it crossed the Danube it was down to about a quarter of its strength.

The river there was broad but shallow, and the girls walked through it up to their waists in icy water, with both hands raised above their heads holding their rifles. The German fire was not heavy and as she emerged on to the other bank Vera was thinking only about how and when she would be able to dry out her wet clothing and boots at least a little. The severe bombardment began only when they reached the shore. Their commander died immediately, and a sniper called Sasha had a finger severed by shrapnel. Some of those around her fell, and the others, crouching down, ran forwards, Vera among them. She was quite unaware of having been wounded until they were a considerable distance from the river and assembled at the line of the German trenches and one of the girls suddenly asked her, horrified, "Vera, what's that?" "What?" "How have you kept going?" Her friends quickly pulled off the shredded greatcoat, bandaged her over her clothes, and carried her on the greatcoat to the field hospital. There they "undressed me and started poking", giving her alcohol as an anaesthetic. Thankfully, her stomach wound turned out to be fairly superficial: the shrapnel had first struck a button on her coat, her "saviour-button" as she dubbed it. After a period lying on her back, Vera Barakina returned to her unit and fought on until the victory, although not as a sniper. Her Anatoly, who the preceding winter had been seriously crippled, wrote to her from hospital that he was waiting for her. Vera wanted only for the war to be over, so she could get back home to him. He was one of very few infantry lieutenants fortunate enough to survive the war. Most of those that did had, like him, been invalided out after being seriously wounded. He was also lucky to have escaped the scourge that pitilessly scythed down the Soviet Army as they advanced through Europe: methyl alcohol. Methyl alcohol, or methanol, was used for a wide range of technical purposes; it was also highly dangerous if ingested. A person who drank it would begin to suffer visual impairment, which could lead to blindness, vomiting and convulsions. If he was lucky he might only be disabled for life, but it was more likely that, after imbibing even very small doses of this alcohol, he would suffer an excruciating death.

Accidents caused by drinking alcohol unfit for consumption occurred both before and after the war. In 1944 and 1945, however, when Soviet troops were fighting on foreign soil, and when among the goods they captured there were so many carboys – and sometimes whole railway tanks – containing unknown liquids, such instances assumed epidemic proportions. Entire units rendered themselves unfit for duty. The orders from above became more and more stern, and the penalties could see you brought before a tribunal that had authority to pronounce the death sentence. The official line was that it was prohibited for troops to consume captured food and drink on the grounds that they might have been poisoned by the Germans. While it is not impossible that there really were cases of that, in practice, almost 100 per cent of poisonings were caused by methyl alcohol. Despite such orders being issued on all fronts, and severe punishment of those who disobeyed them, there was only an insignificant improvement in the situation by May 1945. In a bulletin from the quartermaster service of the First Byelorussian Front on 6 May 1945, instances of poisoning are said still to be on a massive scale. For example, "In 3 Assault Army, the abuse of methyl (wood) alcohol resulted in the poisoning of 251 persons, causing 65 fatalities. In 49 Army, 119 persons were poisoned after drinking spiritous fluids, of whom 100 died. In 46 Army and 5 Artillery Division, 67 service personnel were poisoned after drinking captured fluids, 46 of whom died. The organisers (of the booze-up) were the officers."[442]

But Russian men, as the Russian saying goes, will drink any liquid that is flammable. Even the girls were convinced that in wartime, especially in cold temperatures, it would be hard to get by without alcohol. They did not spurn their "hundred grams". In Klava Loginova's platoon the commander, Anya Matokh, insisted the girls should take a couple of sips, "twenty grams", before going out to hunt in order to keep warm, especially in winter. The remainder Anya kept faithfully, to be used when they came back from their positions for rubbing frozen hands and feet. In the summer they swapped their hundred grams with the men in return for chocolate.[443]

"Did my Anatoly drink it?" was the first thing Vera Barakina asked the soldiers in his wagon when she ran there during a stop. The moment it halted, she heard that many in his company had been struck down. The infantry division had been redeployed from the Karelian Front, up near Finland, all the way to the Third Ukrainian Front, and its troops had whiled away the endless journey as best they could. For the men, as always, that meant doing everything conceivable and inconceivable to get hold of alcohol. The soldier pointed to Anatoly, who was snoring on straw. Vera thought he seemed all right. She gave him a shake but, after muttering something, he fell asleep again.

She heard from the soldiers that they had all got drunk after an older sergeant had given them alcohol he had obtained somewhere. Both soldiers and officers suffered, and several dead bodies were unloaded from the train. A dozen others were at death's door. The more cautious ones drank a little, sensed there was something wrong and did not continue. Anatoly was lucky. One of the soldiers told Vera that, after a couple of sips, he had been sick and that had saved him.

In March 1945, Lida Bakieva, the snipers' deputy platoon commander, was invited to a gathering of the army's best soldiers. Such gatherings had become popular from 1942 onwards and were organised for different types of troops, different military specialities or, like this one, just for outstanding soldiers. As a decorated sniper with a tally of over seventy kills to her name, Lida unquestionably came into that category.

The event was a considerable distance away in East Prussia. Lida first walked, then got a ride in a horse-drawn cart, and for the last part of the journey she sat in the back of a truck covered with tarpaulin with other soldiers on their way to the rally, and a colonel who was on his way home after being wounded. They also had with them a cinematographic technician, who was being sent to film the proceedings. It was terribly cold, and the colonel, who was bringing felt boots home for his daughter, took pity on her. "While we are on our way, my dear, put on these boots," he said. Lida changed her footwear and put her own boots next to the cinematographic equipment. A German aircraft suddenly appeared and began firing at them. In his haste to escape the strafing, the driver took an ill-starred turning in the dark and the truck overturned. Lida groped in the gloom for her boots. When she and the colonel arrived on foot in the town where the meeting was being held, she realised that one of the boots she had put on in the confusion following the crash, a man's size 43, belonged to the truck driver. She managed to find him, to his great joy, because he was finding her own, far smaller, boot highly unsatisfactory.

At the rally, Lida was presented with a brand new sniper's rifle. But why would she need a new one when the old one had been zeroed in perfectly? Lida had no wish to part with a rifle she had had since sniper school. For a couple of weeks she dragged two rifles around, before presenting the new one to her sergeant.

Lida Bakieva raised her tally during the siege of the fortress at Breslau. Her unit was there from February 1945 until the end of the war. They managed to take Breslau only at the beginning of May, after an almost three-month siege. Lida continued shooting for decades after the war and it became her favourite sport. She took part in competitions and travelled all over the U.S.S.R. with various teams, including Kazakhstan.[444]

By early April, the Second Byelorussian Front had succeeded in eliminating the Heiligenbeil Cauldron, where the German 4th Army had been surrounded on the Balga Peninsula. This was the last German stronghold before Köningsberg. On 6 April troops of the Third Byelorussian Front, who were keeping Königsberg encircled, went on the offensive. The assault began with a huge artillery bombardment. Colonel General Kuzma Galitsky recalled, "The earth shook from the roar of the cannons. A solid wall of exploding shells came down on enemy positions along the entire front of the breakthrough. The city was shrouded in thick smoke, dust and fire . . . Through a brown haze you could see our heavy shells demolishing the earthworks covering the defences of forts, and sending wooden beams and lumps of concrete, rocks and the twisted wreckage of military equipment flying into the air. Katyusha missiles roared over our heads."[445] At the beginning of the assault bad weather prevented Soviet aircraft from playing a full part, but in the following days "Ilyushin-2 ground attack aircraft, 'The Black Death'", were constantly overhead.[446] The city garrison and the Volkssturm divisions (a German national militia established during the last months of the Second World War, largely made up of old men and young boys barely into their teens) cut off in Königsberg fought to the last: there was no line of retreat. The townspeople and refugees trapped in the city hid in cellars. Overcoming one line of defence after another, the Russians fought their way to the fortress.

Many official Soviet sources claim the city was taken with minor losses on the Soviet side, but eyewitness accounts do not bear this out. First Lieutenant Anna Saikina of the medical service, an operational dressing nurse in a field hospital in the forest five kilometres from Königsberg, never forgot the "unending stream of the wounded". When she got into the city after the assault, she was struck by the "unfamiliar Gothic architecture" and, despite the huge destruction, the "perfect order and cleanliness to be seen in places that remained intact".[447] She was taken aback by German neatness.

This pronounced neatness and thoroughness, as well as the manifestly robust German economy, evoked not jealousy in the troops, but bafflement and rage – just as it had elsewhere in East Prussia. The commander of an infantry platoon, twenty-year-old Nikolai Chernyshev, related how after the battle he and his soldiers ran from the streets into empty apartments and "from inertia smashed everything to pieces with rifle fire: windows, mirrors, crockery". The soldiers' hands were shaking and, by making mayhem, they "let loose their tension". In those days, the young sergeant saw no point in "taking ordinary soldiers prisoner: they could give us zero information."[448] The only prisoners worth having were staff officers who had been captured in the city's fort. It is not difficult to infer that many German soldiers of no value as squealers ended up in the mass graves at Königsberg.

Some way from the city, 31 Army was advancing on the Frisches Haff lagoon. The weather was bad on those days, the sea rough, the sky overcast, and rain alternated with snow. The German troops that were desperately fighting here were being pushed towards the Baltic Sea. Their situation was desperate, the only hope being to cross the Frisches Haff bay to a narrow spit of land, the Frische Nehrung, and make their way to Danzig. However, the spit had already been cut off from the other side, and this narrow strip of land was packed with frantic troops and refugees. Many of them were doomed.

People had begun to flee along the spit in January when the Red Army entered Prussia. Countless people died without reaching the coast – from cold and hunger on the way, the shelling, or at the hands of the pursuing Russian soldiers. How many more died that winter on the ice of the lagoon from bombing, falling through the ice, or collapsing and freezing to death! Even those fortunate enough to reach Danzig were not yet out of danger: Soviet submarines were waiting for vessels leaving the port. The most appalling tragedy happened on 16 April 1945 when, around midnight, the submarine L-3, under the command of Captain Vladimir Konovalov, sank the German transport ship *Goya* with 7,200 people, including 6,000 refugees, on board.[449] Fewer than 200 people were rescued.

Many years after the war, Klava Loginova and Anya Mulatova learned that they had been taking part in the Königsberg offensive quite close to each other, only in different divisions. Anya's unit had reached the lagoon when their commander called several girls, including Anya, and ordered them, while there was a lull in the fighting, to run to the quartermaster platoon for more magazines for the assault rifles. They went off but were soon lost, having no idea where the quartermaster platoon was. Fierce shelling began, and Anya became separated from the others. She decided to shelter behind the wall of a ruined house and wait for the bombardment to finish before continuing the search or going back. She heard cries to her right, and turned to see a wounded soldier lying in a swamp across the road from her. He was crying out in terrible pain for help, but the firing was too intense for Anya to get to him. She decided she would go over as soon as it was safe, but the wounded man fell silent. "He must have died," she thought. She stood there and cried, not so much from fear, although the situation was certainly frightening, but because someone had been in pain so close to her and had now, apparently, died without her being able to help him. "Oh, Mum, how they are hurting us here!" she murmured repeatedly, weeping.

The shelling stopped and she ran back to the lagoon. Where were Tasya and the other girls from her platoon? Anya Mulatova had no idea, but it did not matter. There was no one she recognised around her. Infantry soldiers were running alongside so she joined them.

The beach was littered with wrecked and abandoned army equipment, and German soldiers whose only retreat was into the sea. The Germans threw themselves in desperation into the icy water to swim out to the spit, or perhaps just to drown – a fate considered preferable to capture. Anya saw one blow himself up with a hand grenade.[450]

When Klava Loginova's regiment reached the lagoon, a major battle was raging. As often happened, when wounded soldiers saw the girls they called to them, "Nurse, help!" Klava and Olga could hardly start explaining that they were not nurses. Together they bandaged wounds and dragged the injured to safety. There was no sign of any other nurses or orderlies. When Klava later watched films about the war where a nurse pulls the wounded from a battlefield, she reflected she had never herself seen one running side by side with the soldiers into combat and helping them after they fell.

They would drag another injured soldier to safety and run on. When the bombardment was heavy, they would fall to the ground and crawl. But where were the troops from their own regiment? Under fire, Klava and Olga realised that they recognised none of the soldiers around them. In front were bushes and pits, and further on up a mound were the German trenches and bunkers. The German fire was heavy and the regiment they were now with had seen its headlong progress halted when it reached the line of trenches near the sea. There had been many wounded and the others lay down, in no hurry to launch a new attack.

Klava and Olga lay there, nudging each other in the ribs and wondering whether to stand up or not. In the end, Klava decided: "Olya, let's go! If we get killed, too bad, but the men will follow us." They did not get up at once, first letting the artillery do its job. Then the commander again called them to attack. Klava and Olga stood and saw that the soldiers behind them had got up too. As they advanced they came to a bunker, and a soldier ran to them and said, "There's people crying out in there!" Soldiers with rifles went and opened it, to find wounded German soldiers. These wounded Germans had not been firing at them and, at least while Klava was there, they remained unharmed. The soldiers drove out the walking wounded: "*Schnell, schnell!*" A young, ginger-haired German soldier, lightly wounded, thin faced, came over to Klava. He raised his hand in the communist *Rot Front* salute and smiled at her anxiously, saying "*Sniper gut, gut!*" He was right to be afraid: Russians had lost faith in the international solidarity of the working class very early on in the war. The German pointed and, as best he could, explained there was a store of some kind, and chocolate there. The soldiers immediately made off in that direction, but Klava and Olga, more disciplined, shouted to them to stop. "Where are you going? There are mines everywhere!" The ginger-haired German shook his head: "Mines – *nein!*" and went into the store himself. He pulled out a big box of chocolate for the girls and opened it: "*Bitte!*" Needless to say, Klava and Olga could not take the box with them, and their knapsacks were in the baggage train, so they just stuffed their pockets with presents for the other girls.

The battle ended, the wounded were collected, and the soldiers told the girls the commander wanted to know which unit they were from. They had ended up in 608 Regiment "and we don't have any girls," the officer explained. He asked who their battalion commander was. They told him and the officer phoned through to their headquarters, where people were worrying about them. It was night, but the commander of 608 Regiment instructed an orderly to escort the girls back to their regiment, and radioed that they should be put forward for an award. Very proud of themselves, they went back, only to be met with a torrent of abuse from the battalion commander. "What if the Germans had got you?" he yelled. Klava knew why he was so concerned about them, and about her. Battalion Commander Mikhail Denishchev had a soft spot for Klava that he made no attempt to hide. She liked him too: he seemed to her very grown-up and mature. He was a sturdy, good-looking man with brown hair and hazel eyes. Just as importantly, he was also a courageous commander.

The girls spent the night in a small room in a house. They were stunned by the decor and furnishings. This was real luxury. For the first time in her life, Klava encountered down pillows and duvets. They opened the wardrobes and admired the beautiful long dresses hanging there. The next day, the unit was shown round Königsberg. The city was badly damaged, and Klava remembered only the church, which had somehow remained untouched.

After the capture of Königsberg their division was taken by train to the First Ukrainian Front, and on the way Battalion Commander Denishchev continued to press his suit. "Well," he said, "Shall we get married?" Klava did not entirely trust him; there were plenty of men eager to take advantage of young girls. They might register their relationship, only for it then to transpire that he had a wife and family in the rear. But Mikhail, when Klava asked him directly whether he was already married, only laughed. "No," he said, "I had no time to get married before the war. I have only my mother in Nizhny Novgorod." "Right. I'll think about it," Klava replied.[451]

Mikhail was no longer alive when, still at the front, Klava was awarded a medal "For Valour". She had to wait for the Order of Glory, Third Class – for setting an example and getting those soldiers to attack – until after the war. When she met Olga later on, Klava heard that she too had been awarded the Order of Glory.

Chapter 20

"Hold on, Kolenka!"

"Girls, some milk for the wounded, please," Regimental Commander Shlikhter requested. Vera Chuikova went off to look for a bucket. She had known how to milk a cow since she was little, and there was no shortage of cows here in the vicinity of Stettin.[452] "From somewhere far away came the plaintive lowing of unmilked cows, like a wail of the dying," the Night Witches, pilots of night bombers, recalled. They were bombing the Germans not far away.[453] Many others later remembered those cows with bitter, redundant milk in their udders, and even Ilya Ehrenburg wrote on 1 March 1945, "If you can feel pity for any of those on the roads of Germany, then only for tiny, bewildered children, the maddened unmilked cows and abandoned cats and dogs: only they bear no responsibility for the atrocities." These cows and other livestock were often killed by soldiers – not always for meat but often for fun. Not infrequently, after killing a pig, they would help themselves to only a couple of kilos of meat from the carcass. A political report on 31 Army mentions, "In villages it is not unusual to see a slaughtered pig weighing 80 or 90 kilograms from which only a portion of the meat has been cut off and used. The remainder has been discarded and left to rot."[454]

Vera Chuikova, who in the twenty years of her life up till that moment had never been either prosperous or well-fed, was amazed here in East Prussia at the wealth on display in the abandoned German houses with their crystal chandeliers, velvet curtains, parquet flooring and carpets. She did not approve of soldiers who took satisfaction in wrecking all this. Soviet power would come to this land, the palaces would be given over to schools or used as orphanages! But, needless to say, she and her friends made up for all their years of hunger. What could be easier than to catch and pluck a chicken? In their knapsacks they had German home-cured ham and sausage, and chocolates. How nostalgically she looked back on these days after the war. Life in her village was even poorer in the late 1940s than it had been before the conflict began.

But in Prussia . . . chicken soup for the patients? No problem! You need milk? I'll just find a cow! Vera had many occupations during the war: rescuing and bandaging wounded soldiers, shifting soil, milking cows, and even operating a searchlight. Despite being a sniper, though, she was never called upon to shoot anyone. And thank God for that, she thought. What a sin to burden your soul with.

At the sniper school in Podolsk, this short, brown-eyed girl with a lovely figure was the best shot in her platoon. In fact, she was so good that they kept her behind in the instructors' company. She and her comrades were taken to the front on 1 February 1945. On the way their train stopped at Kovel where, along with the other soldiers, the girls were taken to see a concentration camp. They were shown the oven in which human bodies were burned, mountains of clothes and shoes, both for adults and children. For a long time Vera could not forget a pair of tiny, well-worn children's shoes.[455] It would be difficult to imagine a more effective propaganda exercise. The girls were told that experiments had also been conducted at this camp into killing people by electrocution.[456]

By the time they arrived at their unit, the First Byelorussian Front had reached Poznan. Their platoon was assigned to 236 Infantry Regiment, and Battalion Commander Bocharov immediately tested them to see how well they could shoot, an assessment supervised by a young lad they were told was a famous sniper. To their regret, neither Vera nor her friends could recall his name in later years, but he was "festooned with medals". "They shot well and will not need a nanny," he reported to the regimental commander Shlikhter. Shlikhter, however, was a kindly man and did not want to put them in harm's way. "Girls, I am going to take good care of you. Why would I want to push you out to the front line?" he once said, and he was as good as his word. They never fired a shot in anger. The middle-aged Battalion Commander Bocharov also treated them as if he were their father.

That is not to say, of course, that all sorts of things did not go on. They had more to put up with than just the misbehaviour of soldiers who, during the advance, would use the stereotelescope to peep at them when they went into a crater to relieve themselves; or harassment from soldiers and officers, especially when they were drunk. As part of 69 Army they would march 30–40 kilometres a day on foot carrying a heavy load. Crossing the Oder was sheer hell. They were on the receiving end of terrible shelling, even, on occasion, from their own Soviet Katyusha rockets and artillery. ("Girls, sit in this crater. A shell doesn't hit the same spot twice," Bocharov instructed them.) One girl was blown up by a mine when, just before the German surrender, she went on to a bridge to wash her hair. Their work with the wounded was endless and could be very trying. To all intents and purposes they became nurses, bandaging and evacuating the wounded during battles. Vera thought it was a pity they had had no medical training at sniper school. What an ordeal she found dressing a terrible leg wound a soldier suffered during the crossing of the Oder, She had first to pull cloth and padding out of it that had come from the warm quilted trousers the soldier was still wearing even though the weather was no longer cold. To cap it all, beside himself with the pain, he lashed out at Vera's head. She often wondered after the war which of the men she had rescued and bandaged survived. Had she actually saved anyone's life?[457]

It was on the Oder that Vera Chuikova became a searchlight operator. In mid-April 1945, the First Byelorussian Front was to storm the Seelow Heights, a heavily fortified ridge on the left bank of the old channel of the Oder and the last obstacle on the road to Berlin. The Germans were prepared to defend it to the last and had assembled 200 guns there to cover a single kilometre of the front line. Marshal Georgy Zhukov, commanding the Front, decided on a night-time assault using searchlights to shock and blind his opponent. In these final days, the demoralised German troops were still clinging to the hope that a much-rumoured miracle weapon would save them. At the same time they were frightened by whispers of a new Soviet armament even more terrible than the Katyusha rocket-launcher system. Part of Zhukov's calculation was that they might well mistake an exceptionally powerful artillery bombardment, accompanied by searchlights, for the mystery Soviet weapon. He had already tried carrying out an operation with searchlights in a counter-attack on the Germans during one of the most difficult moments of the fighting at Stalingrad. That had not proved a great success, but now he decided to try again, this time with a large concentration of aircraft and heavy guns, together with more powerful searchlights, borrowed this time from the anti-aircraft defence forces.

An officer who took part in the assault recalled,

> Water was lapping in our shallow trench, people were standing in mud with assault rifles in their hands. Machine guns were rolled out to their positions. Huge trucks drove up to the trenches, bringing searchlights to the front. We had not seen this kind of armament before and did not know what their role could be . . . Fifty of my guardsmen boarded tanks and were thus detached from the battalion. Suddenly the searchlights were switched on. For a couple of seconds, we saw the enemy's trench and, in the distance, the Seelow Heights, but at that very moment the artillery struck and everything in front of us was shrouded in smoke, through which all we could see was the sparkling of explosions.[458]

Vera Chuikova had no idea what those searchlights were for. Nobody had explained the thinking of the top commanders to the troops. Her platoon was summoned and told they were to give moral and practical support to the girls operating them, as they were very young and had no front-line experience. Vera Kobernyuk's sniper platoon was given the task of supporting searchlight operators from Yaroslavl.

Sniper Raisa Serebryakova recalled how terrible the cannonade was. "It was impossible to hear even what someone standing right next to you was saying." A flare was the signal to activate the searchlights. At three o'clock a white beam, the signal to attack, "shot vertically up into the sky".[459] The monstrously intense barrage seemed to last for ever. The Germans remembered it as having lasted two and a half hours, but in fact it went on for only half an hour.

Vera Kabernyuk later recalled that many of the searchlight operators were killed or injured when the Germans opened fire on them with long-range artillery. The snipers replaced them. Vera and her comrades believed, in line with what they were told by their commanders, that the searchlights had made a great contribution to the success of the attack.[460] "The Germans were in complete panic. They believed walls of fire were coming at them," Raisa Serebryakova claimed. Soviet General Vasiliy Chuikov, in command of 8 Army, was less enthusiastic about them: "I have to say that when we were admiring the power and effectiveness of the searchlights at the test site, none of us could accurately predict how they would work in combat. It is difficult for me to judge their effectiveness on the other fronts. On the sector of the front for which our 8 Guards Army was responsible, I saw the searchlights' powerful beams blocked by the billowing curtain of fumes, smoke and dust raised above the enemy's front line. Not even searchlights could penetrate it . . ."[461]

Zhukov sent two tank armies to support the attacking infantry, but they were not able to break through. It was only late on 17 April that 8 Guards Army succeeded in penetrating the defences of the Seelow Heights. Someone who took part in the assault remembered how "Every 6–10 metres along the length of the enemy trench lay our soldiers and officers who had fallen trying to take the Heights."[462] In the fighting on the approaches to Berlin, the Red Army suffered a third of a million casualties, killed or wounded – as many as the Americans lost in the entire war.

In their memoirs, however, the generals wrote about the success of the offensive, and one of them, Lieutenant General Fyodor Lisitsyn, even mentioned Vera Kabernyuk and her comrades, including Vera Artamonova, whose military career began, along with that of Vera Kabernyuk, at Velikiye Luki, and who ended the war with eighty-nine kills and a number of medals to her name. "The girl snipers came to our aid: Lieutenant Artamonova, Sergeants Kabernyuk, Popova and Vlasova," Lisitsyn wrote in his memoirs. "During our troops' attack on the first line of the enemy defences, the fascists subjected the dazzling searchlights to heavy fire from long-range artillery. Many of the operators were killed or wounded. Nevertheless, the lights continued to shine. Those incapacitated were immediately replaced by girl snipers, who saw their combat mission through to the end."[463]

Articles about Vera Kabernyuk note that for rescuing a vehicle she received a commendation in Order No. 359 of 2 May 1945, signed by Stalin personally, and that her mother, Anisia Petrovna, had a letter sent to her in her Altai village of Zonalnoye by the commander of Vera's unit in which he congratulated her on having such a distinguished daughter. Biographers mention also that Guards Sergeant Kabernyuk and her comrades-in-arms celebrated Victory Day by the walls of the Reichstag.

That is absolutely true. Vera and the other snipers from the Central Women's Sniper School took no part in the battle for Berlin, but nonetheless they were in the city immediately after the German surrender, and wrote their names on the Reichstag. Vera Kabernyuk was the daughter of an "Enemy of the People"* shot in 1937. Her regiment's SMERSH officer, a decent man, gave her strict orders back in 1943 to keep her mouth shut and avoid drawing attention to herself: loose talk, or even just a joke or careless word that others might get away with, could destroy her. Now, standing at the Reichstag as one of the victors, having returned to the ranks after being wounded and suffering concussion, having demonstrated that her parents had brought her up to be a true patriot, she believed that life would be different when she got home and that she would no longer have to be afraid of her own shadow.

★

* The cliché employed during the 1930s to describe the victims of Stalin's purges.

In mid-April 1945, 31 Army was transferred from the Third Byelorussian to the First Ukrainian Front, with whom they were redeployed to Czechoslovakia after participating in the Berlin operation. "Redeployed" is perhaps putting it too grandly. In reality, having travelled as far as they could by rail, they marched for several days through the Carpathian Mountains towards the town of Legnica. At first they proceeded at night, resting during the day and, not permitted to make fires, existing on dry rations. After a while the command evidently decided there was no need for concealment, so they marched during the day too.

Battalion Commander Mikhail Denishchev died on 19 April, when the army had almost completed its redeployment. After a night's march they had all slept together during the day in a single tent: the battalion commander and his orderly, Klava and six of her sniper friends. In the evening they set off again. Klava told the others about a dream she had had, in which the sole came off her left shoe. One of the girls said, "That is a warning that something bad is going to happen." They were all as superstitious as most Russian people are, and even more so because they were young and saw death almost every day.

The sniper platoon was marching uphill behind the main body of the regiment. A column of tanks was coming towards them and suddenly all movement stopped, before starting again. Then Mikhail's orderly came looking for Klava, bearing terrible news. Denishchev had been fighting in the war since 1941, survived his tank being hit, and had returned to action after his injury. Now, with victory in sight, he had died absurdly. The battalion commander had decided to ride a horse that had not been properly broken in, despite his orderly's warnings. Frightened by a tank, the horse reared up and threw him straight under the vehicle's caterpillar tracks, which split his skull open. When Klava ran forward, she wailed at the terrible sight she encountered. Her friends made their way to the scene of the tragedy and comforted her as best they could; they had to keep up with the regiment. Mikhail's body was placed on a cart and, in a daze, Klava walked beside it, the other girls and soldiers behind.

The battalion commander was buried when they reached Legnica. The scouts found some suitable materials in a shed and the girls made an abundance of flowers and wreaths. It was the end of April, but Klava remembered clearly that there had been no real flowers at the ceremony. Mikhail was given a solemn funeral in the presence of the regimental commander and his deputies, and a volley was fired into the air. Klava was heartbroken. She refused to take his watch or any of Mikhail's other belongings, asking for them to be sent to his mother. She kept only his ID photograph. On the ninth day she returned to his grave with the girls, along with the logistics officer and a drill sergeant who had been friends of Mikhail. Klava remembered how comforted she was by the wise, calm words of Anya Matokh: "Stop crying now, Klava. It can't bring him back." Anya's words were perhaps so etched in her memory because, within a few days, Anya was no more.

And the war continued, regardless of Klava's sorrow. The army was tasked with capturing the town of Jablonec, but the Germans were not going to surrender without resistance. Indeed, they carried on fighting fiercely even after the surrender on 9 May. On the night of 25 April, the snipers' regiment took up defensive positions in the village of Javor. The alarm was raised that night. In the room they had been allocated on the first floor of the regimental headquarters building the girls were sleeping almost fully dressed, so when they woke up they had only to put on their tunics and boots. A minute later they were down at the windows on the ground floor. The Germans had broken through on the neighbouring stretch, which was being defended by a penal company, and their unit was surrounded. There were soldiers in trenches. The snipers took up positions at the windows and were soon firing at Germans running around close to the house. Then, just fifty metres away, a German self-propelled gun appeared and Klava, standing by the window with Tanya Markelova, saw the muzzle slowly turning in their direction. "It's going to fire. We're done for," Klava just had time to think. A German stuck his head out from behind the gun and Klava and Tanya both shot at him. They did not see him fall because at that moment the artillery piece fired at them.

They heard afterwards that the shell had hit the wall. The blast threw them aside, the room filled with dust, and bricks fell all around them. They were completely dazed and could hardly hear. Some of the scouts they knew ran into the house to show them which way to run. "Snipers, we're surrounded!" they shouted, pulling Klava and Tanya out of the half-ruined house by the hand. "Where's Anya Matokh?" Klava suddenly remembered. "Over there!" Tanya pointed. Anya's body was sitting by the wall, with her severed head beside it.

Klava and Tanya ran after the scouts, while being shot at from the bushes. "Jump!" the soldiers shouted: ahead of them was a high fence: how they got over it, Klava could not imagine.

They took up a defensive position behind the fence, and soon another unit broke through to relieve them. Klava had no doubt the scouts had saved their lives, and when she met up with them again several days later, ran to say, "Thank you so much, lads!"

Not long after, when the First Ukrainian Front had taken Jablonec, Klava went back to that house in Javor to look for Anya and her own belongings, which had been left behind on the first floor where the girls had been sleeping. Anya's corpse was no longer there, and Klava was unable to find out who had buried her. Of her own belongings, all Klava found was a photo of her sister, Tanya, with a boot print on it. She was very sad to lose her knapsack, which had all her front-line possessions in it, all her photos and letters from her family. The only photos of the war she had left were those she had sent to her sisters and mother, and also the picture of Mikhail, which she kept in her breast pocket.[464]

"Anything could happen in the war. Nina Tolchenitsyna died ridiculously but I survived," Anna Sokolova wrote many years later. Like numerous others, she bitterly regretted the loss of comrades who died in the final few exchanges, and was tormented by feelings of guilt that it was not she who had died. Her regiment had to cross a pontoon bridge over the River Oder near Moravská Ostrava and Germans were shooting from the other side. "The water was icy, it was cold and slippery, and the current was very fast," Anna recalled. In the melee, Nina was lightly wounded, but fell from the bridge and drowned. What a stupid way to die! The river there was very shallow, "hardly up to your ankles". What killed Nina was the fact that they were all completely exhausted after marching "day and night in full kit".[465] They had already seen so many people die, but those deaths in the last days of the war they could never forget.

"Sniper! Sniper!" cried the young soldier everybody called Kolenka. He was dying from a severe stomach wound, suffered on 8 May, and wanted Taya Kiselyova, who was helping out in the hospital as a nurse, to sit with him. Taya sat down and held his hand. "Just be sure not to give him any water!" she was warned by the doctor as he walked along the corridor, as if there was still hope. Tears ran down Taya's face from time to time. She felt so sorry for this young soldier, dying when the war would be over any day now. "Hold on, Kolenka!" What else could she say to him?

Taya liked it in the hospital. She was thinking that when she got back home she would study to be a doctor. She did simple bandaging and helped at operations. A couple of times she fainted after inhaling anaesthetic, which was administered very primitively: they just poured it on a shirt and put the shirt over the patient's face. "What sort of assistant have I been given!" was the surgeon's indignant reaction.

Here, on the border between Poland and Czechoslovakia, the Germans continued to resist furiously, and many wounded were being brought in, even after the official German surrender. Among them was an officer who had been courting Taya, Deputy Battalion Commander Ilnitsky. "Fate has brought you together," one of the nurses murmured. Mstislav Ilnitsky was ten years older than Taya, educated, from a good family in Leningrad, genial and polite. By nature he was no mindless disciplinarian and enjoyed the respect of his soldiers. The girls, seeing him gallantly give her a flower after a battle, were jealous and hissed that he was far too good for her. She knew she loved him, however, only when she saw him lying, severely wounded, in hospital. It was so painful to see grievously injured soldiers die in those days, having lived through a war that was now over.

Ilnitsky too called in his delirium for a girl sniper. When the regimental commander came, he ordered Taya to go and sit with him: "He is calling you. Go!" She sat down by his bed, and the wounded man clutched her hand and would not let go. Taya believed that she had pulled him through. They were together to celebrate the victory in the hospital.[466]

At the beginning of May 1945, the Night Witches were flying from an airfield to the north of Berlin: more precisely, from a meadow near the town of Brunn. There was almost "nowhere to fly to", because everywhere the enemy was surrendering. They were sent to bomb only one group of enemy soldiers, in the region of the port of Swinemünde, where "German troops were hastily getting out on steamers across the Baltic." Reconnoitring the zone of operations, they flew a triangular route in daytime, trying, understandably, to deviate in the direction of Berlin to see for themselves the "lair of the fascist beast". They saw before them "a huge, grey, half-ruined city. Smoke was coming from everywhere, and in places fires were still burning. The sky was almost completely overcast with smoke and the sun shone through it with a thin yellow light."[467] Was the war really coming to an end?

Tamara Rogalskaya's regiment had been turned northwards from Berlin in early May, and it was their task to finish off the Germans on the ground at Swinemünde. They had to row across the water, and although they had massive artillery support from the mainland and also from the air, it was a terrifying and perilous crossing. Everybody knew that the fighting would soon be over, but there was no let-up in the German firing. Going into the water up to their waists, the girls climbed into the boats. Tamara got in first, all too aware that she was a very poor swimmer. When they reached the other side, the girls heard that Pavel Yarygin, a battalion commander in their division, had been killed. He had been a cheery young man who sang beautifully and was greatly liked by the girls. When the port of Swinemünde was taken, they joined up with another regiment from their division. The soldiers were shouting, "Victory! Victory!" and the girls thought they were referring to the taking of the port.

Tamara and her friends were able to join in fraternising with the Allies, who had also reached the town. Almost none of them had seen a foreigner before, or ever would again. They were amazed to find the Americans so varied: some were white, others black. The Americans for their part were shocked by the sight of young women with assault rifles (they did not have their sniper rifles during this advance). Tamara remembered two soldiers, one white and one black, going "Bow-wow!" when they saw them. The girls thought that was very funny. Some of them, like the Russian soldiers, gave the Americans a big hug. They all had a sense of overwhelming happiness.[468] How they had dreamed this day would come, that "we would live to see the end of the war, and see what a great life there would be afterwards . . ."[469]

Chapter 21

"They promise you nothing!"

Vera Chuikova's unit was forty kilometres from Berlin and, like many soldiers, the girl snipers were taken after victory for a tour of the fascist capital. Vera's first impression was that, "our side of the city was completely devastated." In the small town where they were deployed there was a civilian camp for women who were being "filtered". Anyone who incurred the suspicion of the Soviet authorities was being checked. Out of curiosity, the girls went to take a look. The women in the camp, who were Russian, waved to them from far away behind a fence. Battalion

Commander Bocharov, hearing what they were planning, warned them, "You should have nothing to do with those women." He told them the women had been deliberately infected with venereal diseases.[470] The snipers felt disgust and pity, but also anger at them for having "sold themselves" to the Germans. They believed they had no one to blame but themselves.

All Vera and her friends wanted now was to sleep and sleep after all the strenuousness of recent months. They had no time to relax, however, because before the victory they were employed training reinforcements, soldiers born in 1926. Relations were strained at first: the sergeants began teaching the new soldiers the art of square-bashing, and the recruits were not happy about having a lot of women with authority over them. Then, however, when they moved on to train them to use firearms, including captured foreign models, which the girls taught them to disassemble, assemble, and shoot accurately, the new recruits began to feel a grudging respect for them. What the girls really wanted, though, was to just go home. "We had all so much been looking forward to the victory. We so much wanted to get back home to help our parents," Lidia Bakieva recalls.[471] They all talked about what it would be like when they got there, changing into dresses again, what food they would cook, and where they would go out to. Their battalion commander was a kind man and, when he heard this, warned, "Girls, girls, what's all the hurry? There's nothing good waiting for you there . . ." He did not go into more detail, and indeed he was already risking his neck by saying even that. Vera found out just how right he was only after she got home. The letters they received at the front were scrutinised by the censor. "Half of it was blacked out: they only left homely details," so they did not even know that there were still ration cards at the rear, and famine.[472]

They celebrated the victory, but for most of them there was no question of demobilisation. Vera and her friends were sent off to help SMERSH: clerks were needed, people to compile reports on Soviet ex-prisoners of war. Vera remembers only too well the lengthy questionnaires: where people had been captured, where they had been held, and so on and so forth. During interrogations a service dog would be present in the room. "Do you think that's the right way to treat people?" the girls whispered back in their barracks. "They fought in the war, after all. Some got captured because they were wounded or concussed." Now they were being interrogated as if they were enemies, with a dog there. They all agreed, however, that their superiors were in a better position to judge than they were.[473]

Klava Panteleyeva, meanwhile, had already gone back to work at her textile factory. After the victory she and her platoon remained with their unit for only a couple of weeks. In those first days, the girls climbed up on to the parapet by their dugouts to watch the long, long columns of German prisoners being herded along past them. One suddenly pulled a bottle of perfume out of his pocket and gave it to Klava. Where had he got it from? Then the Germans were gone, and, to keep the soldiers from being bored, the army found something for them to do. As they were positioned on the edge of woods, they were set to sweeping the tracks and levelling out their edges. In June, however, the girls were demobilised and sent home with the first train: just like in the films, the girls were going home, and with them the "old", soldiers who were about forty, or even fifty. Klava remembered how many of them had been horse drivers: for the Red Army horse-drawn carts were by far the most common means of transport during that war. To the girls' delight, they were issued with new greatcoats. Klava's old one was ragged and burned. The new ones were grey, English and excellent. (Klava later altered hers into an ordinary coat, and was not alone in doing so.) They were returned home in the same heated livestock wagons that, a little over a year before, had brought them to the front. They were given plenty of food to take back: dried rusks, cakes of millet and the like. Now, with Germany far behind, these items were again a rarity, and how glad Klava's large family were to see them! She also brought them money: while she was at the front, this had been accumulating on her record. It was not a lot, of course, but a great help to her starved parents, brother and sister, enabling them to break their long, involuntary fast.[474]

Just a couple of days after the victory, a wedding was celebrated in Jablonec as Sniper Lyuba Guseva married a nice young man, one of the scouts. They invited an accordionist and Klava Loginova and her friends made lots of Siberian *pelmeni*, dumplings made to a recipe used by almost every housewife in the Urals:

   1 cup of cold water
   a pinch of salt
   1 egg
   1 kilogram of flour
   1 kilogram of meat

Heap the flour on the table, mix the water with the egg and salt and add it little by little to the flour, mixing all the time. (The egg can be dispensed with if need be.) The dough should be firm enough to come off your hands without needing to be helped. The most delicious filling consists of three kinds of meat: beef, pork and lamb. In the olden days, instead of lamb they would have used game, elk or deer. Even after the advent of mincers, the filling for the dumplings would be chopped by hand. The finished *pelmeni* would be frozen by hanging them outside in linen bags. Before taking the dumplings out of their bag to be placed in a saucepan of boiling water, the bag had to be vigorously shaken until the dumplings rattled or they would still be stuck together after they were cooked. In the Urals, *pelmeni* were made for the winter after the frosts were severe. The whole family would join together to make hundreds of the small dumplings. Several generations of women would sit (the men's only role was to chop the meat), and work, sing songs and talk.

Needless to say, in Jablonec Klava did not have the prescribed three types of meat, but the scouts produced a meat filling of some description and flour. The girls fashioned the dumplings, and Klava remembers all their talk was about going home and seeing their mothers again. The wedding was a great success: the accordionist played and they danced and enjoyed themselves. Klava felt some of the tension lifting: soon she would be home with her mother and able to tell her all she had experienced in the war.

On 14 August at Bobyrka station in Lvov Province all the girls from the Urals were loaded into a wagon with hay and straw, and slowly set off in the direction of home. Klava had a considerable supply of food and clothing, which was issued to them as they were leaving the unit: two lengths of material (silk and white staple); two dresses (one of dark blue, heavy material; the other a crêpe-de-Chine summer dress); trousers of a pretty fabric which appeared to be waterproof; and a pair of black, high-heeled shoes. When Klava got married a few years later the trousers proved very useful when converted into a blanket cover. The girls were generously provided with food: 4 kilograms of sugar, 4 kilograms of flour, and in addition oats and dehydrated fruit, to a total weight of 12 kilograms. Klava transported these treasures in a suitcase and rucksack. The journey took two weeks, even though the train stopped infrequently. As they travelled on, and girls got off at each stop, there were fewer and fewer of them left. Many got out at Moscow. It was an enjoyable journey: they were well fed as they travelled, accordionists played, and they sang all their front-line songs. People welcomed them at the stations with flowers, gifts and singing. They brought along their children, looking among the soldiers for their loved ones. They congratulated them, hugged them, laughed and cried.[475]

Tasya Pegesheva was unlucky. She fell in love with a young officer in her regiment but, after several dates, he started avoiding her. He had never had any serious intentions and was tired of her. For Tasya, a girl with a rural background, to lose your virginity and then be abandoned was a shame and a disgrace. She went and told the political officer. He summoned the officer who had used Tasya so cruelly but who, after listening, said coolly, "I never promised her anything. As for our relations, she wanted it too." At that, he shrugged. What more could be said? What more could the political officer do for Tasya? Thank God she didn't get pregnant.

"It's perfectly true: they promise you nothing," Anya thought as she tried to console the weeping Tasya. She too had found love in Czechoslovakia, and while everything so far seemed to be different, she was worried and full of doubt about the future.

At Jablonec, not long before the end of the war, she had again met the captain who had once sworn at her and Tasya and called them "unauthorised" as they stood in their snipers' trench, but then gone on to invite Anya and Roza Shalaeva to tea, and teased Anya by calling her his "Moscow girlfriend". Anya liked him very much but, to the best of her ability, played hard to get. When Anatoly asked, "Are you a maid?" she pretended not to understand and replied, "No, I'm a boy," but did then give herself to him. After the victory, Anatoly took her into his unit and, until demobilisation, she worked there as a clerk. Many of her friends from the platoon were also now living with front-line husbands, many of whom, but by no means all, later became their husbands in peacetime.

Anya and Anatoly were demobilised, and when the contingent for Moscow was being assembled, he told her there was no rush for her to go home to her native Simanshchina in Penza Province. They travelled back to Moscow together. He brought Anya straight from the war to the room in Mariina Roshcha where his parents lived and where he had been brought up.[476]

"I often wonder what kind of reception we army girls will come back to after the war. Will we be met with suspicion, despite the fact that we have risked, and many of us have given, our lives fighting for the Motherland?" Roza Shanina had written as she worried about the future. Anya wondered about that too, but the reaction she got from her fiancé's parents was unexpected.

Anatoly's father was immediately hostile, and right in front of her he chided his son. "So many rich girls are free now, and look what you have brought back!" His mother said nothing, but it was clear that she was far from enthusiastic about Anya. "This is my wife," Anatoly said, and again the objections rained down: he had nowhere to live, no job, and he had brought this woman back in an army greatcoat and boots. They would even have to find something for her to wear. As if Anya had not arrived bearing the fabric she was issued with on demobilisation, and the food! Anatoly's reply was something Anya remembered for the rest of her life: "Our love is cloudless." There was no more debate.

Svetlana Alexievich has written about the tragedy of girls who returned from the war and were treated by their neighbours, and even their own families, as if they had been no better than prostitutes at the front.[477] There is nothing I can add to her exemplary accounts. This turn of events was foreseen by Sasha Yekimova, who in 1944 wrote a story in Roza's diary about three girls:

My very dear Roza, on 20 November 1944 I had the following dream. It was June 1947, a beautiful sunny day. Life in Moscow, the capital of the Soviet Union, was once again as bustling as ever. Two years had passed since the end of a severely testing war. Those who fought in it had returned to their homes. How these people had changed in just two years of peacetime! Today, a Sunday, the streets of Moscow were especially busy. Two girls were walking down Gorky Street and were clearly in a hurry to get somewhere. When they came to a white house, they stopped by the entrance. A few minutes later, a third girl came out of the door, a beaming smile on her face. In a matter of seconds, the three of them continued on their way together. A couple were coming towards them, and the girls' eyes were immediately fixed on them. A slim young man was elegantly dressed in military uniform. In his arms he was holding a baby wrapped in a light shawl. Next to him walked a slender, dark-haired girl. They were chatting happily about something. The young man spotted the three girls. Their eyes met, and in an instant each saw before them their whole life at the front, the friendship between snipers and someone operating a Katyusha rocket launcher.

They did not stop when they met, only nodded a greeting. Two years of peace had dramatically changed these people. Once they had been great friends. The young man evidently felt it beneath him to acknowledge that in the presence of his companion. The three girls went on their way, but now in silence. If you had taken a close look at their faces, you would have had no difficulty in seeing that one of them, in particular, was looking miserable.[478]

Of the inseparable "battle troika", only Kalya Petrova lived to see how life turned out after the war. After the fall of Königsberg, their division was taken to fight against Japan. They travelled in railway wagons for perhaps two weeks before reaching Moscow. The fine, lively city was in striking contrast to the dead, devastated Königsberg. While their train was stopped there, she had time to run out to see her aunt and uncle, and her uncle, who was a general, came back to the station to see her off. He made a big impression on her commander: her friends knew of his existence, but modest Kalya had not boasted about him to the officers. "I didn't know your uncle was a general or I would have courted you!" the commander said. There followed more weeks of travelling. At the stations another sniper, Zoya Mikhailova, who had long been nicknamed "the Actress", organised and presented amateur concerts. They had their sniper rifles with them, polished and still cherished above all else, but in the Far East they never fired them: they worked instead as telephone operators. The war soon ended and they were demobilised.

When she first left school, Kalya had wanted to go to the Institute of Foreign Languages, but when she came back from the war, decided to become a doctor instead. After all she had experienced she wanted to save lives. However, Moscow University was the only place where she could get a bed in the student hostel. So that is where she went, to study hydrology. Her sister clothed her and her life moved in a completely new direction. It was hard, and not particularly prosperous, and there was no place in it for all the horrors of the past. In the 1970s, journalists writing about Shanina beat a path to the door of Kaleria Alexandrovna Morokhovets, an "academic researcher and attractive, self-confident woman" in whom it was hard to recognise the "wide-eyed little soldier" laughing with Roza and Sasha from a front-line photograph. Kaleria showed them photographs of those who had returned from the war and those who had not: Masha Shvarts, Sasha Yekimova, Roza . . . Dusya Shamanova had managed to escape from the Germans who dragged off Tanailova and Nesterova, but then she too died from her wounds. Valya Nikolaeva was wounded in the jaw, Eva Novikova in the eye. Anya Nesterova died in a concentration camp, Lyuba Tanailova was imprisoned in a German concentration camp, then sent by her own side into exile. Nadezhda Minaeva died from her wounds. Anna Lysenkova was killed, as were Masha Fertova, Dusya Kekesheva, Valya Lazorenko, and Posazhnikova, and Kareva . . .[479]

Epilogue

"One day my mother went to fetch water," veteran sniper Irina Izmestieva recalled. "On the way back, she saw in the distance a little soldier had turned in to their street. It was me, in a tunic, in canvas boots, with a half-empty rucksack."[480] The girl snipers were coming home.

Klava Loginova's mother knew from letters that her daughter had been demobilised, and constantly went to the station to meet the trains that brought soldiers home. While Klava was away at the war, her mother always prayed and lit candles for her. Her hope was that Klava would not come back a cripple, because then, she believed, it would be better for her to have been killed. One time she saw a girl in army uniform at the station with a terribly burnt face. She had a terrible fright, thinking it was Klava.

When Klava did get out at their station, it was already evening and she knew she would not be able to get home that night. Instead she went to the factory where her sister worked and phoned her from there since the working day was over. Her sister came to collect her on horseback, and immediately started phoning round all their relatives: "Klava's come back. She's alive!"

Her mother did not immediately let Klava return to work. She wanted her to have time to settle down again. She was right, of course. Magnesium carbonate was mined in the town, and the ore was sometimes blasted out even at night. Often, when she heard the explosions, Klava would jump out of bed and grab her greatcoat, ready to run. Like most who had fought at the front, she wore that greatcoat for many years since it was impossible to buy anything else.[481]

Katya Peredera spent a whole year in hospital and underwent five operations: her heel had been pulped and numerous small bones shattered. There were many other people in the wards with her, and Katya, who was by nature kind and sociable, realised that even though she was ill and could not walk, she could still help them: if not by doing things for them, then by talking to them. She decided to become a doctor, and viewed the future with optimism. Her foot was not always going to hurt, but she found she could only walk with difficulty, using a stick.

In her first months at the hospital in Kropotkin it struck her what a wonderful family she had. Her parents cared for her as if she were a little girl again, all but spoon-feeding her, and not letting her help with household chores. In her home town, however, Katya immediately sensed animosity: animosity towards a sniper seriously wounded at the front, a disabled soldier! "What, did you go there looking for a husband and not find one?" someone who had known her before might ask. (In the south of Russia, people are not always good at guarding their tongues.) She often heard people sniggering behind her back: "Front-line wife!", or "Disappeared without trace!" It made her feel like crying. At the front she had twice fallen in love, but neither time had this led to intimacy. First, at Taman, she had met Lyova, the young sergeant with whom she only once managed to outwit "One-and-a-half Ivans", her ever-vigilant commander, and spend twenty minutes with him.

The second boy was Alexander Vinogradov, and he was the love of Katya's life. Handsome and cheerful, a former pilot who, after being wounded, was retrained as an artillery observer, his unit soon left the quarry and he really did "disappear without trace". After the war, Katya thought of looking for him, but how many Alexander Vinogradovs were there in the U.S.S.R.? Hundreds, thousands?

In Krasnodar, where she went to study at medical school, she also found people looking down on her. They would sometimes not let her go to the front of the queue, even though they could see she could hardly stand, leaning on her stick and in her soldier's greatcoat. Back home, Katya would get into a bath of cold water to ease the pain in her foot, and cry.

Thankfully, she did have some kind classmates, both girls and boys.

Most were younger, and many helped Katya a great deal, doing her laundry, shopping for food, and those who lived locally would bring her some food from home. Her mother bought her a pink synthetic-fibre dress, and her sister Nina also helped with clothes and food when she started working. Katya began to get her life back together.

She even tried to wear high heels, pulling the shoe on to her crippled foot with great difficulty. The trouble was that sockings on that foot wore out quickly and they, like salt, were improbably expensive. When the time came to choose a medical specialisation, Katya saw she could not do work that involved a lot of standing, so she became a medical microbiologist. She married and had two sons, and as she had once promised her friends on the front line, took her boys to Sapun Ridge to show them where she had fought, and where her friend Zhenya Makeyeva had died.[482]

A few years after the victory, a plaque was put up in Taya Kiselyova's old school in Kharkov, listing the former pupils and teachers who had fought in the war. It included all the boys in her class, but she was the only girl. Almost all the boys had been killed.[483]

How many people did the Soviet Union lose in the war? A book edited by Grigoriy Krivosheyev gives figures of 10,008,434 "irrecoverable" losses and 18,190,693 "medical" losses.[484] [485] Historian Yelena Senyavskaya estimates that only 3 per cent of men born in 1923 survived the war.[486] There are other estimates at great variance with these, which is not surprising. The reliability of Soviet statistics is often dubious, they routinely tried to play down the scale of the casualties suffered by the Soviet side, and there are even wildly divergent numbers for the total pre-war population.

The present book has not been about the big picture, but about the particular; it has not been about statistics, but about the people who make up the statistics. In 1943, along with Vera Chuikova, two other girls – both called Tonya – left the village of Prokhorovskoye near Yaroslavl (which no longer exists) for the front. All three returned in the autumn of 1945.

Of the young men who went to the war from this village of seventy-five homesteads, not one returned: no one born in 1923, no one born in 1924, no one born in 1925.

Shortly after returning, Vera and one of the Tonyas went to a dance in the village. The other girls there were younger than them, and had grown up while they were at the front. They danced in some new way that Vera did not know, and sang songs that had become popular while she was away. The boys were all several years younger than Vera and none of them asked her to dance, and she and Tonya felt hurt somehow. Some of the younger girls began insinuating that because they had been in the army they should not be there. Vera rounded on one of them and asked straight out, "What do you think I was doing there? Do you think I was a prostitute?" The girl backed off.

A couple of years later, Vera married a man four years her junior, but before that she kept hoping a boy she had met at the front, a tank driver called Slava Gondar, would come and find her. He had said he loved her, but his unit was urgently marched off and Vera never saw or heard from him again. Had he been killed? Had he lost her address, or found someone else and forgotten her? Vera still had his mother's address in Ukraine, but did not write to her. Somehow she got sucked into the harsh routine of life on a collective farm with no men.[487]

Of the 120 men and boys who had gone from Lida Larionova's village to the war, only five came back. Lida, who had left with a bundle over her shoulder, in a much darned and re-darned skirt, came back in some style by village standards. Now she was wearing warm stockings, a new, tailored tunic and skirt, a jacket and canvas boots that actually fitted. She brought other possessions back with her, and had seen other countries, but the existence awaiting her after the war was just as dreary as before, and now she had almost no hope of getting married. Just as before the war, they were robbed by the state, forced to work for next to nothing and pay unaffordable taxes. Just as before the war, their only salvation was their private plot of land where they planted potatoes and other vegetables, and livestock. Just as before the war, there were years of famine: the late 1940s were yet more terrible than the 1930s. Even after the conflict, village people were not given an internal passport so, like serfs under the tsars, they could not escape from their village to the local town.

For fighting in the war Lida was, for a long time, paid no pension, and before long she saw it was best not to mention she had been a woman at the front.[488]

Male veterans were treated with a degree of respect, but women continued to be regarded with suspicion or hostility; but never with respect. Some were advised by their husbands, others by parents or friends, that the less they mentioned their front-line past the better. They learned to stay silent. Even later, during the era of Brezhnev, who himself was a frontovik, when war veterans were suddenly back in the limelight, when reunions began to be held and they were invited to give talks to school-children, many women who had been at the front preferred to steer clear of it all.

"After the war I tried for a long time to forget all the monstrous sights I had seen. I felt constantly burdened by a sense of irrational guilt towards my fallen comrades: why was I alive when they had been killed?"[489] Many women who fought at the front would identify with these feelings. Still very young, they bore a terrible legacy they could not share. People who had not fought in the war could not understand them, "and somehow you felt very uncomfortable among people who had not the faintest idea of what we had been through," a man the same age as Anya Mulatova recalled.[490]

And yet, some women found it easier to cope than their male counterparts: how could you give way to depression if you had children to bring up, if you had to worry every day about how you were going to feed your family?

Anya Mulatova's mother- and father-in-law soon came to love her as if she were their own daughter: she was hardworking and cheerful and had a warm personality. They all went off to their jobs in the morning, and she would cook for them, keep the place tidy, bring in firewood from the shed and keep the big stove fuelled. While the weather was warm, she and her husband slept in the woodshed: there were a lot of those at that time in Mariina Roshcha. Later in the year there was nothing for it but to move into the single room all together: the parents slept in the bed, and the young couple moved chairs up to the sofa and put a duvet on top. In 1946, their son, Valerik, was born, and in 1947 Anatoly graduated from the military academy and was given an appointment in Byelorussia. They had a grim time there at first, living in hunger and poverty, with an income insufficient to buy even potatoes on the black market. Parcels from Anatoly's parents in Moscow with dried bread rusks and bagels were the saving of them. Anatoly was cashiered under Khrushchev, who purged the army of the old front-line soldiers, and they found themselves back with their parents in their 15-square-metre room. Anya worked as a school administrator. She would have liked to become a teacher, but it never happened. She longed at least to complete her ten-year secondary schooling at night school.

A decade after the war, she did manage to begin studying, but her husband raged that she was not keeping the house tidy and she had to abandon her studies. Anatoly, like the husbands of many of her front-line comrades, was by this time drinking heavily.[491]

Dramatis Personae

Asya (Anastasiya)Akimova, machine-gunner, 123 Infantry Regiment, 31 Army

Sima Anashkina (Vasina), sniper, 33 Army, 344 Infantry Division

Lida Bakieva, sniper, 32 Siberian Infantry Division

Vera Barakina, sniper, 715 Infantry Regiment, 122 Rifle Division

Muza Bulatova, sniper, 125 Infantry Division

Maria (Marusya) Chigvintseva, sniper, 344 Infantry Division, 33 Army

Klava Chistyakova, sniper, 62 Infantry Division, 31 Army

Vera Chuikova, sniper, 236 Infantry Division

Galya Dokutovich, navigator, 46 Guards Night Bomber Regiment

Ziba Ganieva, sniper, 3 Moscow Communist Rifle Division

Rufina Gasheva, navigator, 46 Guards Night Bomber Regiment

Zina Gavrilova, sniper, Komsomol organiser, 344 Infantry Division, 33 Army

Polina Gelman, navigator, 46 Guards Night Bomber Regiment

Golubev, lieutant colonel, regimental commander of 62 Infantry Division, 31 Army

Olga Golubeva, navigator, 46 Guards Night Bomber Regiment

Zhenya Grunskaya, nurse, 19 Cadet Infantry Brigade

Maria (Marusya) Gulyakina, sniper, 344 Infantry Division, 33 Army

Nina Isaeva, lieutenant, commander of sniper platoon, 174 Infantry Division

Taisiya (Taya) Kiselyova, sniper, 125 Infantry Division

Vera Kabernyuk, sniper, 3 Assault Army

Galya Koldeyeva, sniper, 19 Cadet Infantry Brigade

Olga Korotkevich, sniper, 19 Cadet Infantry Brigade

Natasha Kovshova, 3 Moscow Communist Rifle Division

Nikolai Krasavchenko, official from the Central Committee of Communist Youth

Yelena Kulkova (Malyutina), pilot, 587 Dive Bomber Regiment

Afanasia (Faya) Larionova, sister of sniper Lida Larionova

Lida Larionova, sniper, Volkhov Front

Klava Loginova, sniper, 1138 Infantry Regiment, 39 Army

Zhenya Makeeva, 19 Cadet Infantry Brigade

Tonya (Tosya) Makhlyagina, sniper, Third Belorussian Front, 755 Infantry Regiment, 217 Infantry Division, 48 Army

Katya Makoveeva, sniper, 174 Infantry Regiment, 39 Army

Anya Matokh, sergeant, sniper, 174 Infantry Regiment, 39 Army

Pyotr Molchanov, war correspondent

Bella Morozova, sniper, 125 Infantry Division

Rita Moskva, sniper, 152 Fortified District, 39 Army

Anna Nesterova, sniper, 1138 Infantry Regiment, 184 Infantry Division

Yekaterina Nikiforova, commissar, Central Women's School of Sniper Training

Olga Nikolaeva, sniper, 174 Infantry Division, 39 Army

Shura Okuneva, machine-gunner, 123 Infantry Regiment, 62 Division, 31 Army

Nonna Orlova, sniper, 152 Fortified District, 39 Army

Klava Panteleyeva, sniper, 344 Infantry Division, 33 Army

Lyudmila Pavlichenko, sniper, Independent Maritime Army

Vladimir Pchelintsev, sniper, Leningrad Front

Tasya (Natasha) Pegesheva, sniper, 62 Infantry Division, 31 Army

Katya Peredera, sniper, 19 Cadet Infantry Brigade

Kaleriya (Kalya) Petrova, sniper, 1138 Infantry Regiment, 184 Infantry Division

Nina Petrova, sniper, 284 Infantry Regiment, 86 Infantry Division

Masha Polivanova, sniper, 3 Moscow Communist Rifle Division

Rakityansky, lieutenant, commander sniper platoon, 62 Infantry Division, 31 Army

Irina Rakobolskaya, Chief of Staff, 46 Guards Aviation Regiment

Tamara Rogalskaya, sniper, 184 Infantry Regiment, 56 Division

Klava Romashova, radio operator, partisan unit

Captain Sagaidak ("The Beard"), Regimental Chief of Staff, 125 Infantry Division

Olga Sanfirova, pilot, 46 Guards Night Bomber Regiment

Seryogin, captain, platoon commander, 19 Cadet Infantry Brigade

Roza Shanina, sniper, 1138 Infantry Regiment, 184 Infantry Division

Anna Sheinova, sniper, Volkhov Front

Anna Sinyakova (Mulatova), sniper, 62 Infantry Division, 31 Army

Vasily Slavnov, commander of 123 Infantry Regiment, 62 Division, 31 Army

Anna Sokolova, sniper

Nina Solovey, nurse, sniper, 3 Moscow Communist Rifle Division

Alexander Stanovov, war correspondent

Lyuba Tanailova, sniper, 1138 Infantry Regiment, 184 Infantry Division

Lida Vdovina, sniper, 1138 Infantry Regiment, 184 Infantry Division

Valya Volokhova, sniper, 152 Fortified District, later 174 Infantry Division, 39 Army

Anna Egorova, pilot of Il-2 assault aircraft

Sasha Yekimova, sniper, 1138 Infantry Regiment, 184 Infantry Division

Nikolai Zainutdinov, sniper, platoon commander, 19 Cadet Infantry Brigade

Tonya Zakharova, sniper, 143 Infantry Division, 47 Army

Yulia Zhukova, sniper, 611 Infantry Regiment, 88 Infantry Division, 31 Army

Notes

Chapter 1 "You're my little girl! How will you survive there without borshcht?"

1   Kostenkov, *Ukhodili na voinu devchata* (Krasnodar: Krasnodarskoe knizhnoe izdatel'stvo, 1969), p. 48.
2   Ibid., p. 41.
3   Ibid., p. 50.
4   Author's interview with Ekaterina Fedorovna Terekhova, Krasnodar, September 2010.
5   Ibid.
6   Interview with Petr Kravchenko (from a broadcast on Kuban State TV and Radio, 9 October 2013, reporter Iuliia Volkova).
7   Aleksandr Orlov, "Bez vesti propavshie", *Severnyi krai*, 16 May 2012.
8   Author's interview with E.F. Terekhova.
9   Kostenkov, *Ukhodili na voinu devchata*, p. 97. 12 Author's interview with E.F. Terekhova.
10 Author's interview with E.F. Terekhova.
11 Lidiia Iosifovna Burmistrova, interview published on the website www.iremember.ru.
12 L.G. Stepanova, "Kollaboratsionizm na Kubani vo vremia nemetskoi okkupatsii: sotsial'nye istoki i proiavleniia", www.history-kuban.ucoz.ru
13 Author's interview with E.F. Terekhova.
14 Vera Cherepnina, "Okkupatsiia", *Moskovskii Komsomolets – Krasnodar*, 22 May 2013.
15 Kostenkov, *Ukhodili na voinu devchata*, p. 20.
16 Ibid., p. 24.
17 Author's interview with E.F. Terekhova.
18 Ibid.
19 Ibid.
20 Kostenkov, *Ukhodili na voinu devchata*, p. 30

Chapter 2 "Who would think of powdering their nose in a war?"

21 Vladimir Pchelintsev, "Osobaia missiia", Internet version.
22 Liudmila Pavlichenko, *Ia – snaiper. V boiakh za Sevastopol' i Odessu* (Moscow: Veche, 2015), p. 7.
23 Vladimir Pchelintsev graduated from the N.K.V.D. Troops' Sniper School in 1939. Pchelintsev, *Osobaia missiia* (Moscow: Molodaia gvardiia, 1991).
24 Pchelintsev, *Osobaia missiia*, p. 11.

25 For example, "Guerrilla queen at Washington", *Press and Journal*, 29 August 1942.

26 Pchelintsev, *Osobaia missiia*, p. 53.

27 "Lyudmila Pavlichenko speech in New York City", YouTube.

28 Pchelintsev, *Osobaia missiia*, p. 30.

29 "Woman sniper loses tooth", *Gloucestershire Echo*, 17 September 1942.

30 *Time*, 28 September 1942.

31 Ibid.

32 *Soviet Russia Today*, vol. 11, No. 6 (October 1942).

33 Pchelintsev, *Osobaia missiia*, p. 104.

34 "No Chocolates for Miss Pavlichenko", *Evening Telegraph and Post*, 29 August 1942.

35 The above examples are taken from *Soviet Russia Today*, vol. 11, No. 6 (October 1942).

36 Petr Vail', *Genii mesta* (Moscow: AST, 1999), pp. 23–4.

37 *New York Times*, 23 November 1942.

38 This information is taken mainly from speeches and interviews Pavlichenko gave during her tour of America, Canada and the United States in 1942, and from publications about her at the time. As mentioned, after the war Liudmila Pavlichenko did not write about herself or her time at the front, and rarely gave talks.

39 Pchelintsev, *Osobaia missiia*, p. 103.

40 A.I. Begunova in her book *Angely smerti. Zhenshchiny-snaipery. 1941–1945* (Moscow: Veche, 2014), p. 30 actually mentions the number of Pavlichenko's personal file in the Central Archive of the Ministry of Defence (TsAMO): it is 593897.

41 http://novodevichiynecropol.narod.ru/pavlichenko_lm.htm

42 Liudmila Pavlichenko, *Ia – snaiper*, pp. 256–7.

43 Gilbert King, "Eleanor Roosevelt and the Soviet Sniper", 21 February 2013. Online at http://blogs.smithsonianmag.com

44 Pavlichenko, *Ia – snaiper*, pp. 70, 73, 74.

45 Oleg Kaminskii, "Zagadka snaipera Liudmily Pavlichenko", published online at www.proza.ru

46 Pavlichenko, *Ia – snaiper*, p. 131.

47 Kaminsky, "Zagadka snaipera Liudmily Pavlichenko".

48 Ibid.

49 Pavlichenko, *Ia – snaiper*, p. 255.

50 *U chernomorskikh tverdyn'* (Moscow: Voenizdat, 1967), Internet version.

51 Ibid.

52 Ibid.

53 Ibid.

54 A.I. Begunova, Preface to Pavlichenko, *Ia - snaiper*, p. 5.

55 Pchelintsev, *Osobaia missiia*, p. 130.

56 Ibid., p. 129.

57 Pavlichenko, *Ia – snaiper*, p. 17.

58 Ibid., pp. 145, 169, 203, etc.

59   Ibid., p. 78.
60   Ibid., pp. 89, 110, 131, etc.
61   Ibid., p. 292.
62   Ibid., p. 298, etc.
63   Ibid., pp. 324–7.
64   Ibid., pp. 360–61.
65   Author's interview with Vsevolod Vital'evich Mal'tsev, Moscow, 2013.
66   Ibid.

Chapter 3 "Look at the family she's from. And we're just ordinary!"

67   Pchelintsev, *Osobaia missiia*, pp. 80–81.
68   Iozef Ollenberg [Josef "Sepp" Allerberger], *Nemetskii snaiper na Vostochnom fronte* (Moscow: Yauza-press, 2010), p. 153.
69   Vasilii Mizin, *Snaiper Petrova* (Leningrad: Lenizdat, 1988), p. 44 ff.
70   Author's interview with Afanasiia Naumovna Larionova, Babaevo, July 2013.
71   Ibid.
72   Ibid.
73   Nikolai Nikulin, *Vospominaniia o voine* (Moscow: AST, 2015), pp. 89, 90.
74   Begunova, *Angely smerti*, p. 227.
75   Author's interview with Anna Fedorovna Siniakova, Moscow, 2013.
76   Author's interview with Kaleriia Aleksandrovna Morokhovets, Moscow, June 2011.
77   *Leninskii Komsomol v gody Velikoi Otechestvennoi voiny* (Moscow, 1975), quoted from V.S. Murmantseva, *Sovetskie zhenshchiny v gody Velikoi Otechestvennoi voiny* (Moscow 1987), p. 7.
78   Ivan Red'ko, ed., "*Tyl i front ediny*" (Akbulak: Stepnye zori, 2002), pp. 33–4.

Chapter 4 "Mummy, why are there all uncles and only one auntie?"

79   Iuliia Zhukova, *Devushka so snaiperskoi vintovkoi* (Moscow: Tsentrpoligraf, 2006), p. 67.
80   V.A. Chuvilkin, *Devushki v shineliakh* (Moscow: Moskovskii rabochii, 1982).
81   Zhukova, *Devushka so snaiperskoi vintovkoi*, p. 68.
82   Author's interview with Klavdiia Etremovna Kalugina, Moscow, June 2011.
83   Author's interview with Klavdiia Grigor'evna Krokhina, Minsk, August 2012.
84   Author's interview with K.G. Krokhina, August 2012.
85   Chuvilkin, *Devushki v shineliakh*, p. 6.
86   Author's interview with Anna Fedorovna Siniakova, Moscow, 2013.
87   Ibid.
88   Author's interview with K.E. Kalugina, Moscow, February 2011.
89   Author's interview with K.G. Krokhina, Minsk, July 2012.

90   Ibid.

91   A.A. Agafonov, ed., *I v snaiperskom pritsele est' dobro* (Podolsk, 2005), p. 29.

92   Zhukova, *Devushka so snaiperskoi vintovkoi*, p. 79.

93   Ibid.

94   Author's interview with K.G. Krokhina.

95   Zhukova, *Devushka so snaiperskoi vintovkoi*, p. 71.

96   Author's interview with A.F. Siniakova, Moscow, summer 2013.

97   Zhukova, *Devushka so snaiperskoi vintovkoi*, p. 72.

98   Author's interview with A.F. Siniakova, Moscow, 2010.

99   Author's interview with K.E. Kalugina, Moscow, August 2013.

100 Author's interview with A.F. Siniakova, Moscow, June 2013.

101 Author's interview with Taisia Dmitrievna Il'nitskaia, St Petersburg, June 2011.

102 Zhukova, *Devushka so snaiperskoi vintovkoi*, pp. 88, 89.

103 Author's interview with K.G. Krokhina, Minsk, August 2013.

104 Author's interview with A.F. Siniakova, Moscow, August 2013.

105 Author's interview with K.G. Krokhina, 2013.

106 Author's interview with Mariia Antipovna Maksimova, Kaluga, September 2010.

107 Ibid.

108 Zhukova, *Devushka so snaiperskoi vintovkoi*, Internet version.

109 Author's interview with K.G. Krokhina, Minsk, July 2012.

110 Author's interview with Vera Nikolaevna Liubilkina, Moscow, March 2009.

111 The reference seems to be to the Badaev warehouses.

112 Author's interview with Vera Nikolaevna Liubilkina.

113 Author's interviews with A.F. Siniakova and K.G. Krokhina.

114 Author's interview with K.G. Krokhina, Minsk, July 2012.

115 Zhukova, *Devushka so snaiperskoi vintovkoi*, p. 88.

Chapter 5 "Why wash? It's dark, isn't it!"

116 Letters and photographs of Zhenia Makeeva provided to the author by her family.

117 Author's interview with E.F. Terekhova.

118 Ibid.

119 Ibid.

120 Kostenkov, *Ukhodili na voinu devchata*, p. 104.

121 Ibid.

122 G.A. Litvin, *Osvobozhdenie Kryma noiabr' 1943–mai 1944* (Moscow: Krechet, 1994), p. 28.

123 Ibid.

124 Rakobol'skaia and Kravtsova, *Nas nazyvali nochnymi ved'mami*, pp. 265–7. See also author's interview with Ol'ga Timofeevna Golubeva-Teres, Saratov, September 2010.

125 Author's interview with O.T. Golubeva-Teres.

126   Litvin, *Osvobozhdenie Kryma*, p. 34.

127   Author's interview with E.F. Terekhova.

128   Kostenkov, *Ukhodili na voinu devchata*, p. 106.

129   Author's interview with E.F. Terekhova.

130   Kostenkov, *Ukhodili na voinu devchata*, p. 107.

131   Author's interview with E.F. Terekhova.

132   *Operativnaia svodka za 14 noiabria*, www. great-victory.ru

133   Boris Nikolsky, «Kerchensky kapkan. Borba za Krym» (The Kerch Trap. Struggle for the Crimea). Electronic version.

134   *Rozhdennaia voinoi* (Moscow: Molodaia gvardiia, 1985).

135   Information from the website www.timashevsk.ru

136   Author's interview with E.F. Terekhova.

137   G.A. Litvin, *Osvobozhdenie Kryma noiabr' 1943–mai 1944* (Moscow: Krechet, 1994), p. 36.

138   Author's interview with O.T. Golubeva-Teres.

139   Ibid.

140   Ibid.

141   Andrei Kuznetsov, *Bol'shoi desant. Kerchensko-El'tigenskaia operatsiia* (Moscow: Veche, 2011). Internet version.

142   Described by Protsenko. Quoted from Vsevolod Abramov, *Kerchenskaia katastrofa 1942* (Moscow: Yauza Eksmo, 2006), pp. 97, 98.

143   Il'ia L'vovich (ps. Ellii-Karl) Sel'vinskii (1899–1968), poet, playwright, literary critic. In the 1930s and during the Second World War, a correspondent for *Pravda*.

144   Abramov, *Kerchenskaia katastrofa*, pp. 97, 98.

145   Kostenkov, *Ukhodili na voinu devchata*, p. 108.

146   Author's interview with E.F. Terekhova.

147   Ibid.

148   Kostenkov, *Ukhodili na voinu devchata*, p. 112.

149   Author's interview with E.F. Terekhova.

150   Kostenkov, *Ukhodili na voinu devchata*, p. 119.

151   Author's interview with E.F. Terekhova.

152   Kostenkov, *Ukhodili na voinu devchata*, p. 121.

153   On 14–17 July 1943 a summary trial was held in Krasnodar of Germans and their accomplices accused of committing atrocities in Krasnodar and the Krasnodar region. On 18 July 1943, eight collaborators were sentenced to death and the sentence was carried out in the city square.

154   Kostenkov, *Ukhodili na voinu devchata*, p. 122.

155   Author's interview with E.F. Terekhova.

156   Ibid.

157   Kostenkov, *Ukhodili na voinu devchata*, p. 128.

158   Ibid.

159   Author's interview with E.F. Terekhova.

160   Kostenkov, *Ukhodili na voinu devchata*, p. 129.

161   Author's interview with E.F. Terekhova.

162 Ibid.

163 An edition of the newspaper *Zaria Eniseia* dedicated to the 65th anniversary of victory.

164 *Krest'ianka*, No. 20, 1941.

165 Kostenkov, *Ukhodili na voinu devchata*, p. 131.

166 Author's interview with E.F. Terekhova.

167 Ibid.

168 Kostenkov, *Ukhodili na voinu devchata*, p. 134.

169 The offensive conducted by the Independent Maritime Army in January 1944 did, however, inflict such heavy losses on enemy forces that it would have been impossible for them to undo the damage by marching in reinforcements. To have any chance of retaining Crimea, the enemy had, in the second half of February, to hastily redeploy its 73 Infantry Division from Odessa. The division, flown in on transport aircraft, landed at the airport at Dzhankoi and, tasked with reinforcing the troops at Kerch, took up defensive positions at the end of February on the main line of defence at Kerch.

170 Kostenkov, *Ukhodili na voinu devchata*, pp. 134, 135.

171 *Boets-snaiper Natasha Kovshova* (Moscow: Glavnoe arkhivnoe upravlenie, 2010), p. 133.

172 Vera Murmantseva, *Zhenshchiny v soldatskikh shineliakh* (Moscow: Voenizdat, 1971), Internet version.

173 *Boets-snaiper Natasha Kovshova*, p. 165.

174 Ibid., p. 321.

175 Ibid., p. 179.

176 Ibid., p. 198.

177 From the memoirs of the artist, Taira Salakhova about Ziba Ganieva, www.1news.az

Chapter 6 "Klava, I beg you, don't take up smoking there!"

178 I. Tikhonov, ed., *"My znaem, chto znachit voina." Vospominaniia, pis'ma, dnevniki universantov raznykh let* (St Petersburg University, 2010), p. 59.

179 Unpublished memoirs of A.F. Siniakova (given to the author).

180 Author's interview with K.E. Kalugina, Moscow, 2011.

181 Traditionally read three times. The prayer "A Living Refuge" (Psalm 90) is considered in folk medicine to have power as a talisman. It is recited over a sick person in an attempt to drive out illness.

182 *Krest'ianka*, March 1944.

183 Author's interview with A.F. Siniakova, Moscow, 2012.

184 Author's interview with Mariia Antipovna Maksimova, Kaluga, September 2010.

Chapter 7 "That was somebody's father, and I have killed him!"

185 Author's interviews with A.F. Siniakova, 2010, 2012.

186 Regimental Doctor S.S. Aboev (mentioned in Slavnov).

187 Author's interview with A.F. Siniakova, August 2013.

188 *Zhenshchiny Slavy* (Moscow: Izd. Tsentr MOF "Pobeda - 1945 god", 1994), p. 71.

189 Interview with K.E. Kalugina, on the website www.iremember.ru

190 Ibid.

191 Ibid.

192 Memoirs of Serafima Anashkina (Vasina), published in Agafonov, ed., *I v snaiperskom pritsele est' dobro*, p. 117.

193 Author's interview with K.E. Kalugina, Moscow, 2012.

194 Interview with Klavdiia Lukashova (Romashova), published on the website www.iremember.ru

195 Author's interview with A.F. Siniakova.

196 Unpublished memoirs of A.F. Siniakova, author's personal archive.

197 Alternate rows of logs covering a dugout are stacked horizontally across each other.

198 Author's interview with A.F. Siniakova.

199 Unpublished memoirs of A.F. Siniakova.

200 Author's interview with A.F. Siniakova.

201 Author's interview with Antonina Vasil'evna Borodkina (Makhliagina), Gomel, August 2012.

202 Antonina Vasil'evna remembered this German clearly, although in 2012 when we met she was suffering from memory loss and could not remember how old she was or where she lived.

203 Author's interview with Lidiia Efimovna Bakieva, Alma-Aty, 2010.

204 Author's interview with A.F. Siniakova.

205 Author's interview with K.E. Kalugina, 2010.

206 Interview with V.G. Selin, published online at www.iremember.ru

207 Author's interview with K.E. Kalugina, February 2010.

208 Interview with K.A. Morokhovets, Moscow, July 2012.

Chapter 8 "Your daughter died for the Motherland. It has not been possible to bury her"

209 Rakobol'skaia and Kravtsova, *Nas nazyvali nochnymi ved'mami*, Internet version.

210 Kostenkov, *Ukhodili na voinu devchata*, pp. 139–140.

211 Published online at www.soldaty-pobedy.ru

212 Kostenkov, *Ukhodili na voinu devchata*, p. 141.

213 Ibid, p. 140.

214 Interview with I.Ia. Shpak online at www.iremember.ru

215 Kostenkov, *Ukhodili na voinu devchata*, p. 146.

216 *Kirovets* (a newspaper), 22 April 2010.

217 Interview with M.F. Ivashchenko, published online at www.iremember.ru

218 Eduard Asadov, "Moia zvezda", *Polnoe sobranie stikhotvorenii v odnom tome* (Moscow: Eksmo, 2015), p. 691.

219 *Kirovets*, 22 April 2010.

220 Author's interview with E.F. Terekhova.

221 Ibid.

222 Kostenkov, *Ukhodili na voinu devchata*, p. 175.

223 Of the forty-seven girls who in 1943 left Medvedovskaia for Kuban to drive out the Germans, thirteen were killed and twenty-five wounded. Many, like Katia Peredera, were permanently disabled.

Chapter 9 "The girls behave with exceptional modesty and discipline"

224 TsAMO RF, fond 1138 SP.

225 V. Mamonov and N. Poroshina, *Ona zaveshchala nam pesni i rosy* (Ust'ianskii kraevedcheskii muzei, 2001, p. 27.

226 Ibid.

227 Ibid.

228 Mamonov and Poroshina, *Ona zaveshchala nam pesni i rosy*, p. 19.

229 Lidiia Bazhenova (Vdovina) in *Zhenshchiny Slavy*. Quoted from http://airaces.narod.ru/snipers/w1/bajenova.htm

230 Ibid.

231 In fact, Zinaida Karmysheva.

232 *Rozhdennaia voinoi*, p. 134.

233 Author's interview with A.F. Siniakova, February 2010.

234 This is how Vladimir Il'iashenko recalls the power of the Katyusha, more correctly, the BM-13 Guards rocket mortar launcher. Published online at www.iremember.ru

235 Klavdiia Efremovna Kalugina, interviewed by Artem Drabkin. Online at www.iremember.ru

236 Author's interview with K.E. Kalugina, Moscow, June 2010.

237 Ibid. See also interviews with K.E. Kalugina online at www.iremember.ru

238 1156 Regiment of 33 Army, 344 Infantry Division.

239 Author's interview with K.E. Kalugina, Moscow, June 2011.

240 Interview with K.E. Kalugina, online at www.iremember.ru

241 Author's interview with K.E. Kalugina, Moscow, June 2011.

242 Author's interview with Elena Mironovna Kul'kova, Moscow, August 2013.

243 M.A. Kazarinova and A.A. Poliantseva, eds., *V nebe frontovom. Sbornik vospominanii i ocherkov* (Moscow, 2009), Internet version.

244 Author's interview with E.M. Kul'kova.

Chapter 10 "Hey, was that you who whacked him? Well done, now go and wash yourself!"

245   Author's interview with A.F. Siniakova, Moscow, February 2011.
246   Ibid.
247   Ibid.
248   Author's interview with A.F. Siniakova, Moscow, July 2013.
249   Tikhonov, *My znaem, chto znachit voina* . . . (illustration on the insert).
250   The Swiss gold watch is working to this day.
251   Author's interview with A.F. Siniakova.
252   Mansur Abdullin, *160 stranits iz soldatskogo dnevnika* (Moscow: Molodaia gvardiia, 1990), p. 121.

Chapter 11 "I knew nothing about him and I had just killed him"

253   Author's interview with K.G. Krokhina, Minsk, July 2012.
254   Tsentral'nyi arkhiv Ministerstva oborony (TsAMO), 164 OPAB, opis' 1, delo 6, korobka 26-34.
255   Author's interview with K.G. Krokhina, Minsk, August 2012.
256   Author's interview with A.F. Siniakova.
257   Author's interview with A.F. Siniakova and K.G. Krokhina.
258   Author's interview with A.F. Siniakova.
259   V.P. Slavnov, *Skol'ko bylo proideno* (Moscow: Voenizdat, 1984), p. 122.
260   In his memoirs Slavnov mistakenly calls Ania Mulatova "Shura Mulatova", on p. 123.
261   Ibid.
262   www.moy-polk.ru
263   Samuil Rozenberg, interview on the website www.iremember.ru
264   Author's interview with K.E. Kalugina, Moscow, March 2011.
265   Author's interview with K.E. Kalugina, Moscow.
266   Author's interview with A.F. Siniakova, July 2013.
267   Author's interview with A.F. Siniakova.
268   Slavnov, *Skol'ko bylo proideno*, p. 5.
269   Ibid., pp. 75, 76.
270   Ibid.
271   Author's interview with A.F. Siniakova.
272   Author's interview with K.E. Kalugina, Moscow, June 2011.
273   Author's interview with A.F. Siniakova.
274   Author's interview with K.E. Kalugina, Moscow.
275   Movsha Samuilovich Muler. Interview published on www.iremember.ru
276   Author's interview with L.N. Larionova, Babaevo, 2013.
277   Author's interview with K.E. Kalugina, Moscow.
278   Svetlana Aleksievich, *U voiny nezhenskoe litso* (Moscow: Vremia, 2015), pp. 44, 45.
279   Author's interview with K.G. Krokhina, Minsk, July 2012.

Chapter 12 "How will I live without them when the war is over and we all go off in different directions?"

280 Author's interview with V.N. Liubilkina, Moscow, February 2010.
281 "Dedovskie memuary", online at http://partisan-p.livejournal.com/10831.html
282 Author's interview with V.N. Liubilkina.
283 Author's interview with T.D. Il'nitskaia, St Petersburg, June 2011.
284 "Dedovskie memuary".
285 Author's interview with T.D. Il'nitskaia.
286 Ibid.
287 "Dedovskie memuary".
288 Mamonov, *Ona zaveshchala nam pesni i rosy*, pp. 52–3.
289 Author's interview with K.A. Morokhovets.
290 A. Drabkin interviews Antonina Kotliarova.
291 Galya Dakutovich, *Sertsa i kryly. Dzennik shturmana zhanochago aviiatsyinaga palka* (in Byelorussian) (Minsk, 1957), p. 72.
292 Author's interview with K.A. Morokhovets.
293 Mamonov, *Ona zaveshchala nam pesni i rosy*, p. 44.
294 Author's interview with K.E. Kalugina, Moscow.
295 TsAMO, fond 31 Armii, politdoneseniia.
296 Ibid.
297 Author's interview with K.E. Kalugina, Moscow.
298 Ibid.
299 Slavnov, *Skol'ko bylo proideno*, p. 154.
300 Ibid., p. 155.
301 Author's interview with K.A. Morokhovets.
302 Ibid.

Chapter 13 "Where's Tosya?" "Dead"

303 Author's interview with K.A. Morokhovets.
304 Author's interview with A.F. Siniakova.
305 Author's interview with K.G. Krokhina.
306 Author's interview with A.F. Siniakova.
307 In the memoirs mentioned above, Liudmila Pavlichenko writes that she was assigned to provide sniper fire cover for scouts going out on a mission: another surprising fact in her biography.
308 Author's interview with A.F. Siniakova.
309 Ibid.

Chapter 14 "I no longer have a heart. I am cold-blooded"

310 *Unichtozhim vraga*, 17 and 24 September 1944.
311 For confidentiality in letters and documents, and when talking on the phone, "black" meant killed and "red" meant wounded.
312 Mamonov, *Ona zaveshchala nam pesni i rosy*, p. 33.

313 Leonid Rabichev, *Voina vse spishet* (Moscow: Tsentropoligraf, 2009), pp. 141–2.

314 I.G. Erenburg, *Ubei!* (no place: Voenizdat NKO SSSR, 1942).

315 Alexander Werth's definition.

316 A.M. Sologubov, *Vestnik Baltiiskogo federal'nogo universiteta im. I. Kanta*, 2011, issue 12, pp. 76–82.

317 Ibid., vol. 16, p. 161.

318 Daniil Granin, *Prekrasnaia Uta*, Internet version.

319 A.M. Sologubov, *Vestnik Baltiiskogo federal'nogo universiteta im. I. Kanta*, 2011, issue 12, pp. 76–82.

320 Sologubov, ibid., vol. 7, pp. 216–17.

321 Leonid Moiseevich Shmurak, Interview published on www.iremember.ru

322 Ekaterina Sazhneva, "Poteriaesh' chest' – s fronta ne vozvrashchaisia", *Moskovskii Komsomolets*, 7 May 2004.

323 Ibid.

324 Roza's letter to Petr Molchanov is published in *Snaipery* (Moscow: Molodaia gvardiia, 1976).

325 Mamonov, *Ona zaveshchala nam pesni i rosy*, p. 34.

326 Memoirs of Captain Medvedev (Retd.), who took part in the battle, in *Ona zaveshchala nam pesni i rosy*, p. 35.

327 Ibid.

328 Mamonov, *Ona zaveshchala nam pesni i rosy*, p. 34.

329 Ibid. Roza initially wrote Anya Kuznetsova in her diary, but changed her to Zina Shmelyova in the letter to Molchanov.

330 Roza's letter to Petr Molchanov in *Snaipery*.

331 Ibid.

332 Ibid.

333 Agafonov, ed., *I v snaiperskom pritsele est' dobro*, pp. 117–18.

334 Ibid.

335 Author's interview with K.A. Morokhovets.

336 Mamonov, *Ona zaveshchala nam pesni i rosy*, p. 45.

337 Author's interview with K.A. Morokhovets.

338 "Tsena pobedy". *Rossiiskie shkol'niki o voine* (Moscow: Memorial, 2005), pp. 242–3.

339 Anna Timofeeva-Egorova, *Nebo, shturmovik, devushka* (Moscow: Yauza, Eksmo, 2007), pp. 297–302.

340 Mamonov, *Ona zaveshchala nam pesni i rosy*, p. 62.

Chapter 15 "Well, what are you here for? To fight or . . . ?"

341 Rakobol'skaia and Kravtsova, *Nazyvali nas nochnymi ved'mami*, pp. 295–8.

342 Many years after the war, P.M. Silkin read Rufina Gasheva's article and wrote to her. He remembered that night, and told her the name of the soldier who lent his boots to her was Moroz. He died six weeks or so after Ol'ga Sanfirova. Quoted from *Nazyvali nas nochnymi ved'mami*, pp. 295–8.

343 Quoted from Elena Seniavskaia, "Soldaty Krasnoi armii na pol'skikh zemliakh", *Istoriia*, August 2001, Internet version.

344 Ibid.
345 Ibid.
346 Ibid.
347 TsAMO, *Donesenie Politotdela 19 Armii*.
348 V.P. Slavnov, *Skol'ko bylo proideno*, p. 161.
349 TsAMO, fond 31 Armii, *Politdoneseniia*.
350 Zhukova, *Devushka so snaiperskoi vintovkoi*, p. 103.
351 Ibid., pp. 110, 111.
352 Ibid., p. 116.
353 Telephone interview with Yu.K. Zhukova.
354 Ibid.
355 Zhukova, *Devushka so snaiperskoi vintovkoi*, pp. 118–22.
356 TsAMO, fond 31 Armii, *Politdoneseniia*.
357 Ibid.

Chapter 16 "Aryan flesh"

358 Author's interview with K.G. Krokhina.
359 Ibid.
360 *Muzhestvo, otvaga i . . . liubov'* (Moscow: Paleia, 1997).
361 Author's interview with K.G. Krokhina.
362 Author's interview with K.E. Kalugina.
363 Ibid.
364 Author's interview with L.E. Bakieva.
365 TsAMO, fond 31 Armii, p. 155.
366 Mamonov, *Ona zaveshchala nam pesni i rosy*, p. 43.
367 Ibid.
368 The reference is to an attack by German tank troops.
369 Author's interview with L.E. Bakieva.
370 Mamonov, *Ona zaveshchala nam pesni i rosy*, p. 34.
371 Author's interview with L.E. Bakieva.
372 Vasilii Grossman, *Gody voiny* (Moscow: Pravda, 1989), pp. 250–1.
373 Published online at http://articles.gazeta.kz/art.asp?aid=59250
374 *Krest'ianka*, Nos. 19–20, October 1942.
375 Ibid.
376 Zhukova, *Devushka so snaiperskoi vintovkoi*, p. 133.
377 Ibid., pp. 134–5.
378 Author's interview with A.F. Siniakova.
379 It was probably these which inspired the printing of Soviet New Year greetings cards, which first appeared just after the war.
380 Author's interview with A.F. Siniakova.
381 Aleksievich, *U voiny nezhenskoe litso*, pp. 212, 213.
382 Author's interview with V.V. Chuikova.
383 Author's interview with A.F. Siniakova.

384 Mamonov, *Ona zaveshchala nam pesni i rosy*, p. 39.

385 Hans Kinschermann, *Ia - pulemetchik Vermakhta. Krovavo-krasnyi sneg Vostochnogo fronta* (Moscow: Yauza, 2013), pp. 64–5.

386 Author's interview with A.F. Siniakova.

Chapter 17 "Maybe it's for the best that Roza has died . . ."

387 Mamonov, *Ona zaveshchala nam pesni i rosy*, p. 65.

388 Ibid., p. 66.

389 Ibid., p. 44.

390 Ibid., p. 45.

391 Ibid., p. 33.

392 Ibid., p. 45.

393 Ibid., p. 57.

394 Ibid., p. 38.

395 In connection with Roza Shanina's diary, the author consulted Vasilisa Elizarova, a psychologist.

396 Mamonov, *Ona zaveshchala nam pesni i rosy*, p. 30.

397 Ibid., p. 31.

398 Ibid, p. 58.

399 Ibid.

400 Ibid., p. 31.

401 TsAMO, fond 1156 sp, opis' 37104, delo 1.

402 Mamonov, *Ona zaveshchala nam pesni i rosy*, p. 41.

403 Ibid., p. 29.

404 Ibid, p. 37.

405 Ibid.

406 Ibid.

407 *Snaipery* (Moscow, 1976).

408 Mamonov, *Ona zaveshchala nam pesni i rosy*, p. 55.

409 Ibid., pp. 55–6.

410 Ibid., p. 47.

411 Ibid., pp. 47–9.

412 Ibid., pp. 49, 50.

413 Iosif Utkin, *Izbrannoe* (Moscow: Khudozhestvennaia literatura, 1975), p. 286.

414 Mamonov, *Ona zaveshchala nam pesni i rosy*, p. 56.

415 Ibid., p. 42.

416 Ibid., p. 58.

417 Ibid., p. 44.

418 Author's interview with K.A. Morokhovets.

419 Mamonov, *Ona zaveshchala nam pesni i rosy*, p. 59.

420 Ibid.

421 Ibid., p. 11.

422 Ibid.

Chapter 18 "We did not want to bury them looking like that"

423 Zhukova, *Devushka so snaiperskoi vintovkoi*, p. 136.

424 Ibid., p. 138. Iuliia Zhukova mentions only Dusia (Evdokiia Andreevna) Filippova, but according to other sources (cf. www.forum_kenig.ru), two other girls from the platoon, Antonina Aleksandrovna Shabanina and Mariia Mikhailovna Kulikovich, were also captured by the Germans and brutally murdered.

425 Author's interview with K.G. Krokhina.

426 Zhukova, *Devushka so snaiperskoi vintovkoi*, p. 143.

427 Ibid.

428 Mamonov, *Ona zaveshchala nam pesni i rosy*, p. 51.

429 Author's interview with K.A. Morokhovets.

430 Ibid.

431 Author's personal archive. Interviews recorded in Leningrad by E.N. Nikiforova. The record was given to the author by T.D. Il'nitskaia.

432 Karl-Heinz Schmeelke, "Der Untergang von Ostpreussen und das Ende der 4. Armee", published online at http://www.klee-klaus.de/der_untergang_ostpre-ussens.htm

433 Tamara Rogal'skaia's testimony was recorded at a snipers' reunion in Leningrad by E.N. Nikiforova. The record was given to the author by T.D. Il'nitskaia. Author's personal archive.

434 Mizin, *Snaiper Petrova*, p. 48 ff.

435 Mizin does not mention this in his documentary novella about Petrova.

436 Mizin, *Snaiper Petrova*, pp. 98–101.

437 Author's interview with T.D. Il'nitskaia.

438 "Dedovskie memuary", online at http://partisan-p.livejournal.com/10831.html

439 Author's interview with T.D. Il'nitskaia.

440 "*Dedovskie memuary.*"

Chapter 19 "Oh, Mum, how they are hurting us here!"

441 Author's interview with V.N. Liubilkina.

442 V.O. Bogomolov, *Zhizn' moia, il' ty prisnilas' mne?* (Moscow: Knizhnyi klub 36, 6, 2014), pp. 39–42.

443 Author's interview with K.G. Krokhina.

444 Author's interview with L.E. Bakieva.

445 K.N. Galitskii, *V boiakh za Vostochnuiu Prussiiu* (Moscow: Nauka, 1970), p. 385.

446 Script for an oral magazine for the 6th Study Course on the Königsberg Operation, 26 March 2015 [no location] (prepared by teaching trainer and organiser, O.N. Kolegaeva).

447 Published in the online journal *Letopis' – novosti arkheologii i istorii*, 16 May 2015.

448 "Kaliningradskie veterany vspominaiut shturm Kenigsberga", *Komsomol'skaia Pravda-Kaliningrad*, 9 April 2009.

449 Khans Shoifler, Vil'gelm Tike (Hans Scheufler and Wilhelm Tieke), *Marsh na Berlin 1944–45* (Moscow: Eksmo, 2005), Internet version.

450 Author's interview with A.F. Siniakova.

451 Author's interview with K.G. Krokhina.

Chapter 20 "Hold on, Kolenka!"

452 Author's interview with V.V. Chuikova.

453 Rakobol'skaia and Kravtsova, *Nazyvali nas nochnymi ved'mami*, p. 32.

454 TsAMO, fond 31 Armii, opis' 8599, delo 218.

455 Author's interview with V.V. Chuikova.

456 "After the liberation, in Pit No. 1, length 100m, width 10m, and depth 4–5m, there were discovered 8,000 bodies of women and children, stripped naked. On some there were no traces of wounds. This confirms that citizens were exterminated using electric current." http://kovelyaka.ru/ukr/history/vijna/index.html

457 Author's interview with V.V. Chuikova.

458 "Memoirs of Hero of the Soviet Union, Guards Major Tsitovskii", quoted from http://www.inberlin.ru/proriv/Zeelovski/

459 Aleksei Isaev, *1945. Poslednii krug ada. Flag nad Reikhstagom* (Moscow, 2009), Internet version.

460 Interview with Vera Korneevna Zubchenko (with the assistance of Viacheslav Dranitsa), Zonal'noe, Altai region, summer 2011.

461 Bogomolov, "Zhizn' moia, il' ty prisnilas' mne?", *Nash sovremennik*, Nos. 10–12, 2005; No. 1, 2006.

462 Interview by Aleksandr Arapov of Nadezhda Sakharovskaia, Ren TV, 11.27 hrs, 21 April 2015.

463 F.Ia. Lisitsyn, *V te groznye gody* (Moscow: Voenizdat, 1978).

464 Author's interview with K.G. Krokhina.

465 Agafonov, ed., *I v snaiperskom pritsele est' dobro.*

466 Interview with T.D. Il'nitskaia.

467 Rakobol'skaia and Kravtsova, *Nas nazyvali nochnymi ved'mami*, p. 312.

468 Tamara Rogal'skaia's tale, written down by E.N. Nikiforova.

469 Author's interview with L.E. Bakieva.

Chapter 21 "They promise you nothing!"

470 The myth of specially infected women tasked with sapping the strength of the Red Army was used to explain the widespread incidence of venereal disease in the army in 1944–5. The women in the camp were probably Soviet citizens forcibly transported to work in Germany.

471 Ibid.

472 Author's interview with V.V. Chuikova.

473 Ibid.

474 Author's interview with K.E. Kalugina.
475 Author's interview with K.G. Krokhina.
476 Author's interview with A.F. Siniakova.
477 Aleksievich, *U voiny nezhenskoe litso*, pp. 103, 104, etc.
478 Mamonov, *Ona zaveshchala nam pesni i rosy*, p. 40.
479 Author's interview with K.A. Morokhovets.

Epilogue

480 Agafonov, ed., *I v snaiperskom pritsele est' dobro*.
481 Author's interview with K.G. Krokhina.
482 Author's interview with E.F. Terekhova.
483 Author's interview with T.D. Il'nitskaia.
484 The sick and wounded who later died in hospital were included under "medical" losses.
485 Grigorii Krivosheev, ed., *Velikaia Otechestvennaia bez grifa sekretnosti. Kniga poter'* (Moscow: Veche, 2014), p. 69.
486 E.S. Seniavskaia, *Psikhologiia voiny v XX veke: istoricheskii opyt Rossii* (Moscow: ROSSPEN, 1999), Internet version.
487 Author's interview with V.V. Chuikova.
488 Author's interview with L.N. Larionova.
489 Semen Markovich Polonskii, online at www.iremember.ru
490 Nikolai Inozemtsev, *Frontovoi dnevnik* (Moscow: Nauka, 2005), Internet version.
491 Author's interview with A.F. Siniakova.

Bibliography and Other Sources

BOOKS

Abdullin, Mansur, *160 stranits iz soldatskogo dnevnika* (160 Pages from a Soldier's Diary) (Moscow: Molodaia gvardiia, 1990)

Abramov, Vsevolod, *Kerchenskaia katastrofa 1942* (The Kerch Disaster of 1942) (Moscow: Yauza Eksmo, 2006)

Agafonov, A. A. (ed.), *I v snaiperskom pritsele est' dobro* (There is Good in a Sniper's Sight, Too) (Podolsk, 2005)

Aleksievich, Svetlana, *U voiny nezhenskoe litso* (The War's Unwomanly Face) (Moscow: Vremia, 2015)

Allerberger, Josef, *Nemetskii snaiper na Vostochnom fronte* (German Sniper at the Eastern Front) (Moscow: Yauza-press, 2010)

Asadov, Eduard, *Moia zvezda* (My Star) (Moscow: Eksmo, 2015)

Begunova, A. I., *Angely smerti. Zhenshchiny-snaipery. 1941–1945* (Angels of Death. Women Snipers. 1941–1945) (Moscow: Veche, 2014)

Boets-snaiper Natasha Kovshova (Soldier Sniper Natasha Kovshova) (Moscow: Glavnoe arkhivnoe upravlenie, 2010)

Bogomolov, V. N., *Zhizn' moia, il' ty prisnilas' mne?* (My Life, Were You Just a Dream?) (Moscow: Knizhnyi klub 36. 6, 2014)

Chuvilkin, V. A., *Devushki v shineliakh* (Girls in Greatcoats) (Moscow: Moskovskii rabochii, 1982)

Dakutovich, Galina, *Sertsa i kryly. Dzennik shturmana zhanochago aviiatsyinaga palka* (Heart and Wings. Diary of a Navigator of a Female Aviation Regiment [in Byelorussian]), (Minsk, 1957)

Erenburg, I. G., *Ubei!* (Kill!) (Voenizdat NKO SSSR, 1942)

Galitskii, K. N., *V boiakh za Vostochnuiu Prussiiu* (In the Battles for East Prussia) (Moscow: Nauka, 1970)

Granin, Daniil, *Prekrasnaia Uta* (The Beautiful Uta) (Moscow: Sovetskaya Rossiya, 1974)

Grossman, Vasilii, *Gody voiny* (The Years of War) (Moscow: Pravda, 1989)

Inozemtsev, Nikolai, *Frontovoi dnevnik* (The Front Diary) (Moscow: Nauka, 2005)

Isaev, Aleksei, *1945. Poslednii krug ada. Flag nad Reikhstagom* (The Last Circle of Hell. Flag over the Reichstag) (Moscow: 2009)

Kazarinova, M. A. and Poliantseva, A. A. (eds), *V nebe frontovom. Sbornik vospominanii i ocherkov* (In the Skies of War. Collection of Memoirs and Essays) (Moscow, 2009)

Kinschermann, Hans, *Ia – pulemetchik Vermakhta. Krovavo-krasnyi sneg Vostochnogo fronta* (I Was a Machine-Gunner for the Reich. The Blood-Red Snow of the Eastern Front) (Moscow, Yauza, 2013)

Kostenkov, Afanasii, *Ukhodili na voinu devchata* (Girls Were Leaving for War) (Krasnodar: Krasnodarskoe knizhnoe izdatel'stvo, 1969)

Krivosheev, Grigorii, (ed.), *Velikaia Otechestvennaia bez grifa sekretnosti. Kniga poter'* (The Great Patriotic War. The Full Story) (Moscow: Veche, 2014).

Kuznetsov, Andrei, *Bolshoi desant. Kerchensko-Eltigenskaia operatsiia* (The Big Landing Force. Kerch-Altigen Operation) (Moscow: Veche, 2011).

Litvin, G. A., *Osvobozhdenie Kryma noiabr 1943–mai 1944* (Liberation of the Crimea, November 1943–May 1944) (Moscow: Krechet, 1994)

Mamonov, V. and Poroshina, N., *Ona zaveshchala nam pesni i rosy* (She Bequeathed to Us Songs and Dew) (Ustianskii kraevedcheskii muzei, 2001)

Mizin, Vasilii, *Snaiper Petrova* (Sniper Petrova) (Leningrad: Lenizdat, 1988)

Murmantseva, Vera, *Zhenshchiny v soldatskikh shineliakh* (Women in Soldiers' Greatcoats) (Moscow: Voenizdat, 1971)

Murmantseva, Vera, *Sovetskie zhenshchiny v gody Velikoi Otechestvennoi voiny* (Soviet Women During the Years of the Great Patriotic War) (Moscow, 1987)

Muzhestvo, otvaga i . . . liubov (Courage, Audacity and . . . Love) (Moscow: Paleia, 1997)

Nikulin, Nikolai, *Vospominaniia o voine* (Memoirs of the War) (Moscow: AST, 2015)

Pavlichenko, Liudmila, *Ia – snaiper. V boiakh za Sevastopol' i Odessu* (I Am a Sniper. In the Battles for Sevastopol and Odessa) (Moscow: Veche, 2015)

Pchelintsev, Vladimir, *Osobaia missiia* (Special Mission) (Moscow: Molodaya gvardiia, 1991)

Rabichev, Leonid, *Voina vse spishet* (The War Will Write Everything Off) (Moscow: Tsentropoligraf, 2009)

Rakobol'skaia, Irina and Kravtsova, Natalia, *Nas nazyvali nochnymi ved'mami* (They Called Us the Night Witches) (Moscow: MGU, 2005)

Redko, Ivan, ed., *Tyl i front ediny* (Rear and Front Are United) (Akbulak: Stepnye zori, 2002)

Rozhdennaia voinoi (Born in the War) (Moscow: Molodaia gvardiia, 1985).

Sagaidak, *Dedovskie memuary* (Grandpa's Memoir), online at http://partisan-p. livejournal.com/10831.html

Scheufler, Hans and Tieke, Wilhelm, *Marsh na Berlin 1944–45* (The March towards Berlin) (Moscow: Eksmo, 2005)

Schmeelke, Karl-Heinz, *Der Untergang von Ostpreussen und das Ende der 4. Armee* (The Doom of East Prussia and the Ruin of the 4th Army), published online at http://www.klee-klaus.de/der_untergang_ostpreussens.htm

Seniavskaia, E.S., *Psikhologiia voiny v XX veke: istoricheskii opyt Rossii* (Psychology of War in the Twentieth Century: Russia's Historical Experience) (Moscow: ROSSPEN, 1999).

Slavnov, Vasilii, *Skol'ko bylo proideno* (We Have Walked So Far) (Moscow: Voenizdat, 1984)

Stepanova, L. G., *Kollaboratsionizm na Kubani vo vremia nemetskoi okkupatsii: sotsial'nye istoki i proiavleniia* (Social Origins and Manifestations of Collaborationism in the Kuban During the German Occupation), www.history-kuban.ucoz.ru

Tikhonov, ed., *My znaem, chto znachit voina. Vospominaniia, pis'ma, dnevniki universantov voennykh let* (We Know What War Is. Memoirs, Letters, and Diaries of University Students of the War Years (St Petersburg University, 2010).

Timofeeva-Egorova, Anna, *Nebo, shturmovik, devushka* (Sky, Assault Aircraft, Girl) (Moscow: Yauza, Eksmo, 2007)

"Tsena pobedy". Rossiiskie shkol'niki o voine (The Price of Victory. Russian School Children Discuss the War) (Moscow: Memorial, 2005).

U chernomorskikh tverdyn' (The Strongholds by the Black Sea) (Moscow: Voenizdat, 1967), Internet version.

Utkin, Iosif, *Izbrannoe* (Selected Verse) (Moscow: Khudozhestvennaia literatura, 1975)

Vail, Piotr, *Genii mesta* (The Genius of a Place) (Moscow: AST, 1999).

Zhenshchiny Slavy (The Women of Glory)(Moscow: Izd. Tsentr MOF "Pobeda – 1945 god", 1994).

Zhukova, Iulia, *Devushka so snaiperskoi vintovkoi* (Girl with a Sniper Rifle) (Moscow: Tsentrpoligraf, 2006)

ARTICLES

Cherepnina, Vera, "Okkupatsiia", in *Moskovskii Komsomolets* – Krasnodar, 22 May 2013

Script for an oral magazine for the 6th Study Course on the Königsberg Operation, 26 March 2015 [no location] (prepared by teaching trainer and organiser, O. N. Kolegaeva)

Online journal *Letopis'* – *novosti arkheologii i istorii*, 16 May 2015

"Kaliningradskie veterany vspominaiut shturm Kenigsberga", *Komsomol'skaia Pravda-Kaliningrad*, 9 April 2009

Kaminskii, Oleg, *The Mystery of Sniper Liudmila Pavlichenko*, published online at www.proza.ru

Kirovets, 22 April 2010

Krest'ianka, Nos. 19–20, October 1942

Krest'ianka, March 1944

Memoirs of Hero of the Soviet Union, Guards Major Tsitovskii, quoted from http://www.inberlin.ru/proriv/Zeelovski/

Operativnaia svodka za 14 noiabria (Summary of Operations, 14 November), www. great-victory.ru

Orlov, Aleksandr, "The Ones That Went Missing", *Severnyi Krai*, 16 May 2012

Sazhneva, Ekaterina, "Don't Bother to Come Back from the Front If You Have Lost Your Honour", *Moskovskii Komsomolets*, 7 May 2004

Seniavskaia, Yelena, "Soldiers of the Red Army on Polish Territory", *Istoriia*, August 2001

Sologubov, A. M., "Pomerania through the Centuries", *Vestnik Baltiiskogo federal'nogo universiteta im. I. Kanta*, 2011, issues 12,16

Unichtozhim vraga (army newspaper), 17 and 24 September 1944

ARCHIVE DOCUMENTS

Central Archive of the Ministry of Defence of the Russian Federation (TsAMO), 164 OPAB, opis' 1, delo 6, korobka 26–34

TsAMO RF, fond 1138 SP

TsAMO, *Donesenie Politotdela 19 Armii*

TsAMO, fond 31 Armii, *Politdoneseniia*

Unpublished memoir by Anna Siniakova, private archive of A. Siniakova

Letters of Zhenia Makeeva, private archive of Aleksandr Khovantsev

INTERVIEWS

Author's interview with Lidiia Bakieva. Alma-Aty, 2010.

Author's interview with Antonina Borodkina (Makhliagina). Gomel, August 2012.

Lidiia Burmistrova, published online at www.iremember.ru

Author's interview with Vera Chuikova. Kormilitsyno, Yaroslavl Oblast. Summer 2013

Author's interview with Olga Golubeva-Teres. Saratov, September 2010

Author's interview with Taisia Ilnitskaia. St Petersburg, June 2011

Interview with M. F. Ivashchenko, published online at www.iremember.ru

Author's interviews with Klavdia Kalugina, Moscow, 2011, 2012, 2013 and 2014

Artyom Drabkin interviews with Antonina Kotliarova

Interview with Petr Kravchenko (from a broadcast on Kuban state TV and radio, 9 October 2013, reporter Iuliia Volkova)

Author's interview with Klavdia Krokhina. Minsk, August 2012

Author's interview with Elena Kulkova. Moscow, August 2013

Author's interview with Afanasia Naumovna Larionova. Babaevo, July 2013

Author's interview with Lidia Larionova. Babaevo, 2013

Author's interview with Vera Liubilkina. Moscow, March 2009

Interview with Klavdia Lukashova (Romashova), published online at www.iremember.ru

Author's interview with Maria Maksimova. Kaluga, September 2010

Author's interview with Vsevolod Maltsev. Moscow, 2013

Author's interview with Kaleryia Morokhovets. Moscow, June 2011

Interview with Semen Polonski, published online at www.iremember.ru

Testimony from Tamara Rogal'skaia, recorded at a snipers' reunion in Leningrad by E.N Nikiforova

Interview with Samuil Rozenberg, published online at www.iremember.ru

Interview by Aleksandr Arapov of Nadezhda Sakharovskaia. Ren TV, 21 April 2015

Interview with V. G. Selin, published online at www.iremember.ru

Interview with Leonid Shmurak, published online at www.iremember.ru

Interview with I. Shpak, published online at www.iremember.ru

Author's interview with Anna Fedorovna Siniakova. Moscow, 2013

Author's interview with Yekaterina Terekhova

Interview with Vera Korneevna Zubchenko (with the assistance of Viacheslav Dranitsa), Zonal'noe, Altai region, summer 2011

Picture Credits

akg-images: 37 (image number)

akg-images / Pictures From History: 38

akg-images / sputnik: 8, 30, 32

akg-images / Voller Ernst / Chaldej: Back cover

From R.G.A.K.F.D. (the Russian State Documentary Film and Photo Archive, Krasnogorsk): Front cover, 1, 16, 17, 20, 24, 26, 31, 34, 35, 36, 39

From the private archive of the author: 41

From the private archive of Anna Sinyakova (Mulatova): 9, 40

From the private archive of Kaleriya Petrova (Morokhovets): 6, 21, 22, 23, 27, 28, 29, 33

From the private archive of Klavdiya Kalugina (Panteleeva): 10

From the private archive of Klavdiya Krokhina (Loginova): 4, 15, 42

From the private archive of Lidiya (Lida) Bakieva: 7, 25

From the private archive of Taisiya Ilnitskaya (Kiselyova): 11, 12, 13, 14, 44

From the private archive of Vera Lyubilkina (Barakina): 5

From the private archive of Yekaterina Terekhova (Peredera): 18, 19

Acknowledgements

I am extremely grateful to Klavdia Kalugina (Panteleyeva) who was until 2012 the head of the Moscow group of veterans of the Podolsk women's snipers school. Not only did she share contacts of other snipers, but also her personal recollections of the front and of her dead friend Marusya Chigvintseva. Without her I would have achieved very little.

Taisiya Ilnitskaya (Kiselyova) in St Petersburg also put me in touch with her former comrades-in-arms and gave me some precious photographs and documents from her archive. I will hand all of this over to a museum of Soviet female soldiers as soon as such a museum is set up.

The families of some of my heroines were extremely kind to me. Despite very late notice Yuri and Irina Morokhovets found photographs of Kaleriya and her friends in the family archive. Aleksandr Khovantsev has given me precious relics from his family archive: photos and letters of his great aunt Zhenya Makeeva.

I am grateful to historians Anatoly Chernobaev and Viktoriya Petrakova for their invaluable advice. My colleague and friend Artem Drabkin was, as always, extremely generous with materials and contacts. Journalist Vyacheslav Dranitsa in Altai made several attempts to interview Vera Zubchenko for me before, eventually, he succeeded. My cousin Nadya Trofimova found Vera Chuikova's house in a village near Yaroslavl and finally persuaded her to speak with me. And Marina Chertilina from the Russian State Archive of Film and Photo Documents has helped me to find some really great photographs.

Many thanks to Arch Tait for the clever translation and the title, which was his idea! Thanks to Josh Ireland for making the text digestible for the western audience. To Katharina Bielenberg for taking care of the whole publishing process. And I am forever grateful to my agent and friend Andrew Nurnberg for his attention, encouragement and support, and for his patience in providing answers to any tricky questions that I might have.

L.V.

Index

DR LYUBA VINOGRADOVA was born in Moscow and graduated from the Moscow Agricultural Academy with a PhD in microbiology. In 1995 she was introduced to Antony Beevor and helped him research *Stalingrad*. Since then she has worked on many other research projects, and is the co-author (with Beevor) of *A Writer at War: Vasily Grossman with the Red Army*. Her book about Russian women fighter pilots, *Defending the Motherland*, was published by MacLehose Press in 2015.

DR ARCH TAIT has translated many of the leading Russian writers of today, notably the late Anna Politkovskaya. For her book *Putin's Russia* he was awarded the PEN Literature in Translation Prize.